DEFYING EVIL

DEFYING EVIL

HOW THE ITALIAN ARMY SAVED CROATIAN JEWS DURING THE HOLOCAUST

By Benjamin Wood

History Publishing Company
Palisades, New York

Published in the United States by
History Publishing company LLC
Palisades, New York
www.historypublishingco.com

ISBN-10: 1-933909-27-7
ISBN-13: 9781933909-27-1

LCCN: 2012933032
SAN: 850-5942

Wood, Benjamin, 1964-
    Defying evil : how the Italian Army saved Croatian
Jews during the Holocaust / by Benjamin Wood.
    p. cm.
    Includes bibliographical references and index.
    LCCN 2012933032
    ISBN 9781933909271 (pbk.)
    ISBN 9781933909288 (e-book)

    1. Holocaust, Jewish (1939-1945)--Croatia. 2. Italy.
Army--Officers.   I. Title.

    D804.3.W66 2012   940.53'18
                                 QBI12-600031

Printed in the United States on acid free paper

9 8 7 6 5 4 3 2 1

First Edition

For my father and step-father, both of whom loved history.

TABLE OF CONTENTS

INTRODUCTION

THE STORY OF ITALY'S RESCUE AND DEFENSE OF CROATIAN JEWS IS unique in the history of World War II and the Holocaust. Officials at the highest level of Fascist Italy defied their ally Nazi Germany to protect Jews who were not even citizens of their own country. Unquestionably, thousands of Croatian Jews would have been murdered had it not been for the heroic efforts of members of the Italian Military and Foreign Ministry between April 1941 and July 1943. Why and how did Italians in positions of power risk their careers, reputations, and, in some cases, their very lives to protect a persecuted minority?

In occupied Croatia in the summer of 1941, individual Italian soldiers found themselves intervening to save the lives of Jews and Serbs who were being murdered by Croatian Fascists. Over the next two years, these isolated acts would develop into a conspiracy at the highest levels of the Italian government and military to save Jews from deportation and death at the hands of the Nazis.

Benito Mussolini's officers and statesmen were able to rescue Jewish men, women, and children first from the Ustasha (the Croatian Fascists) and then from the Nazis for several reasons. Unlike Adolf Hitler, who rarely took the advice of his generals or allowed subordinates to disagree with him on matters of policy, Mussolini could be influenced by members of the *Commando Supremo* (Supreme Command) which included the army's most senior generals as well as civilian officials. Significantly, Mussolini was far from an anti-Semite (although, ever the political opportunist, he did pass anti-Jewish laws in 1938 in an effort to draw closer to Germany). Mussolini had known and respected Jews including many who had served in the Italian army. In the end, he would not allow himself to become involved in the evil of the Holocaust.

Of additional assistance to the Italians' efforts was the fact that the Nazis permitted Italy a free hand over the areas of Europe it occupied during the war. Until 1943, Italy was treated as a full partner rather than as a puppet regime. Hitler had always had great respect for *Il Duce* ("the Leader," as Mussolini was known), and viewed Mussolini as a mentor and key theorist of Fascist philosophy. This admiration allowed the Italian dictator a degree of freedom unequalled in Nazi dominated Europe.

Throughout the period from 1941 to 1943, the German Foreign Ministry, led by Joachim von Ribbentrop, continually pressured the Italian government to surrender Jews who had fled into Italian areas of occupation. The Jews would have been sent to Auschwitz, the same destination to which the Germans were already deporting thousands from their zone of occupied Croatia. The mercurial Mussolini allowed himself to be swayed by subordinates in the Army and Foreign Ministry to resist Germany's demands. Hitler, while undoubtedly annoyed, nevertheless did not violate *Il Duce's* "sphere of influence" by moving troops in to seize the refugees who sought Italian protection.

The fact that Italian soldiers and statesmen saved Jews in Croatia does not of course absolve Italy of the atrocities it committed against civilians prior to and during the Second World War. The 1935 Italian invasion and subsequent rule of Ethiopia were brutal. Within the Balkans, Slovenes and Communists partisans suffered terribly at the hands of the Italians.

Yet Italy deserves great credit for its actions on behalf of the Jews. Approximately 3,500 Jewish men, women, and children owe their lives to the Italians. Although the motivations for some Italians were somewhat questionable, the overriding tenet was a sense of humanitarianism. Many Italian officers, when told by their

German counterparts that they would have to hand over Jews, simply refused, declaring that such an action was beneath the dignity of the Italian army and a violation of Italian honor. The courage and compassion the Italians displayed in challenging Nazi authority and standing up for a powerless minority provide a true bright spot in a very dark chapter of history.

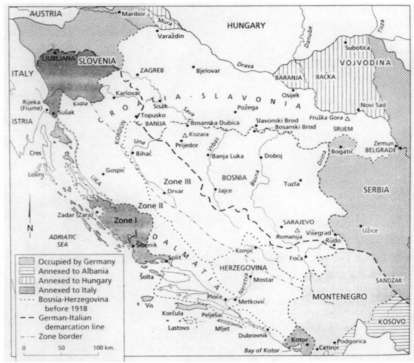

1

WAR COMES TO CROATIA

By the spring of 1941, Adolf Hitler was the master of Europe. A year and a half earlier, after Hitler signed a nonaggression pact with the Soviet Union, his armies had begun the Second World War by annihilating Poland with a *Blitzkrieg* (lightning war) attack. The next year France fell to the *Wehrmacht* (army forces of Nazi Germany). What the German Army had been unable to do in four years of fighting during the First World War, it accomplished in six weeks in 1940. The countries of Belgium, Holland, Luxembourg and Norway fell in quick succession. Following a desperate air battle in the fall, England alone held out against the Nazis.

Fascist Italy too had been aggressively expanding its control over foreign lands. Benito Mussolini sought to create a new Roman Empire and in 1935 attacked Ethiopia. This was followed in 1939 by the invasion of Albania and in 1940 by a much more difficult campaign against Greece. By March of 1941, the eyes of the two dictators were fixed upon the Kingdom of Yugoslavia.

The "Kingdom of the Serbs, Croats and Slovenes" had been established in 1918 at the end of World War I (the name changed to Yugoslavia in October 1929[1]). The country was formed through the

Treaty of Versailles by stripping each of the defeated Central Powers (Germany, Austria-Hungary, and Turkey) of territory. The former Austro-Hungarian provinces of Slovenia, Croatia-Slavonia, Dalmatia, and Bosnia-Hercegovina, were united with Montenegro and the Kingdom of Serbia, (including Macedonia, Vojvodina and Kosovo) to form the new nation. The capital was established at Belgrade and the Serbian king became the titular head of state.

Yugoslavia therefore was comprised of a patchwork of nationalities and ethnic groups. The population numbered approximately 16 million in 1941 and included some 6.5 million Serbs, 3.75 million Croats, 1.5 million Slovenes, 900,000 Macedonians, 800,000 Muslims, 400,000 Hungarians, 250,000 ethnic Germans, 400,000 Montenegrins and some 400,000 additional minorities including Czechs, Slovaks, Romanians, Jews and Gypsies.[2]

From the beginning, many Croats resented Serbian economic and political domination and yearned for independence. As a result, a Croatian terrorist movement, the Ustasha (from the verb *Ustati* meaning "to rise up"), sprang up in 1929 and in 1934, its members succeeded in assassinating the Yugoslav King Alexander I. Following the King's murder his son ascended to the throne as King Peter II. Since Peter was only eleven years old at the time, his cousin, Prince Paul, became Regent and head of state until the Axis invasion of 1941.

On March 25, 1941, under enormous pressure from Nazi Germany, the Yugoslav government of Prime Minister Diagisa Cverkovich was forced to become a signatory to the Tripartite Pact. Originally signed by the governments of Germany, Italy, and Japan on September 27, 1940, this treaty bound the three states together economically, politically and militarily. The three nations acknowledged spheres of influence; Germany was to be master of Europe, Italy would take control of the Mediterranean, and Japan would create a new order in the Far East. Should any one of the three be attacked by a nation not already involved in the European war or the Sino- Japanese conflict, the other two were honor bound to aid the third. Between November 1940 and March 1941, the countries of Hungary, Romania, and Bulgaria also joined the Tripartite Pact.

On March 26, one day after Prime Minister Cvetkovich added his signature to the Pact, huge demonstrations, organized mainly by the Communist Party, erupted in Belgrade condemning the government's actions. The following day, a small group of Yugoslav air force officers in a bloodless *coup d'etat*, ousted the regent, Prince Paul. In the wake of the removal of his cousin, King Peter II assumed control of the government and named a new Prime minister

Adolf Hitler, upon hearing of the Serbian public's opposition to being drawn into the Axis orbit and seeing an opportunity to destroy a creation of the German-loathed Treaty of Versailles, began planning the invasion of Yugoslavia. Strategically the destruction of Yugoslavia as a political entity would secure the German southern flank and enable the *Wehrmacht* to aid the Italians in their Greek campaign. On a more personal level, Hitler viewed the Serbian demonstrations against an alliance with his country as a personal insult. Following the events of late March 1941, the stage was set for the Axis invasion and dismemberment of Yugoslavia.

Although Mussolini had his hands full fighting the Greeks, he nevertheless welcomed the events occurring across the Adriatic. He viewed the situation as offering a golden opportunity to seize Yugoslav territory. Like Hitler, he blamed the Serbs for making hostilities necessary, comparing their actions to the assassination of the Austrian Archduke Franz Ferdinand in Sarajevo in 1914 that led to the First World War.[3]

The Nazi attack on Yugoslavia began on the morning of April 6, 1941 with an air raid on Belgrade. German troops, along with the Fascist armies of Italy, Hungary, and Bulgaria, poured across the borders. With some 52 divisions arrayed against it, the Royal Yugoslav Army was outmatched and overwhelmed. After only eleven days, the Yugoslav government surrendered and the young King Peter was forced to flee to London where he created a government in exile. Immediately, the five victors set about tearing Yugoslavia apart, like thieves eager for their shares of the loot.

Germany annexed northern Slovenia, while Italy annexed southern Slovenia (renaming it the Lubiana Province). Italy also annexed the Dalmatian coast, occupied Montenegro, and awarded its vassal state Albania the entire province of Kosovo and much of Macedonia. The regions of Bachka and Baranya in the north went to Hungary and Bulgaria received that portion of Macedonia that lay east of the Vardar River. Germany seized Serbia proper, including the fertile Banat region, and within days set up a military government. Finally, Croatia-Slavonia, the parts of Dalmatia that had not been taken by Italy, and Bosnia-Hercegovia were combined to form *Nezavisna Drzava Hrvatska* or the NDH (the Independent State of Croatia).

German troops entered Zagreb, Croatia on April 10, 1941. They were welcomed by the majority of citizens who were overjoyed to be free from "Serbian domination." Accompanying the Germans was Slavko Kvaternik, a former Lieutenant Colonel in the Austro-Hungarian army and a representative of the Ustasha organization. Kvaternik read a statement over Radio Zagreb proclaiming the existence of the new nation:

Croats!

God's providence and the will of our ally, as well as the hard centuries—long struggle of the Croatian people and the great efforts of our Poglavnik [Leader] Dr. Ante Pavelic and the Ustasha movement both at home and abroad, have determined that today, the day before Easter, our independent Croatian state arise.

I call upon all Croats wherever you may be, and especially all officers, non-commissioned officers, and privates of the entire armed forces and public security forces, to maintain perfect order, to report to the commander of the armed forces in Zagreb or the place where you are now stationed, and to take an oath of allegiance to the Independent State of Croatia and its Poglavnik.

As Plenipotentiary of the Poglavnik I have today taken control of the entire government and command of all armed forces.[4]

With this declaration, and the unconditional support of the Italians and Germans, Kvaternik seized power until Ante Pavelic, the founder of the Ustasha movement in 1930, arrived in the city.

The Ustasha (from the verb *Ustati* meaning "to rise up")[5] movement had but one goal: an independent Croatia.[6] To achieve that end, they employed violent tactics both within and outside of Yugoslavia. In addition to rejecting all association with other Yugoslavs, the Ustasha asserted Croatian sovereignty over any and all lands in which Croats had ever lived. They believed that only Croatian Catholics should have a voice in government and that minorities should have no rights whatsoever.

Before founding the Ustasha, Pavelic was associated with the outlawed Internal Macedonian Revolutionary Organization (IMRO) which sought Macedonian Independence. He was forced to flee to Austria, and from there to Italy, when the Yugoslav king Alexander created a special tribunal to deal with IMRO threats to the state. In 1929, Pavelic was tried in absentia and sentenced to death by a Yugoslav court. That year also marked the beginning of Italian sponsorship of Pavelic, as Mussolini, in a bid to destabilize Yugoslavia, gave 25 million Lire to IMRO.[7] In addition, the Italian dictator allowed IMRO and later Ustasha training camps to be established in Italy in which extremists were trained in the use of small arms and explosives.[8] In 1934 the Pavelic's Ustasha struck a major blow to Yugoslavia with the assassination of King Alexander as he arrived on a state visit to France. On October 9, Alexander and the French Foreign Minister Jean-Louis Barthou were shot to death as they drove through the streets of Marseille, by a Macedonian revolutionary named Vlada Chernozemski. The police immediately killed the assassin and arrested three Ustasha accomplices who were sentenced to life in prison (although they would be freed in 1940 by the Germans).

The French government quickly determined Pavelic and Eugen Dido Kvaternik, another Ustasha leader, were responsible for planning the attack. The French demanded their extradition from Italy. Although Mussolini denied the request, he was embarrassed by the international incident. He ordered the two leaders sent to prison for a year and a half. Pavelic was then placed under house arrest and monitored by the police once released. In addition, Mussolini ordered the disarming of Ustasha members within Italy.[9]

The Ustasha philosophy, which was first publicly expressed in 1932, was one of extreme nationalism mixed with unbridled hatred of Serbia as well as all "foreign elements" within Croatia. Foreign elements included three minority groups: Serbs, Gypsies, and Jews. Only "pure" Croats would have rights within the Ustasha's desired new state.

In 1941 as the "Independent State of Croatia" (NDH) was created, its population numbered approximately 6,700,000. This included 3,300,000 Catholic Croats, 2,200,000 Orthodox Serbs, 750,000 Muslims[10] (mostly located in Bosnia-Hercegovina), 170,000 ethnic Germans,[11] 40,000 Jews,[12] and 25,000 Gypsies.[13] For centuries, religious tension had existed between the Catholic majority and the Serb minority who were Orthodox Christians. Taking their cue from the Vatican, most Croats had always regarded Serbs as something less than true Christians. Partially due to Germany's growing influence in the Balkans, the ethnic German community or *Volksdeutsche* was tolerated, but more surprisingly, so too was the Muslim minority. The Ustasha actually made a special effort to win over this population; Bosnia was considered an integral part of the new state. It was dubbed the "heart of Croatia" while its people were known as the "flower of the Croatian nation." The inclusion of Bosnian Muslims, who hardly fit the criteria of "pure" Croats, was a cynical attempt by the Ustasha to set these people against the neighboring Serbs.

A new era had begun in Croatia, one that would see some of the worst atrocities committed during the Second World War and would be remembered as one of the darkest chapters in Croatian history. Pavelic arrived in Zagreb on April 15, having traveled from Italy with approximately 300 Ustasha loyalists. An additional 300 joined him in his new capital having returned from exile in Germany and Hungary. Overnight, this one time lawyer from Bosnia, who only days earlier had been merely the head of a small band of terrorists, now found himself the dictator of a nation. He immediately took the title of *Poglavnik* (leader), and assumed the posts of prime minister and foreign minister.

Over the next few weeks, Pavelic and his followers moved swiftly to consolidate their power. They banned all rival political parties, outlawed all non-governmental newspapers, seized all printing presses, and named deputies to the *Sabor* (Croatian Parliament). Throughout the war years, the *Sabor* would have no real power and would act simply as a rubber stamp for the Pavelic and his policies. Overjoyed at the prospect of independence, most Croatian people, especially those less educated, welcomed Pavelic with open arms. By May, some 100,000 new members had joined the Ustasha movement[14]

Even though Ustasha party membership had dramatically increased, the majority of Croatians continued to identify with the more moderate Croatian Peasant Party. Unfortunately, during the war years, this organization was ineffective as an opposition party having been outmaneuvered and left politically isolated by it's more ruthless rivals. Unlike the Ustasha, the Croatian Peasant Party, under the leadership of Vladko Macek, was never willing to become a tool of Germany or Italy in order to acquire a Croatian state separate from Yugoslavia. Throughout the 1930s, Macek's philosophy had been one of compromise. He and his party had striven toward establishing an autonomous Croatian region within the framework of the Yugoslav state. Following the events of early April 1941, this plan was obviously no longer feasible. With his options limited and despite his dislike of Pavelic, Macek ordered his people to cooperate with the new authorities once the Ustasha were in power. This action notwithstanding, Macek was still seen as a threat to the regime and was arrested and sent to the Jasenovac concentration camp. Unlike most inmates, however, he was not executed or worked to death because he was such a well known political figure. Eventually, Macek was released and placed under house arrest. Vladko Macek survived and, following the war, moved to France and then to the United States.

Even though most Croats had long dreamed of independence, and despite the public's exuberance at finally achieving that goal, the Ustasha never enjoyed widespread support within Croatia, primarily due to their violent methods. Many historians have argued that had it not been for the Germans and Italians, Pavelic would never have come to power. Over the course of the next few years, the Ustasha would lose what support they did have among the population due to several factors: the extreme measures taken against minorities; the persecution of political opponents; the leading of the nation into a disastrous war on the side of Nazi Germany; and the crippling of the economy by agreeing to bear the expenses of the occupying German and Italian forces stationed in the NDH.

The Ustasha government lost much of its public favor on May 18, 1941, when it was forced to cede practically the entire Dalmatian coast to Italy. This included most of the islands (except Pag, Brac and Hvar) and all of the major towns and ports (with the exception of Dubrovnik in the south).[15] The Ustasha had no choice as Mussolini had long sought to claim Dalmatia for Italy and the NDH was no match for the Italian military. A year earlier, on April 9, 1940, the Italian dictator raised the subject in a meeting with his Foreign Minister (who was also his son-in-law), Count Galeazzo Ciano. Ciano recorded in his diary, "When we were alone, the Duce talked about Croatia. His hands fairly itch. He intends to quicken the tempo, taking advantage of the disorder that reigns in Europe. But he didn't specify, except to say that he is convinced that an attack against Yugoslavia will not lead France and England to strike at us."[16]

Though the Ustasha government viewed Croatia's Jews as a foreign and alien people, Jews had in fact lived in Croatia since the Roman era. The Ashkenazi (Jews of Central and Eastern Europe) first came as traders during this period, while the Sephardim (Jews from Spain and Portugal) arrived in the early 16th century following their expulsion from the Iberian Peninsula. On the Dalmatian coast, the small Jewish communities of Split and Dubrovnik could trace their origins back to the 14th century. In Bosnia- Hercegovina, which had been part of the Ottoman Empire since 1463, the Turkish authorities welcomed Jewish refugees and valued their knowledge of business, and expertise in arms and ammunition manufacturing.[17]

Despite the fact that Jews had been present for centuries, the Ustasha were determined to create a Croatia for Catholic Croats only. In the minds of Ustasha leaders, Croats were considered "Aryans" and therefore much closer to Germans than to Jews or Serbs. On April 30, 1941, following Hitler's example, Pavelic's government passed the Law Decree on Racial Belonging. This law explained in minute detail how people were to be classified according to race. Those considered "Aryans" would, of course, be included as citizens of the new Croatian state. Jews and Gypsies however, were placed outside of this newly elite group. A person was considered to be a member of the Jewish race if he or she had three or more Jewish grandparents. A Gypsy was classified as such if that person had two grandparents who were Gypsies. This became the basis for all future anti-Jewish legislation. A mere two months later, those considered non-Aryans were stripped of their citizenship. The Law Decree on the Protection of Aryan Blood and Honor of the Croatian People was based in large part upon Germany's Nuremberg Laws of September 15, 1935. As in Germany, Jews were forbidden to marry or have sexual relations with Aryans. The employment of Aryan women under 45 in Jewish households was outlawed. Jews (and Serbs) were forbidden to serve in the military. Jews, but not other minorities, had to register with, and report their movements to, the authorities.

Worse was to come. Over the next two months, the Jews of Croatia were segregated, restricted in their contact with others in society, and publicly humiliated. Perhaps the most degrading law to be enacted was that which required the wearing of a symbol on the outer clothing marking the person as a Jew. This applied to everyone over the age of 14. Although this sign was standardized on June 4, 1941, as a yellow round metal plate with the center marked with the letter "Z" for *Zidov* (Jew), some local Ustasha leaders had already implemented their own version of this policy in late April and symbols varied from one community to another. In Zagreb, Jews were forced to wear two rectangular pieces of yellow cloth—approximately 5 inches by 3 inches, with a large letter "Z" in the center. One was to be worn on the front left side of the chest, and the other on the back at all times while in public. In the city of Osijek, Jews were identified by the wearing of a yellow ribbon.

In order to publicize the new laws, the government printed them in newspapers throughout the country. In May, the official NDH paper, *Hrvatski List* (Croatian Page), informed the population of Osijek of the new rules pertaining to Jews:

WARNING TO THE JEWS CONCERNING THEIR MOVEMENT IN THE CITY OF OSIJEK AND THE VICINITY

Without the ribbons Jews are not allowed to be outside their own houses.

Those Jews who failed to pick up the ribbons, must do so immediately at the Ustasha Headquarters, where they will be fined for negligence.

They may be in the city and the vicinity only between 6 am and 9 pm.

It is forbidden for Jews to frequent theaters, movies, restaurants, coffee shops, and buffets.

They may not walk in the parks or sit on public benches.

They may not meet and gather in their houses, and on the streets there may not be more than two together at the same time.[18]

On May 16, an Ustasha police official ordered the newspaper to print that "On work days they [Jews] may shop at the markets for groceries only from 10 am to noon. For other supplies they may shop from 3 pm to 5 pm. Those non compliant with these directives will be fined for the first offense 5,000 Dinars, second offense 10,000 Dinars, and 8 days in jail, and the third offense 25,000 Dinars and one month in jail."[19] Jews throughout the country were beginning to feel the first affects of government policies that, like those of Nazi Germany, were designed to isolate and humiliate them.

Jewish business owners were not only required to register their companies with the Ministry of the Treasury, they were also forced to post signs in the windows stating "Jewish shop" or "Jewish office." The government had determined that having even one Jew on a board of directors made that business a "Jewish company." The declaring of property applied to both men and women regardless of foreign nationality, as well as to their non-Jewish spouses. As for the disposition of such property officials made their position quite clear:

GUIDELINES FOR THE SALE OF JEWISH PROPERTY
Notice from the Ustasha Headquarters in Osijek
The sale of Jewish property is forbidden without the permission of the Ustasha Headquarters. Jews who wish to sell their property must have the list of properties for sale and the market value for each item. This list must be approved by the Ustaha Headquarters.
Jews who have already sold their property must declare in writing what was sold and to whom. Non -compliance with this order will result in severe punishment. It is strictly forbidden for Jews to sell any property without written permission from the Ustasha Headquarters.
Osijek, 23 May 1941
Croatian Ustasha Headquarters[20]

Over the next four years Ustasha officials would move from a position of strictly regulating the sale and transfer of Jewish property to outright seizure of such valuable assets.

Additional laws were passed aimed at segregating and controlling the Jewish population. All over the NDH, Jewish children were expelled from school, or if they were allowed to stay, they were seated at special desks. In order to restrict their access to non-government broadcasts, Jews, as well as Serbs, were required to turn in their radios.[21] In mid May, the Jews of Osijek were shocked by the news that they were to be thrown out of their homes. The Chief of Police issued the following instructions, "I order that all Jews from the upper town must relocate within one month. ... [They] must relocate outside the city limits within the given time. They may not inhabit the main road leading into the city. In the event they are unable to remove all their property and furniture from their houses they may store the furniture in one room. The keys to the house ...must be turned in to Ustasha Headquarters in Osijek."[22] A similar order was issued in Zagreb. Following the war, a witness named Slavko Radej testified before the State Committee for the

Investigation of War Crimes of the Occupiers and Their Collaborators. He stated:

> From May 6, 1941, Jews in Zagreb were prohibited from living in the Northern part of the city. Those who did not relocate within a certain time limit were immediately thrown out of their houses, and their property was seized. Beside that there were many cases where a single Ustasha walked into the houses of Jews in the permitted part of town, threw the owners out, and simply took their property away. I clearly remember these cases: One day two Ustasha walked into the family Weiss home, on Bukonjicevoj street, threw old Mrs. Weiss out, along with three other members of the family, prohibiting them from taking any of their property with them, they wouldn't even let Mrs. Weiss take her dentures with her. The same scenario happened to Mrs. Benedik, an old lady over 80... This kind of "relocation" was accomplished within a few minutes.[23]

In addition to being expelled from their homes, and having numerous restrictions placed on their daily lives, Jews were also vilified in the press. The government controlled radio stations constantly fed the population a diet of anti- Semitic propaganda. As in Germany, Jews were portrayed as parasites living off of the body of the nation. In the official media, Jews were depicted as a minority who contributed nothing to the country, its culture, or its people. As a result, from time to time groups of Jewish men were arrested, and as "punishment" were forced to perform manual labor. The authorities sought any excuse to implement such actions. In mid summer 1941, the following appeared in *Hrvatski List*:

JEWS ON FORCED LABOR
From the lower town Vrbnik to the rowing club "Drina" the new road is being built. [It] is being built by Jews who have demonstrated anti-German attitudes. They are punished by having to work as the forced labor building the road for 8 hours a day. Sometimes there are as many as 30

Jews, among them there are known to be wealthy Jews who have spent their entire lives in luxury. Now the rich Jews are digging, pounding, and pawing the road, so in the future they will perhaps appreciate the sweat and work of the working class. [24]

Members of the Ustasha were not above resorting to extortion. In May, several prominent Zagreb Jews were arrested. As Mr. Radej later explained, "The purpose of the arrests was to intimidate Zagreb's wealthy Jews and to force them, in the name of the Constitution, to surrender to the Ustashas 1,000 kilograms of pure gold (2,200lbs.) or equivalent value, in gold jewelry, precious stones, ...and foreign currency." He described the chilling experience of one hostage, "Julio Konig told me that Britvic [an official with the Ministry of Internal Affairs] put a revolver to his chest, and in a threatening voice asked him, 'Where is the Jewish gold?' Konig replied that there was no stashed pile of Jewish gold. ... Britvic then said that he would free them and let them go with the task of collecting [the gold], and that if they didn't there would be trouble. But if they did, then they would treat Jews with silk gloves." Fearing for their lives, the men formed a "Committee for Jewish Donations" which eventually raised the required amount. The Ustasha, however, were determined to get more, "At the same time, also at Britvic's request, ... the 'Committee for Jewish Donations' had to collect the best furniture for furnishing the offices of the Treasury, the offices of Marshall Kvaternik, for a German general, for Ustasha camps I and II, for police offices, and for the offices of the Ministry of the Military."[25] In effect, the Jews of the capital city had become hostages of their own government. Not surprisingly, even after the "ransom" was paid, the officials did not live up to the agreement, and the persecution continued.[26]

Not satisfied with simply robbing the Jews, the Ustasha next called for the total destruction of Jewish, as well as Serbian, culture within the NDH. The Cyrillic alphabet (used by Serbs) was banned, and the government, in a ludicrous move, attempted to "purge" the Croatian language of Serbian words (an almost impossible task since the two languages are almost identical). Nor were the houses of worship of the two groups spared. Throughout 1941, synagogues and Orthodox churches were destroyed all over Croatia. In some cases, small groups of Ustasha set fire to the structures, while in others the authorities found creative excuses to justify their actions. Many were demolished for "reasons of town planning." On October 12, the newspaper *Hrvatski Narod* (Croatian People) carried a brief piece entitled "Demolition of the Jewish Temple in Zagreb." The paper announced, "Yesterday afternoon, by order of the mayor Ivan Warner, demolition was begun of the Jewish temple in Zagreb. This decision was made because the temple was not in accord with the regulations of the city of Zagreb concerning architecture and décor."[27] The once beautiful synagogue lay in ruins, and in a cynical twist, the site on which it had stood was later turned into a parking lot for German military vehicles.

The Ustasha men were indeed a sinister lot. Pavelic's chief lieutenants included two members of a fiercely nationalistic family, the Kvaterniks. Slavko Kvaternik was named head of the armed forces. He was a vain man who took the title of Croatia's first Field Marshall. His son, Eugene "Dido" Kvaternik, was placed in charge of the secret police and of the concentration camps that were soon to be constructed throughout the NDH. Other top officials included Andrija Artukovic (also known as the Yugoslav Himmler), the Minister of the Interior, and Mile Budak, appointed Doglavik (Deputy Leader), as well as Minister of Religion and Education.

Budak had previously been known as a writer of novels with fiercely nationalistic themes. Now, in his new role, he saw to it that students were taught to revere the medieval Kingdom of Croatia, whose emblem, the red and white checkerboard was resurrected in the form of the country's new flag. In fiery speeches, he attacked Serbs as *"Vlaches"* (strangers or foreigners) who had no place in the NDH. On June 22, while speaking in Gospic, Budak went further when he declared that a third of the Serbs would have to convert to the Roman Catholic Church, a third would have to leave the country, and a third would have to die. His words were prophetic, for by

1945, the Ustasha regime had come very close to accomplishing this goal. The Justice Minister, Milovan Zanitch, was equally clear in stating the government's intention, "This state, our country, is only for Croats, and not for anyone else. There are no ways and means, which we Croats will not use to make our country truly ours, and to clear it of all Orthodox Serbs. All of those who came into our country 300 years ago must disappear."[28] With top officials espousing such positions in public, it is no wonder that when Italian Foreign Minister Count Ciano first encountered these men on April 25, he described them in his diary as a "band of cutthroats." Unfortunately, the ideas expressed by the leadership would soon inspire their followers to commit unspeakable acts of brutality and barbarism rivaling those perpetrated by the Nazis.

Death at the Hands of the Ustasha

In late April 1941, Pavelic unleashed the Ustasha militia on the Serbs, Jews, and Gypsies of the NDH. Over the next four years, the "wild men of the Ustasha," as the German and Italian troops called them, would murder hundreds of thousands of men, women, and children. In June, Hitler gave his seal of approval when he advised the Croatian leader to be ruthless when dealing with minorities. He went on to suggest that the best way to make sure the new state was successful was to pursue a "fifty-year-long policy of intolerance."[29] The first attack against a civilian target took place on April 27. In retaliation for the death of a Croatian soldier by persons unknown, 196 Serbian men from the town of Gudovac (55 miles east of Zagreb) and the surrounding area were murdered. On May 9, 400 Serbian peasants from the village of Veljun were slaughtered, and shortly thereafter, 260 Serbs from Glina were killed.

The tactics employed by the Ustasha throughout the summer of 1941 were both simple and effective. One favorite method was to summon a segment of the population under the pretext of serving the state on public works projects. The people were forced to gather at a specific time and place. Once assembled, the Ustasha would surround their victims and force them to march outside of the village where they would be murdered. At other times, the militia would quietly encircle a town and move through it indiscriminately killing every inhabitant.

The list of Serbian towns and villages that were annihilated is staggering. In Crevarevac, approximately 600 people were burned alive in their homes. In the town of Otocac, 331 residents, including the Orthodox priest and his son, were forced to dig their own graves. The people were then hacked to death with axes and their bodies thrown into the trenches. The priest's son was killed in front of his father and lastly the priest himself was tortured to death; his hair and beard were torn out, his eyes gouged from their sockets and finally he was skinned alive.[30] In another horrific act, after killing most of the townspeople of Susnjari, the militia locked twenty Serb children in a barn and set it on fire. Most burned to death and the few that managed to escape the flames were shot. Generally using primitive weapons, the Ustasha carried knives, hatchets, and hammers with which to crush their victims' skulls. In Dubrovnik, Italian soldiers were shocked to see a militiaman wearing a string of tongues that had been torn out of the mouths of murdered Serbs.[31]

Jews by the thousands were killed during this explosion of violence. Many were shot to death in raids, or taken as hostages, robbed of their possessions and subsequently murdered. In one instance, the Ustasha issued a written summons to a group of 107 men and boys who were told they were needed on a public works project in Koprivnica. Those men who refused the summons and chose not to report at the appointed time were arrested in their homes. Instead of being used for manual labor, Slavko Radej stated that the Jews were killed near Gospic in the following manner, "They were tied together with wires and placed at the rim of some ravine. The first one was pushed down into the hole, and the rest followed. After that Ustashas threw hand grenades into the hole. According to one native, and I heard this from his cousin, several days after the massacre, cries from the ravine below could still be heard."[32]

The ferocity of the Ustasha surprised even the Germans. The plenipotentiary to Croatia, General Edmund Glaise von Horstenau, himself no friend of the Jews or Serbs, observed that, "the Ustasha have gone raging mad."[33] He advised Pavelic to rein in the militia, not out of any sense of humanity, but for practical purposes. He argued that these actions, if left unchecked, would foment rebellion on the part of the Serbs, thus making it much more difficult to control the countryside.

Despite Hitler's advice to Pavelic on handling ethnic minorities, the German diplomats stationed in Zagreb recognized that it was in their country's interest to have peace restored to the NDH. This would allow agricultural products and raw materials to be exported to the Third Reich without interruption. To that end, the German ambassador Seigfried Kasche objected numerous times to the actions of the Ustasha. Pavelic finally took action. On June 26, 1941 he issued an Extraordinary Law Decree and Command which was designed to control Ustasha excesses, mainly against Serbs, and restore order to the countryside. It had little effect as many militia units simply ignored the order. With regard to the entire Jewish population, the document stated, "Since Jews spread false reports in order to cause unrest among the people and since by their speculation they hinder and increase the difficulty of supplying the population, they are considered collectively responsible. Therefore the authorities will act against them ... they will be confined in assembly camps under the open sky."[34] This "internment" of Jews was the first step in a process that would lead to the deaths of thousands of people in concentration camps. As Pavelic sought to control his rampaging militia he was clearly more comfortable with murdering Jewish victims in an organized methodical way; concentration camps would soon be established throughout Croatia.

Those Serbs, Jews and Gypsies that could flee, made desperate attempts to leave the NDH. Most tried to cross the border into Serbia and by the middle of 1942, some 200,000 people had done so. This pleased the Croatian authorities as they hoped to expel as many Serbs as possible. For Jews, however, flight offered no guarantee of safety. Serbia was occupied by the German army, and led by the collaborationist regime of General Milan Nedic. Within a week of the fall of Belgrade, the Germans had begun to register Serbian Jews. In August of 1941, thousands of Jewish men were interned in one of three camps (located on the outskirts of Belgrade, Nis and Sabac). In the fall, the German army began mass executions, and by mid November some 5,000 men had been murdered in these camps. In December, thousands of women and children were interned and shot soon thereafter.[35]

The internment and execution of Jews in Serbia took place in the wake of the German invasion of the Soviet Union where special *Einsatzgruppen* (special action squads of the SS that followed the German army) had already begun to murder Jews. This was prior to the *Gross Wannsee* conference of January 20, 1942 at which the decision was made to implement the "final solution" to the Jewish question. The phrase "final solution to the Jewish problem" was used by the Nazis throughout the war to denote the physical destruction of the Jews of Europe.

The execution of Jews in Serbia increased as new political events unfolded in the country. Following the German attack upon the Soviet Union, on the morning of June 22, 1941, the Yugoslav Communist Party issued a formal call to arms against the Germans, Italians and Ustasha. Since all Communist parties looked to Moscow for leadership the fact that the Soviet Union was now in the war against Germany energized and inspired young Communists to join resistance movements throughout Yugoslavia.

The Yugoslav Communist Party, led by the Croatian born Josip Broz (who had adopted the alias "Tito" in 1934), was to become the primary military force opposing the Germans and their collaborators both in Serbia and Croatia. Partisan attacks on Fascist positions and outposts began in earnest in the autumn of 1941. In response, German soldiers executed scores of Jews and Serbs.

On September 16, Hitler issued a particularly barbaric order that was meant to combat uprisings in the occupied lands. The directive, which was strictly complied with in Serbia, called for the execution of 100 hostages for every German soldier killed and 50 for every soldier wounded. The Germans made sure to include as many Jews as possible in these executions. By mid 1942, the fate of Serbian Jews was sealed. With the exception of those who had gone into hiding or joined the Communists, the vast majority, approximately 15,000, were killed.[36]

Within the NDH, as the Ustasha continued their murderous activities throughout the summer of 1941, Serbs were offered a chance to save their lives by converting to Catholicism. Thousands were "persuaded" to change religions in this manner. Catholic priests working with Ustasha units conducted mass conversions in predominately Orthodox towns and villages all over the country. During the war years approximately 300,000 people were baptized. The vast majority of those who were forced to accept the Catholic faith were peasants, while members of the intelligentsia, teachers, wealthy merchants, and the Orthodox clergy, were deemed "unacceptable." In fact some 700 Orthodox priests were murdered between 1941 and 1945.[37]

Yet the offer of conversion to Catholicism was not extended to the Jews. NDH laws stipulated that Jews were not a religious group but rather a race and were not allowed the option of converting to save their lives.[38]

Although the Vatican officially opposed forced conversions, many priests supported this and other policies of the Ustasha regime. Father Dionizio Juric, Pavelic's confessor, stated, "Any Serb who refuses to become a Catholic should be condemned to death"[39] and in a shocking pronouncement which clearly advocated mass murder, one Father Srecko Peric advised, "Kill all Serbs. And when you finish come here, to the Church and I will confess you and free you from sin."[40] In the summer of 1941, the Ustasha bloodlust was so great that even Serbian peasants who had converted were not safe. In numerous villages the Ustasha swept in and massacred the inhabitants despite their conversions. Of the senior Church leaders in Croatia, only the Bishop of Mostar, Alojzije Misic, openly criticized the government and advocated friendship with Serbs. The other dozen Bishops either remained silent or actually supported the goals of Ante Pavelic and his henchmen.

With regard to the slaughter in Croatia, the most senior official of the Catholic Church, Alojzije Stepinac, the Archbishop of Zagreb, had a decidedly mixed record. Stepinac had always been a staunch Croatian nationalist and publicly stated his support for the new Ustasha regime on April 12, 1941. Two weeks later, he issued a circular letter that called upon all priests to cooperate with the new state. The archbishop believed that Croatia was threatened from all sides. Orthodox Serbs represented a challenge to the Catholic Church within the country; Communists and Freemasons represented a threat from outside the country due to their support for a unified Yugoslavia in the interwar period. At first Stepinac remained silent in the face of the bloodshed taking place around him. In mid 1942, he tried to justify his silence by stating that if he were to condemn the actions of the government, the Vatican would order him into a monastery (most likely just an excuse). Should that occur he explained he would be unable to defend the thousands of orphaned children, many of them Serbs, then in his care. Whether or not the Pope would have taken such action against Stepinac is uncertain. Throughout the war, the Holy See retained good relations with the Croatian government, despite the fact that it opposed the idea of forced conversions and never officially recognized the Ustasha regime. The lack of formal diplomatic relations was in line with the Vatican's tradition of not recognizing new governments that emerge during wartime.

To his credit, however, the Archbishop did intervene on several occasions with government officials to save the lives of individuals, including Jews in mixed marriages. In one instance, Stepinac saved fifty-five elderly residents of a Jewish old age home, and sheltered them on a church-owned estate near Zagreb.[41] By 1943, with the Allies making progress on all fronts, Stepinac gradually came to realize that Germany was losing the war and that the Croatian state may not survive. At this point he began to criticize Nazi policies publicly, and by extension those of the Ustasha.

In October 1943 an event occurred that had a profound impact upon the Archbishop. His brother Misko, a member of the Partisan Liberation Committee of his home village of Krasic, was captured and executed by the Germans. The Archbishop responded in his sermon:

> The Catholic Church cannot admit that one race or one nation, because it is more numerous or better armed, may do violence to a smaller nation with fewer people.... The

system of shooting hundreds of hostages for a crime, when the person guilty of the crime cannot be found, is a pagan system which only results in evil.... We condemn all injustice; all murder of innocent people; all burning of peaceful villages; all killings; all exploitation of the poor. We sorrow for the miseries and the sadness of all who today suffer unjustly, and reply: the Catholic Church upholds that order which is as old as the Ten Commandments of God.[42]

From this point until the end of the war, the Archbishop continued to be closely associated with the NDH. Had he spoken out sooner and more forcefully, he would surely have saved lives with his great influence as both the highest ecclesiastic official in the land and as Pavelic's Apostolate Vicar of the Ustasha Army. Yet since the Archbishop had refused to discipline clergymen involved in atrocities, many considered him to be complicit in the murder of hundreds of thousands of people.

Death in the Croatian Concentration Camps

Following Hitler's example, the Ustasha established a network of concentration camps throughout the country to control so-called "undesirables" and "enemies of the state" (such as Jews, Serbs, Gypsies, and dissident Catholics). The first concentration camp in Croatia was created on April 29, 1941 at Danica, approximately 50 miles northeast of Zagreb. Twenty more soon followed. Though the camps were scenes of torture and mass murder, they were referred to in typical bureaucratic terms as "collection" or "purifying" camps. The worst included Jadovno near Gospic, Loborgrad, Sisak, Slano on the island of Pag, and Tenje near Osijek. The largest and most infamous of all was Jasenovac. This complex consisted of a series of five camps located near the confluence of the rivers Una and Sava that were constructed between August 1941 and February 1942.

The Jasenovac camp system was massive, extending over 120 square miles from Stara Gradiska in the east (a former prison converted into a concentration camp for women and children) to the village of Kraplje in the west. Jasenovac was strategically located

along the Zagreb-Belgrade railway. This allowed for the easy movement of prisoners to the camp, although thousands would also arrive
by wagons and on foot. Bordered by three rivers, the Sava, Una, and
Velika, the entire area was a swampy plain, which made escape
extremely difficult.

The poor living conditions at Jasenovac ensured that many prisoners did not last long in the camp. Those who were not murdered
upon arrival suffered from a combination of a poor diet, lack of proper sanitation, and cruel and sadistic treatment by the guards. The
only times conditions improved, albeit temporarily, were prior to the
rare visits of international organizations such as the Red Cross.

The camps came under the jurisdiction of, and were the responsibility of, the Ustasha Surveillance Service headed by Vjekoslav
"Maks" Luburic. The blame for the atrocities committed within
them thus must be placed on the Croatians themselves and not the
Germans. Although the Germans did maintain a small group of ten
soldiers as a "liaison" with the Ustasha at Jasenovac, the camp was
strictly under Croatian authority. In the broader context, however,
the Nazi camp system did serve as a model for the Croatian camps.
In early October, Luburic, at the direction of Pavelic and Kvaternik,
visited Germany. While there, as a guest of the Nazis, he was given
a tour of German concentration camps. Upon his return, he set
about reorganizing Croatia's camps, modeling them upon those he
had seen in Germany.

As in Germany, the arrest and deportation of individuals to concentration and labor camps was conducted in a "legal" manner
through the issuing of a number of decrees. The Law Decree on the
Deportation of Undesirables and Dangerous Persons to Detention
and Labor Camps was implemented on November 25, 1941. On
July 10, 1942, another decree was issued that increased the state's
power and led to an influx of prisoners to the camps. The Law
Decree on the Suppression of Punishable Acts against the State,
Individuals, or Property allowed for people accused of such crimes
to be sentenced to terms between six months and three years in a
camp.[43] The law went on to state that should the individual responsible fail to be apprehended by the authorities, other family mem-

bers would be taken in place of the perpetrator. In addition, all property of those arrested could be, and often was, nationalized.[44]

The prisoners who arrived at Jasenovac consisted of Serbs, Jews, Gypsies, and opponents of the Ustasha regime. Although Jews were occasionally sent to this death camp directly from their native towns, they were more often first assembled in Zagreb or Sarajevo from other parts of the country before being shipped to the camp.

Most Jewish victims were murdered soon after their arrival at special execution sites that had been erected on the right bank of the Sava, near the village of Gradina. While the idea of using gas chambers to kill prisoners was briefly considered, none were ever built at Jasenovac. Instead, the methods of execution were simple and typical of the brutality and viciousness demonstrated so often by the Ustasha. At times the guards killed their victims by stabbing them to death or by crushing their skulls with blows from axes and hammers. In some cases, groups of people were hanged or shot and their bodies then thrown into the Sava.

Between 1941 and 1945, there were between 3,000 and 6,000 prisoners in Jasenovac at any given time. Few lasted longer than three months, after which time, according to camp rules, they were murdered to make room for new arrivals. Camp officials allowed those who belonged to certain professions or who possessed specialized skills to live-at least temporarily. Doctors, Nurses, shoemakers, electricians, and gold and silversmiths were put to work within the camp. They remained alive only as long as they remained useful to their Ustasha overlords. Inmates died from many causes including the periodic typhus and cholera epidemics that ravaged the camp. The torture and executions that occurred were condoned and encouraged not only by Luburic, but also by the various camp commanders, including two of the most notorious, Miroslav Majstorovic and Dinko Sakic. In one of the most grotesque events of the entire war, a contest was held on the night of August 29, 1942 in which the guards competed to see who could kill the largest number of prisoners. After several hours, one Petar Brzica was proclaimed the winner. Using a specially designed knife dubbed the *srbosjek* or Serb-cutter he is reported to have cut the throats of 1,360 people. While this figure is undoubtedly an exaggeration, (it was put forth by Dr. Nikola Nikolic, a prisoner serving as a camp doctor), the fact remains that the event did take place. The actual number of those murdered is probably several hundred.[45] As a reward for this "achievement," Brzica was proclaimed the "King of Cut-Throats" and awarded a gold watch, a silver service, a roasted suckling pig and wine.

In the summer of 1942, officials at Jasenovac prepared to receive thousands of new prisoners. In June and July, the Germans and Ustasha launched combined military operations against the Communists in the area of Mount Kozara in northwest Bosnia. As the Fascists swept through the region, approximately 40,000 Serbian villagers were rounded up and deported. Most of the men were killed in Jasenovac, while many of the women were separated from their children and transferred to Germany to work as slave laborers. Even children were shown no mercy. Of some 23,000 taken along with their families, 11,000 were murdered, and many others were dispersed throughout the country to be adopted by Catholic families or raised in orphanages.[46]

One eyewitness who lived to tell his tale was Ilija Ivanovic. Ivanovic, then a boy of thirteen, realized that he would only survive in Jasenovac by mastering skills that the Ustasha deemed useful. He soon became apprenticed to a locksmith and a barber. He described how the peasants' terrifying ordeal began even before they reached the concentration camp, "Black [uniformed] Ustashas were walking around and watching young women and maidens. The young girls were hiding in wagons, pretending to be ill and dressed as old people. The Ustasha took Milka from the neighbor's wagon. After some time, Milka came back in tears with a torn skirt and blouse. Her mother went to her—crying, ...and quietly cursing the Ustasha." The horrified youth went on to say, "That night many maidens and women were raped. One woman never came back. What happened to her, we have never heard."[47]

Dr. Nikolic described how the guards at the camp used some inmates to kill others to make room for the newly captured Communists and their families. Groups of Gypsies were stationed in the village of Gradina where they were forced to dig graves for, and then murder, the prisoners. "German people would amass Serbs from Kozara and give them to these degenerates of our people (Ustasha) for liquidation…. [Those seen as unfit for work] were taken across to Gradina. They were liquidated until 11:00 at night."[48] Once the Gypsies were no longer needed they too were killed.

Ivanovic also would not forget the horrors he saw and experienced in Jasenovac. He noted that the guards were especially brutal to prisoners working in the Clay pits:

> Prisoners the Ustasha thought were more dangerous because of their politics worked in the *baer*…. Conditions for work were incredibly hard and inhumane. Men worked all day digging wet clay and loading it in special carts that a special engine with iron chains pulled into the producing hall. They had to work in all kinds of weather conditions— muddy, wet. Skinny and with chains on their legs, they looked like phantoms. The Ustasha had whips in their hands all of the time. They were watching these poor people and were whipping them for any reason…. They tortured prisoners in countless and merciless ways. They were always trying to make the prisoners' lives more miserable. Boards were placed in the hole, across which wheelbarrows full of clay were pulled. Ustasha guards would put mud and water on these boards so people would fall down in the mud. Then the guards would hit them with shovels and … prevent them from coming out of the mud. But when a man somehow managed to stand up, the guards would push him back, laughing at him sarcastically and sadistically enjoying his attempts to save his life.[49]

Although gas chambers were never employed[50] at the camp, another German innovation was put to use. Within Camp III there was a large oven that was used to bake the clay bricks, but following the Nazi example, it was converted into a crematorium for disposing of many of the bodies of murdered inmates.

At various times, the camp administrators turned their atten-

tion specifically to Jews. Following the war, several survivors reported the systematic methods used by the guards. One witness stated,
"For three days Ustasha supervisors were collecting sick, weak, and
old Jews from the barracks, thus picking some 800 Jews working in
Jasenovac on November 17, 18, and 19, 1942. First they collected
them in a special collective chamber, and then they transported
them over the Sava to Gradina on [sic] one night. Here they had to
dig their own graves, to be killed and buried by Gypsies." Another
camp survivor described how in late 1942 several Jewish women and
children who had recently arrived from the women's camp in
Djakovo were killed in Gradina. In yet another incident "At the end
of December 1942, night, the Ustasha [went] to all the barracks,
took the Jews from their beds and drove them out of the barracks in
the bitter cold" Most were killed that night, those that remained
were murdered soon thereafter.[51]

To the outside world, Jasenovac was portrayed as a work camp.
Like their Nazi counterparts stationed in death camps scattered
throughout Europe, officials at Jasenovac carefully concealed the
fact that people died of starvation, disease, and exhaustion brought
on by overwork. One such "work project" involved the building of
a large earthen dam. Since the complex was located in a low lying
plain subject to floods when heavy rains caused the Sava to rise, the
decision was made to transform the existing smaller dams into one
large protective barrier. As Ilija Ivanovic recalled, many who were
forced to build this structure did not live to see it completed:

> The prisoners called it the 'dam of death.' All day, exhausted
> and hungry prisoners were digging the ground, loading it
> into wheelbarrows, and with their last strength, pushing
> them to the dam. Almost all of them were barefoot and in rags
> that were hanging on their skinny bodies—live skeletons.
> Every day the hard job with little food was exhausting pris-
> oners to the extreme that many of them were falling down
> . . . and they couldn't get up. First, Ustashas would try to
> make one get up with whips, and when they saw that the
> poor man couldn't stand up, an Ustasha would order the rest

of them to put dirt on him and bury him. That's how live people were buried and built into the dam.[52]

Although the Ustasha touted the importance of such construction projects it quickly became apparent to the inmates that the cost of such "improvements" would be their very lives.

To the Jews of Croatia, it seemed as if the whole country had become one giant slaughterhouse. By early 1942, it had become quite clear that they were targeted for annihilation. Thousands were dying in concentration camps, or being massacred in government sponsored raids.

In a desperate effort to save their lives, those who could still flee saw only one hope: escape into the Italian zone of occupation. It was a desperate gamble since the Italians were also Fascists and officially allied to Germany and the NDH. There was no guarantee that the Italians would not hand over the Jews to the Ustasha upon their arrival. But there was simply no alternative. The terrified refugees hoped and prayed that they would be treated humanely by the Italians.

1   N. Thomas and K. Mikulan, Axis Forces In Yugoslavia 1941-5 (Oxford: Osprey Publishing Ltd.1995), p.3.
2   Ibid.
3   Richard West, Tito And The Rise And Fall Of Yugoslavia (New York: Carroll and Graf Publishers, Inc. 1994), p.70.
4   Jozo Tomasevich, War and Revolution in Yugoslavia, 1941-1945: Occupation And Collaboration (Stanford: Stanford University Press, 2001), p.53.
5   John Cornwell, Hitler's Pope: The Secret History Of Pius XII (New York: Viking, 1999), p.249.
6   The idea of Croatian separatism can be traced to the mid 1800s when Croatia was still part of the Austrian empire. The Croatian Law Party proposed a "Greater Croatia" which was also to include Bosnia-Hercegovina, and Dalmatia.
7   Avro Manhattan, Terror Over Yugoslavia: The Threat To Europe (London: Watts and Company, 1953), p.42.
8   Rebecca West, Black Lamb And Gray Falcon: A Trip Through Yugoslavia (New York: Penguin Books, 1940), p.19.

9   Tomasevich, p.35.

10 Cornwell, p.250.

11 Tomasevich, p.282.

12 Ibid., p.592.

13 Ibid., p.609.

14 Ivo Goldstein, <u>Croatia: A History</u>, trans. Nikolina Javanovic (London: Hurst and Company, 1999), p.134.

15 Ibid.

16 Hugh Gibson, ed., <u>The Ciano Diaries 1939-1943: The Complete, Unabridged Diaries Of Count Galeazzo Ciano Italian Minister For Foreign Affairs 1936-1943</u> (Garden City, New York.: Doubleday and Company, 1946), p.234.

17 Centropa, "Excerpts from Jews in Yugoslavia- Part 1," Centropa Reports [home page on-line]; available from <u>http://www.centropa.org/reports</u>; Internet; accessed May 26, 2005.

18 State Committee for the Investigation of War Crimes of the Occupiers and Their Collaborators, July 21, 1947 (Zagreb) p.1, Trans. [from Serbo-Croatian] George Radich, Croatian State Archives.

19 Ibid.

20 Ibid., p.2.

21 Although other Croatians were allowed to keep their radios, they faced the death penalty if caught listening to banned stations such as Partisan radio, or the BBC.

22 State Committee, p.3.

23 Ibid., May 21, 1947, p.2.

24 Ibid., July 21, 1947, p.5.

25 Ibid., May 21, 1947, p4.

26 In September 1943 the SS would use the same tactic on the Jews of Rome.

27 State Committee, July 21, 1947, p.62.

28 Manhattan, p.60.

29 West, <u>Tito</u>, p.79.

30 Cornwell, p.252.

31 Manhattan, p.66.

32 State Committee, May 21,1947, p.4.

33 Cornwell, p.254.

34 Tomasevich, p.593.

35 Lucy Davidowitcz, <u>The War Against the Jews 1933- 1945</u> (New York: Bantam, 1975), p.392.

36 Tomasevich, p.588.

37 Avro Manhattan, <u>The Vatican's Holocaust</u> (Springfield, Missouri.:

Ozark Books, 1986), p.88.

38 Chief Librarian Julija Kos,—Jewish Community of Zagreb, interview by author, Zagreb, Croatia, July 13, 2005.

39 Manhattan, <u>The Vatican's Holocaust</u>, p.69.

40 Ibid. p.68.

41 Goldstein, p.139.

42 Tomasevich, p.557.

43 Ibid. p.399.

44 Ibid.

45 Curator Dorde Mihovilovic, - Jasenovac, interview by author, Jasenovac, Croatia, July 12, 2005.

46 West, Tito, p.129.

47 Ilija Ivanovic, <u>Witness to Jasenovac's Hell</u>, trans. Aleksandra Lazic (Mt. Pleasant, Texas: Dallas Publishing Company, 2002), p.31.

48 Ibid. p.56.

49 Ibid. p.69.

50 Ibid. p.131.

51 Ibid.

52 Ibid. p.81.

2

REFUGE IN THE ITALIAN ZONE OF OCCUPATION

From the outset of World War II, the "independent" state of Croatia was far from an independent country and was in fact heavily influenced by both Germany and Italy. Although in the latter years of the war Germany's power in the Balkans surpassed Italy's, in 1941 the Axis partners viewed each other more or less as equals in the region. Foreign ministers Joachim von Ribbentrop of Germany and Count Galeazzo Ciano of Italy signed an agreement in Vienna on April 22, 1941 that divided Croatia between the two nations. A demarcation line was drawn roughly down the middle of the new country with the German military controlling the northeastern sector and the Italian Army occupying the southwestern sector.

The Germans enjoyed friendly cooperation with the Pavelic regime and had the Axis forces triumphed, it is not difficult to imagine Hitler withdrawing his troops and leaving Croatia in his hands. Italian—Croatian relations on the other hand were never as smooth. Despite Croatia's public expressions of friendship and ideological solidarity, Croatian officials resented Italy's attempt to dominate the Adriatic and seizure of much of the Dalmatian coast. They especially resented Italy's annexation of two key cities: Trieste, which had been

43

officially taken following the First World War, and Fiume (Rijeka), which had been handed over to Italy by treaty in January 1924. These difficulties not withstanding, Pavelic traveled to meet Mussolini in Rome in May 1941. With high profile ceremonies in both countries, a series of agreements was signed on May 18 which theoretically laid the foundations for harmonious relations between the two states.

The May 18 agreements finalized the borders and, with a strange twist, created an Italian-style monarchy for Croatia headed by a member of the Italian royal family. A search was conducted in order to find a suitable candidate to hold the purely symbolic title of "King of Croatia." After some time, the Italian government selected Aimone d'Aosta the Duke of Spoleto. Interestingly the Duke never actually set foot in Croatia due to the fact that the Italians could not guarantee his safety.

The Italian zone of occupation, into which Jews and Serbs fled for their lives, extended approximately eighty miles inland from the Adriatic coast. It was divided into three sectors known as Zones I, II, and III. Zone I comprised that portion of the Dalmatian coast that was formally annexed by Italy. This area included the coastal cities of Sibenik and Split and contained a population of some 380,000 people, the vast majority of whom had no desire to become Italian citizens. Zones II and III extended to the demarcation line, east of which the Germans occupied. In these areas it was understood that military matters were controlled by the Italian army, while the Croatians were permitted to retain authority over civil affairs.

Throughout the war years, the Italian Second Army, the army that had participated in the initial invasion and destruction of Yugoslavia, was the army of occupation in western Croatia as well as southern Slovenia. Although its numbers fluctuated during the war, in 1941 its total strength consisted of twelve infantry and two mobile divisions, or approximately 100,000 soldiers. For most of the war, the command headquarters was located in the coastal city of Susak with a succession of three commanding generals: Vittorio Ambrosio, Mario Roatta, and Mario Robotti. All three men thought it had been a mistake to allow the creation of a Croatian state that, in their view, was hostile to Italy and Italian interests. In addition, the three generals were to a greater or lesser degree sympathetic to the plight of the Jews and Serbs. On May 9, 1942, the Italian Second Army was renamed the Superior Command for Slovenia-Dalmatia (*Comando Superiore delle Slovenia-Dalmazia*) or Supersloda.[A]

Following the May 18 agreements that defined the boundaries between Croatia and territory claimed by Italy, the Italian army withdrew to Zone I, the coastal area that had been formally annexed by Italy. This withdrawal did not last long, however, as in mid-August, Italian civilian and military officials unilaterally decided to reoccupy Zones II and III. Giuseppe Bastianini, the Governor of Dalmatia, put forth the argument to Mussolini that it was necessary to extend Italian military control inland. The excesses of the Ustasha had forced the Serbs to organize to defend themselves and the threat of civil war was imminent. The Italian coastal zone was thus in danger.

After meeting with Pavelic to inform him of the plan, General Ambrosio issued the order for Supersloda to reoccupy Zones II and III on September 7, 1941. Ambrosio felt the reoccupation (a word which Croatian officials avoided using in public speeches) was necessary for political, military, and humanitarian reasons. He believed Italian political control must be firmly established throughout their entire sphere of influence in such a way as to make clear to the Zagreb government who controlled this region. Like most Italian military officers, Ambrosio had no love for the Ustasha. From a strategic point of view, this redeployment of forces made sense as Tito's partisans were increasing their activities. Although the size of Tito's army was growing it would not pose a serious threat to the Axis forces for another two years.[1] Finally, from a humanitarian perspective, it was becoming apparent that Ustasha units were moving across the border from the German controlled zone and committing atrocities against Serbs, Jews and suspected Communist sympathiz-

---

[A]Tito's partisans became a potent force in 1943 because by then they had the numbers, were being supplied with weapons by the British and Russians, and Italy had dropped out of the war.

ers within Zones II and III. It did not go unnoticed that these atrocities served to drive more people into the ranks of the Communists, for as the war progressed and life became more difficult for the average Croatian, those who came to oppose the Ustasha saw the Communists as the best hope of overthrowing the regime and driving out the Germans and Italians.

As the Italian army moved toward the demarcation line, it was welcomed with open arms by those minorities that had been persecuted and terrorized by the Ustasha. In Bosnia-Hercegovina, Serbs, who had fled their towns and villages to escape Ustasha raids, began to return to their homes. In Mostar an extraordinary incident occurred. After several thousand people had assembled in the main square to welcome the Italians, a young girl, whose parents had been murdered by the Ustasha, stepped forward, presented the commanding officer with flowers, and begged him in the name of all those assembled for the protection of the Italian army.[2] Protection from the Italian army could not have come soon enough.

As a result of the carnage witnessed, the sympathies of large numbers of Italian soldiers now lay with the brutalized minority civilians. After elements of the 6th Bersaglieri Regiment of (an elite infantry regiment) witnessed an Ustasha attack upon the village of Gracac, their commander, Umberto Salvatores, appalled by what he had seen, compared it to scenes in Dante's Inferno. The soldiers' sympathy concerned the Italian military authorities to such a degree that on August 17, an Italian commander, one General Ferrari Orsi, felt it necessary to send a message to all commands reminding them that, "The Serbs are our enemies...the Croatians are our allies...In a situation like the actual one it is possible to make a mistake."[3] It was becoming clear to the higher ranking officers that many of their men were showing signs of compassion toward people that were deemed to be their enemies. This is the "mistake" to which the general is referring.

At first it was junior officers (and in some cases even non-commissioned officers) who took matters into their own hands in order to stop the slaughter of Jews and Serbs by the Ustasha militia. Salvatore Loi, a young second lieutenant, along with a handful of men, intervened to stop the massacre of 400 Serbs who were about to be killed near Gracac. They then proceeded to protect another column of fleeing Serbs and Jews.[4] Another enterprising lieutenant devised a unique way to save the lives of a group of Jews by carrying them past the Ustasha—in Italian tanks. The Croatians were informed that a number of tanks were being sent to engage partisans who were thought to be operating in the area. Instead, the Italian soldiers proceeded to take the Jews aboard the tanks and drove right past the militia. Although the Ustasha members were suspicious, they did not confront the Italian soldiers directly at the time. Some time later however, a letter of protest was sent by the Ustasha to Second Army headquarters. The officers involved were court-martialed, found guilty, and sentenced- to two days house arrest.[5]

There is no doubt that top army officials knew of the efforts of their subordinates to save Jews and Serbs. As a result these same officials were quite lenient when it came to disciplining their men for such unauthorized behavior. Following the war, General Ambrosio stated in a report to the General Staff (the most senior military men of the army) that "The Command of the Second Army, being fully informed of everything that was happening in the Second and Third Zone…not only acquiesced in all that its officers, N.C.O.'s and men were doing to save the lives of thousands of Serb[s] and Jews, but did nothing to hinder them using military transport for this purpose."[6]

Naturally, not all Italian soldiers went out of their way to aid minority refugees. There were certainly those who were indifferent to the plight of Jews and other minorities. However, the fact that many Italian soldiers took action with the tacit approval of their superiors demonstrates great humanity on the part of Italian troops during the war. While the average soldier felt more or less indifferent toward Jews and Serbs upon arrival in Croatia, the shear brutality of Ustasha compelled many to take action to stop such horrific acts of violence.

One would be hard pressed to find similar examples of sympathy toward persecuted minorities among German troops. After years of Nazi propaganda, most German soldiers considered Jews and

Communists their mortal enemies to be dealt with in the harshest possible terms. Unlike that which was occurring in Italian occupied Croatia, in lands conquered by Germany in 1941 such as Lithuania, Estonia, or the Ukraine, and Western Russia German soldiers had already begun to slaughter Jews on a massive scale.

In an effort to escape the Ustasha and save their own lives, some Croatian Jews hoped to escape north into Italy itself. It was a long and harrowing journey and there was no guarantee that they would be allowed to cross the border once they reached the Italian frontier. One such refugee was Ivo Herzer. The boy and his family, along with a few other Jews, while desperately trying to stay one step ahead of the Ustasha, temporarily stopped to rest in a small town. There they found help from an unexpected source. He recalled:

> The situation seemed hopeless. But by chance, a few Italian soldiers who were garrisoned there passed the house where we were staying, and my father, just on intuition, approached them and told them two words. He did not know that much Italian but he said simply, "Ebrie paura" [Jews fear]. The soldiers immediately reacted and answered, "Niente paura," which means fear nothing." Soon their sergeant arrived. He spoke a little French and told us that he would try to get us on an Italian Army train bound for Italy and thereby, of course, save our lives.

> We didn't believe him, but at midnight that night he came with a few soldiers, none of whom we had seen before, who did not demand money… but escorted us to the railroad station and put us on an Italian Army train. They actually boarded the train with us.

> The train was full of Italian soldiers, surprised to see this bunch of 12 or 15 bedraggled civilians running away. But somehow, he was able to explain to them, probably using the words "refugees," "poor people," or even "Jews." I don't know how he did it. I didn't speak Italian at the time, but he managed to get us across the border into the Italian city of Fiume.

But the sergeant didn't stop there. He went to the authorities, asked that we be given food and drink, which was promptly given, and then he took leave. I don't know his name, but I do know that hundreds of Croatian Jews were helped to escape from Croatia, where only death awaited them, into the Italian zone by men like this sergeant.[7]

This is yet another example of the benevolent attitude of many Italian soldiers toward Jews who, desperate to save their own lives, had nowhere else to turn.

General Orsi's communiqué to Italian soldiers warning against showing undo compassion for persecuted minorities and keeping in mind that the Communists were the real enemy is indeed telling. It was becoming apparent that the Ustasha, nominally Italy's ally, were increasingly being viewed by Italians as adversaries if not actual enemies. This aided Jews and Serbs in that whenever possible the Italian army sought to restrain the murderous activities of the Ustasha. One husband and wife who were grateful for the presence of the Italians were the Hirschls. Trapped in a village in Hercegovina during a battle between the Ustasha and the partisans, Julia Hirschl remembered, "Fortunately the Italians arrived, naturally to help the Ustasha, but at the same time they helped us refugees." Following the military engagement the army protected and aided the couple in their efforts to reach Kupari, near Dubrovnik on the Dalmatian coast.[8]

While happy to have the Ustasha militia assist them against the Communists, the Italians were increasingly becoming fed up with their brutal actions against civilians. In the wake of the reoccupation, the Italian military finally banned all Ustasha, and most Croatian army units, from its territory. While the government in Zagreb was privately outraged at having its soldiers removed from what it still considered Croatian territory, diplomatic niceties were observed and publicly it accepted the Italian military's decision. Notwithstanding what Pavelic viewed as "a humiliating" decree, both the Italians and Ustasha continued as before with the business fighting the Communists in their respected areas.

In addition to the Communists, the other opposition to the Fascist occupation of the former Yugoslavia came from the Chetniks. This organization had been created soon after the Axis invasion of Yugoslavia by Royalist army officers who were loyal to the exiled King Peter. The Chetniks were led by the Serbian nationalist Dragolyub (Draza) Mihailovic. Although in theory the Chetniks and the Communists were fighting on the same side, in reality they had entirely different goals. Tito's partisans hoped to drive the Fascist Germans and Italians out and establish a Communist state modeled on the Soviet Union, while Mihailovic wished to see a revived Yugoslavia, led by the young King Peter and dominated by Serbia. Although the two leaders met three times in late 1941, they could not reach an understanding. Mihailovic soon came to view the Communists as a greater threat than the Germans and Italians. After a few early clashes with Axis troops, Mihailovic changed course and began collaborating with the Germans and Italians.

In February and March 1942, several agreements were signed between the Chetniks and Pirzio Biroli, the Italian military governor of Montenegro (one of the major regions that constituted the kingdom of Yugoslavia), as well as with individual Italian division commanders. In accordance with the agreements, the Chetniks in Montenegro would cooperate closely with the Italian army in joint operations against the Communists. The Italians, who were undermanned in this theatre of operations, welcomed the assistance from the Chetniks. (Montenegro which encompasses some 5,000 miles was garrisoned by only 8 divisions of the Ninth Army then headquartered in Tirana, Albania.)

For the next year and a half, Italy armed and supplied their new partner, the Chetniks. Chetnik units were considered auxiliary troops and fought with the Italians and Germans in most areas of the former Yugoslavia, including the NDH.

This new collaboration between the Italians and the Chetniks was yet another cause of friction between the Italians and Ustasha officials. While the Communists remained the Ustasha's primary foe, the Ustasha also viewed the Chetniks as a dangerous new threat to their hold on power. The Italians, on the other hand, sought to use Chetnik fighters against the Communists and were not greatly concerned if this upset the Croatian government.

The German military command was never as comfortable with the Chetniks as the Italians were, as the Germans believed that they could not be trusted. In fact, an unsuccessful effort was made in early 1943 to pressure the Italians to disarm these Serb nationalists.

Although Great Britain initially supported the Chetniks, by May 1943, they had reluctantly established contact with Tito's headquarters. While the British and Americans much preferred the Chetnik idea of a post-war Yugoslavia controlled by the royal family, it was the Communists that were bearing the brunt of the fighting and gaining the support of the common people. By the middle of the war, Allied strategists had determined that the Chetniks were of little value in the battle against the Axis. The following year, the Allies decided that because of the Chetniks' collaborationist activities with the Italians and Germans, they could no longer support the Chetnik cause. For the rest of the war, despite the wishes of the Yugoslav government in exile (which was being led from London by King Peter), all aid from the Allies, including money and weapons that had been earmarked for the Chetniks, was instead redirected to the Communists. The Soviet Union followed suit and sent supplies to the Communists. Thus, as the war progressed, the strength of the Communists continued to grow while that of the Chetniks slowly declined.

The conflict that raged between 1941 and 1945 within the former Yugoslavia was one of the most complicated of any in Europe during World War II. Axis forces were pitted against resistance fighters, both Communist and non-Communist; what we would today term "ethnic cleansing" occurred within Croatia, and a civil war erupted between Tito's Communists and Mihailovic's Chetniks.

While the populations of all ethnic groups in the former Yugoslavia suffered at one time or another during the war, the Jews had an especially difficult time. While Jews in Serbia were marked for death by the Nazis (In 1941 and 1942 the Germans interned and then shot almost all 12,000 Serbian Jews) those in Croatia were being targeted by the Ustasha.

In accordance with Communist ideals, Tito welcomed all who

would fight for the Communist cause, including Jews. This idea of inclusiveness not only increased the ranks of Tito's troops, but it also allowed the partisans to make use of Jews with specialized training (e.g. doctors, nurses, and engineers who would be of great value to any army in wartime). The Chetniks, however, did not accept Jews from the beginning and actually turned some away who tried to join. This situation was reminiscent of that which had occurred during the Russian Civil War that followed the October Revolution of 1917. In that instance too the Tsarist or "White" Russian forces did not welcome Jews, whereas the Bolsheviks or "Reds" happily accepted into their ranks members of the various minorities of the former empire. As with his Communist predecessors in the Soviet Union, Tito's policies of inclusion and superior organizational skills would eventually see the partisans emerge victorious.

Flight to the Dalmatian coast

In the first months of the war, those Jews and Serbs who could frantically tried to evade the bloodthirsty Ustasha by escaping to Italian occupied Dalmatia. They arrived by train, cart, wagon, and on foot. Thousands sought to cross the boundary to that part of the Croatian coast that had been formally annexed by Italy. This formerly Croatian territory offered hope to the fleeing refugees since the Ustasha had no authority there and could not pursue them into territory that was now considered part of Italy proper.

One such refugee was Desiree E. Originally a native of Zagreb, she had been living with her husband in Belgrade at the time of the Axis invasion. Since she spoke German fluently, she boldly went to Gestapo headquarters and, after denying she was Jewish, invented a story about needing to visit her sick uncle in Susak, Dalmatia. A travel permit was granted and the couple departed for Dalmatia. Other members of her family managed to escape to Portugal, although her father, a World War I veteran, perished in Jasenovac. Looking back on the experience, she said of the Italians, "They were occupiers but they were very nice and kind, human, they were *mensches* [people of quality]."[9] After having to register with the local officials every day for eight months, Desiree's husband was ordered to be deported to the internment camp at Ferramonti Tarsia in Italy proper. Following Italy's entry into the war, a number of camps had been created to imprison enemy aliens. Any foreign national with an anti-Fascist past was subject to arrest and incarceration. At this point the couple was offered a choice: Desiree's husband would be sent to the camp or they could remain together under the Italian system of enforced residence. This policy, which was employed throughout the war, consisted of the individual in question being placed under light police surveillance and confined to a small town or village. Although he/she was required to register frequently with the police, movement within the town was unfettered. Not surprisingly, the couple chose to be sent to a village in the Alps north of Milan.

Upon their arrival, Desiree and her husband found that 250 Jews were also living there under the same conditions. In January 1943, the local authorities became concerned for the safety of these people as more German troops moved into the area and advised them to move on. Unsure of what to do or where to go, the refugees were again assisted by Italian soldiers. Desiree recalled, "The Italian army walked with us through the Alps in the snow for two days and three nights and brought us to Switzerland."[10] Upon arrival of the refugees at the border, the Swiss guards initially refused the group entry until after much discussion over the telephone, an Italian officer persuaded officials to allow the band into Switzerland. The fact that Italian soldiers concerned themselves with the wellbeing of a few desperate refugees in the middle of a war is extraordinary. Thankfully, the lives of Desiree and many others were saved by such compassion.

Unfortunately, due to geography, not all Jews were in a position to escape into the Italian zone of occupation. Before the war, the vast majority of Croatian Jews lived in what would become the German occupied zone. Zagreb contained the largest number, approximately 12,000, followed by Sarajevo with 8,000. Only between 800 and 900 Jews lived in what would become the Italian occupied lands. After the war began, Jews saw how much better conditions were for them in the Italian zone. Entry visas were required not only to move into Dalmatia, but also the Italian annexed area surrounding the city of Fiume (Rijeka) and the Lubiana District of Slovenia. Many Jews and Serbs who lacked the necessary document nevertheless attempted to slip across the borders. Those who succeeded in the early days had to live with the knowledge that if caught they could be sent back to the NDH and into the waiting hands of the Ustasha.

Originally Giuseppi Bastianini, Governor of Dalmatia, was reluctant to allow masses of people to enter his territory. For reasons of internal security, politics, and finances, he did not wish to take in and care for thousands of Jews and Serbs. He therefore ordered the army to refuse entry to any more refugees and to expel those already in the province. Fortunately for those refugees, the order was never implemented. Bastianini apparently realized that they would be killed if returned to the NDH and had a change of heart. One event that surely must have influenced Bastianini's decision was the discovery of the bodies of murdered Jews and Serbs on the Island of Pag in September 1941. The Croatian government had ordered the creation of temporary internment camps there to hold Jews and Serbs. Some Serbs were to be transported to Serbia proper, while many of the prisoners were to be shipped to other camps including Jasenovac. As word spread of the Italian army's reoccupation of its sphere of influence (zones II and III), the Ustasha massacred the prisoners rather than let them be taken by the Italians. The Italian troops were shocked by what they found. They unearthed the bodies of almost 800 Jews, including 407 men, 293 women, and 91 children.[11] There was evidence that some people had been buried alive. Some four thousand Serbs had also been brutally butchered. The news of this atrocity was quickly communicated to the Italian government, the Italian King Victor Emmanuel III, Second Army Headquarters, and the governor's office.

Over the next few months, the question of what to do with the refugees in Zone I, where most of the Jews had fled, remained unanswered. Within the Italian army, there was disagreement over the issue. General Renato Contturi, Commander of the Fifth Corps (assigned to the northern coastal sector), had no great sympathy for the Jews, and pressed for their expulsion. Fortunately for the refugees, he found no support for this idea among staff members at Second Army headquarters. In May 1942, representatives of the Italian army, Governor Bastianini, and the Foreign Ministry each advocated various plans only to have them rejected by the others.

Bastianini at first wanted to settle the Jews in an area of Croatia, to be selected in consultation with the Croatian Government. According to his proposal, the Foreign Ministry would first have to elicit from the Ustasha a guarantee that no harm would come to these people. The Croatians would also have to pledge that the refugees would be treated humanely and that they would be provided with proper housing. Foreign Ministry officials, as well as Bastianini himself, realized that this was unrealistic in the face of mass murder that was taking place within the NDH.

The Italian diplomats in Zagreb conceived of a plan which was supported by Foreign Minister Ciano and that called for the army to concentrate and care for the refugees in Zones II and III. Army commanders were less than enthusiastic about the idea since by mid 1942 they had their hands full dealing with Communists. General Roatta stated that the army was already protecting some 300 Jews, which was proving difficult since the Ustasha were constantly demanding that they be turned over to them.[12] The general had resisted these demands in part because rumors had begun to circulate about the brutality occurring at the Jasenovac concentration camp. Roatta felt that whatever course of action was ultimately decided upon, refugees should not be turned over to the Ustasha. In a message to the governor, Roatta stated, "We have guaranteed them [the Jews] a certain protection and have resisted Croatian pressure to deport them to a concentration camp. It is my opinion that if Jews who have fled to [Italian] annexed Dalmatia were consigned to the Croatians, they would be interned at Jasenovac with well-known consequences."[13] The "guarantee" that Roatta spoke of stemmed from the final segment of General Ambrosio's order of September 7, 1941 in which he had stated, "All those who for various motives have abandoned their country are herewith invited to return to it. The Italian armed forces are the guarantors of their safety, their liberty and their property."[14]

General Roatta put forth the suggestion that since many Jews were already in Zone I they should be allowed to remain there, with the provision that they be sent to one of the islands off the Dalmatian coast where they would be safe. Bastianini rejected this idea, as he feared that caring for a large number of Jews and Serbs would be an expensive and time-consuming responsibility, and the various officials continued to search for a solution.

The influx of Jews and Serbs into Dalmatia continued. In a report sent to Mussolini on November 17, 1941, Bastianini stated that his officials had determined that at the time of the initial occupation in 1941, 1,000 Jews had been living in Split (the city was referred to as Spalato by the Italians), but that the population had since swelled to 4,000.[15] Other cities experienced similar population increases. By the middle of 1942 the number of Jews in Dubrovnik had mushroomed from 150 to 1,000 and that of Mostar had grown from 50 to 200.

Bastianini went on to report that some 500 people had been transferred from Dalmatia to internment camps in Italy. Bastianini wanted to relieve himself of the responsibility of caring for these Jews and the Jews were happy to get farther away from the Ustasha. The governor also reported that the Jews had written to their families expressing their gratitude to the Italian authorities for the move. In addition, the vice president of the Jewish community had met with the prefect of Split and asked him to continue with the relocation of Jews to Italy.[16]

The Germans were well aware of the influx of refugees into Italian occupied territory (including Zones I, II, and III) and naturally were becoming concerned with the situation. Especially galling to them was the fact that Italian soldiers were getting along well with Jewish civilians. In December 1941 one *Oberleutnant* (First Lieutenant) Weiss reported to his superiors that in Dubrovnik:

> The relationship between Italian officers and Jews and Serbs, is an absolutely undeniable fact. Italian officers are often seen with Jewish women in the Café Crodska. ... In Dubrovnik there are about 500 Jews. Most of them came

from Sarajewo and were brought here with Italian help. 10,000 to 15,000 *kune* is the normal price for smuggling across the border with false passes. . . . In Mostar things are cruder still. The Italians simply revoke all Croatian orders and let the city overflow with Jews. . . . The director of the German Academy in Dubrovnik, Herr Arnold was invited . . . to a reception . . . and was outraged by the arrogance of the Italian General [Giuseppi] Amico. . . . With regard to Croatia he said that the Italians were there to protect the poor and persecuted—Jews and Serbs—from brutality and terror.[17]

Clearly relations were not harmonious between the supposed allies.

While in German-occupied Croatia and Serbia Jews were being exterminated, in the Italian zone, no actions had been taken against Jews. Attacks by the Ustasha had been thwarted by the Italian military. In fact, there were a few instances in which the Italians actually prevented Croatian civil authorities from imposing discriminatory measures. As had occurred in cities and towns throughout the German occupied zone of Croatia, the Ustasha government sought to impose discriminatory laws aimed at degrading Jews. Such was the case in the city of Karlovac. The mayor complained to the German Ambassador Siegfried Kasche that Jews were housing Italian officers and, as if that were not bad enough, when he attempted to pass anti- Jewish ordinances, the Italians prevented the laws from taking effect.

Many German officers assumed the Italians were taking bribes in exchange for helping Jews. This offered the only possible explanation as to why Jews were allowed to enter Italian territory and treated well thereafter. In some cases, of course, this was true. It was not uncommon for refugees to pay bribes to cross at checkpoints. On the other hand, there were cases in which Italian soldiers and police simply looked the other way and allowed people to enter without the proper documentation.

One man who was able to bribe his way into Italian territory was Dr. Edo Neufeld, a Jewish lawyer from Zagreb. He spoke of his experiences in Croatia after escaping with his family to Switzerland. Neufeld, after having been arrested and sent to a prison camp at Kerestinec, was soon transferred to the concentration camp near Gospic (at which some 8,000 Serbs were murdered). After working as a cook in the camp, he was eventually transferred and was able to bribe an Italian driver to take him into Zone I. From there he fled to Switzerland in November 1942.[18] While Neufeld admired the Italian position of allowing Jews to live unmolested along the coast, he still believed the Italians could have done more to stop the murders of Jews and Serbs committed in the first few months after the initial invasion of April 1941. The doctor also observed what the Ustasha really thought of their Italian partners.

Neufeld noticed the subtle resentment and low -level hostility on the part of the Ustasha directed toward the Italians. He recalled, "They were treated insultingly by the Ustasha. If an Italian officer dared to stroll with a local girl, she was arrested immediately by the Ustasha, taken to their headquarters, had her hair shorn as punishment, and was then thrown out onto the street." The absurdity of the situation was not lost on him, as he further observed, "At the same time, the press of both countries overflowed with professions of friendship."[19]

To the world it appeared the fascist nations of Croatia and Italy were standing shoulder to shoulder, whereas the reality was, and always had been, quite different. The Ustasha despised the Italians as land grabbing interlopers while the Italians considered the Ustasha to be murderous barbarians.

As in the Independent state of Croatia, in Serbia too, Jews were being murdered at an astonishing rate. In Serbia, however, it was the German army, aided by collaborators, that was committing mass murder. The step by step process that led to the elimination of the Jews was very similar to that which had been set in motion by the Ustasha. In April 1941 the Jews of Serbia were forced to register with the German authorities, as well as to begin wearing a Star of David badge for easy identification. In May the German military commander issued regulations forcing Jews to register their property, additional orders were designed to force them from the economic life of the country. In August, the Germans carried out the first internment of Jews. Three concentration camps were eventually built, but even before they were operational, mass shootings of men, women and children had begun. By the middle of the war, the vast majority of Serbia's Jews were dead. Very few saw the danger early enough and had the means and opportunity to escape.

One family that did manage to escape was that of Dr. Alex R. from Belgrade. Alex was a boy of seven when the Germans invaded. He remembered thinking of himself more as a Serb than a Jew at the time, a distinction that would have been lost upon the Germans. At first no one knew what to expect from the invaders. He remembered his grandfather trying to put a group of Jews at ease by saying, "Don't worry these are the people of Bach and Beethoven…and there is no way they are going to do evil things to you."[20] Shortly after the surrender of the Royal Yugoslav Army, three *Wehrmacht* officers were quartered with Alex's family. The officers were polite, well educated and got along quite nicely with the family. Knowing that the SS would soon arrive, the officers advised their hosts to leave the country as soon as possible. The SS *(Schutzstaffel)* was the Nazi Party's military unit and was in charge of carrying out Adolf Hitler's plan for the liquidation of Europe's Jews. Responding to the question "Where can we go?" the Germans stated, "America, that's the only place you'll be safe."[21] A tremendous sense of anxiety gripped the family as their world, which had seemed safe and secure, was quickly becoming very dangerous.

Once the SS appeared anywhere in occupied Europe, including Serbia, they immediately began to assemble lists of the names of Jews. Alex described their callous brutality, "I saw babies being shot and killed by the SS just for the hell of it . . . In the market place a woman was carrying a baby, a very small baby . . . and the German said bist du Jude? [Are you a Jew?], and the woman said nein [no] and he said du bist ein Jude [You are a Jew] and took her baby and killed it on the spot."[22] Rather than waiting for the Nazi storm to blow over (as so many others were prepared to do) Alex's family decided it was time to flee. Unfortunately his Grandparents were caught and sent to Jasenovac where they died, while his Aunt, Uncle and their baby managed to cross into Hungary. After escaping to Split, Alex's father bribed one of the train's Italian coachman to help move his wife and son into the Italian zone. As mother and son hid in a locked compartment, Gestapo agents searched the train for Jews and Communists. The Gestapo (an acronym for *Geheime Staatsspolizei* or Secret State Police) was one of the most powerful and feared organizations during the war. As the German agents reached Alex's compartment, the Italian begged the men not to make him open the door, as he was secretly smuggling liquor. He agreed to pay them two cases of the illegal alcohol and the boy and his mother remained undiscovered. Once they arrived on the Dalmatian coast the family was reunited. The atmosphere that had so recently been one of fear changed immediately, "The Italian soldiers were wonderful, they gave us candy . . . and talked to us." Alex further observed that, "there was no visible anti-Semitism on the part of the Italians, there was on the part of the Croats."[23] After a short time the family was able to bribe its way onto a cruise ship bound for Italy and from there they flew to Spain then on to Cuba. Eventually Alex was able to make his way to the United States.

Those few Jews who were able to move into the Italian zone or to Italy itself were truly the lucky ones (Jews and Serbs moved into the Italian zone but only Jews tried to move on to Italy. The Serbs could avoid the Ustasha and ultimately move to Serbia). Although they still faced an uncertain future that included possible deportation and death, for the moment they were safe and a semblance of normalcy could return to their lives. The fact that the Italians did not confiscate the refugees' money and valuables made life easier. In some cases, Jews were even assisted by the Italian Jewish relief organization DELASEM *(Delegazione Assistenza Emigranti Ebrei)*.

As for Jews who could not reach Dalmatia, their prospects for survival were grim. The Ustasha did its job well and by the end of 1942, of the approximately 39,400 Jews who had been living in the Independent State of Croatia (which included Bosnia-Hercegovina and Dalmatia),[24] only 12,000 remained alive.[25]

The persecuted Jews of the NDH would soon find a much needed friend in the man who assumed command of Italian forces in

Croatia. On January 20, 1942, General Mario Roatta took command of the Second Army replacing General Ambrosio. The new commander would prove to be a pivotal figure in the rescue of Croatian Jews. At age 55, General Roatta was young for the position, but as a career military man, he already had a wealth of experience. Prior to the war, Roatta had served as chief of military intelligence. He had seen action in 1936 during Spain's civil war as field commander of Italian "volunteers" sent by Mussolini to fight with the Fascist troops of General Francisco Franco. Roatta had also spent time in Berlin as a military attaché. He spoke German and was admired and respected by Italian and German officers alike. One German officer described him as "very sharp witted" and Edmund Glaise von Horstenau, the German plenipotentiary in Zagreb, was impressed by his thoroughness and his knowledge of mountain and guerrilla warfare.[27]

The general and his wife moved in high social circles and, according to a secret service report, enjoyed a "luxurious life style" as well as an open marriage of "free principles."[26] Their marital arrangement was not unique among Italy's powerful couples, Foreign Minister Count Ciano and Edda Mussolini lived in much the same way.

The area (Zones I, II, and III) over which Roatta assumed command was far from peaceful. The Italian army was dealing with a serious rebellion in occupied Slovenia and with Communist partisans in Zones II and III. To make matters worse, there was a shortage of manpower as Italy also had troops in North Africa. Italian soldiers were assigned the task of patrolling major roads and defending towns and strong points known as *presidios*. Many of these isolated mountain garrisons made easy targets for Tito's partisans. It was clear to Roatta that the overstretched Italian army was incapable of fully occupying the half of Croatia which Italy controlled on paper. To add to his worries, Roatta had to deal with cross-border incursions by the Ustasha as well as perform a balancing act by working with the Chetniks (who were despised by the Croatian government since they were Serbs, while retaining good relations with Pavelic's regime.)

It was thus decided to consolidate the Italian Army's power by withdrawing most units back into Zone I. An agreement to that end was signed on June 19, 1942 between Supersloda and the Croatian government. The document, which was signed by Roatta and Pavelic, stated that the Croatians would assume all civilian and military power in Zone III and civilian and police power in Zone II.

Although the Croatian government was in general thrilled, as they had long pressed for Italian withdrawal, they accepted certain provisions reluctantly. These stipulations included the official recognition of the Chetniks and agreement not to attack them as well as leaving the railroads in Italian hands. Additionally, although Ustasha units would be allowed to operate in the two zones, they were forbidden to launch military operations without the permission of Supersloda. The Italian military had the right to countermand any Croatian civil measures taken in the two zones and, most importantly, the Italian Army had the right to reoccupy the territory at any time for security purposes.

Although General Roatta withdrew his forces into Zone I, he had no intention of allowing the Croatian government to completely replace Italian influence in Zones II and III.

Of course the people that benefited the most from the Italian withdrawal were the Communists. In southeastern Bosnia and northeastern Hercegovina, prior to June, the Communists had been constantly fighting German, Italian, Croatian, and Chetnik soldiers. The June 19 agreement gave them time to regroup and, more importantly, it allowed them to move into northwestern Bosnia, located in Zone III, from which they could launch new attacks on Fascist lines of communication.

The Germans influence events in Dalmatia

The persecution and murder of Croatian Jews (as well as other minorities) by their fellow countrymen lasted from May 1941 until August 1942. Thereafter, a policy shift took place in which it was decided to allow the Germans to deal with the remaining Jews in Croatia. In May 1942, a request was made by the Ustasha to the German government to have the German authorities deport the

Jews to Eastern Europe. What happened to these "undesirables" following their deportation was of course of no concern to the Ustasha government. The proposal was accepted and was implemented in the middle of August. Almost immediately, some 5,000 Jews in the German sphere of influence were arrested and sent to concentration camps in Eastern Europe.[28]

The Italians first became aware of this decision, which affected all Jews in the NDH, including those in the Italian zone, by sheer accident (The Germans did not see the need to inform the Italians of this plan at first). On June 20, 1942, a group of German officers and engineers working for Todt passed through the city of Mostar in the Italian Zone II. Todt was a construction company and semi-military organization involved in several large government building projects throughout the war years and was overseeing the mining of bauxite in the surrounding area. The Todt men were invited to join Italian General Paride Negri for lunch. During the course of conversation, the topic of where the German personnel were to be accommodated was brought up. The head of the German delegation, General Schnell, stated that there was no need for concern as there would soon be plenty of space once the local Jews were deported. A surprised Negri immediately responded, "Oh, no this is totally impossible, because the deportation of Jews goes against the honor of the Italian army."[29]

The two generals soon reported the incident to their respective superiors. A dispute had thus begun that would pit Italians and Germans against each other and would decide the fate of 3,500 Jews. Over the next year, several Italian Foreign Ministry officials working with senior military officers would seek to buy time through a number of delaying tactics in order to save the lives of the Jewish refugees. These men included Blasco Lanza d'Ajeta, Chief of Staff to Count Galeazzo Ciano, Italy's Foreign Minister; Count Luca Pietromarchi, the Head of the Occupied Territories Department; and Vittorio Castellani, the Foreign Ministry's liaison officer with the Second Army. The German Foreign Ministry, however, was not about to let the Jews escape. Those most insistent in their demands were Foreign Minister Ribbentrop, his Under-Secretary Martin

Luther, and the German ambassador to Croatia Siegfried Kasche.

The Ustasha apparently believed that in order to carry out their plans of ridding their country of Jews, German help would be needed to pressure the Italians into cooperating. Resisting German pressure would not be easy for the Italians. It was one thing for them to reject Croatian demands regarding the Jews; it would be quite another to refuse to cooperate with their closest and most important ally. Two years earlier it had become clear to most observers (although Mussolini would not have admitted it at the time) that Italy was the junior partner. German force of arms had come to Mussolini's aid in Greece and, as the wider war ground on, German economic aid (e.g. coal shipments) proved vital in attempting to stave off the inevitable collapse of the Italian wartime economy.

It was only natural that the Ustasha government would request German assistance, as their Fascist ideology, with its emphasis on race and blood, was much closer to Nazism than to Italian Fascism. While Mussolini did allow, and at times even encouraged, anti-Semitism in the press, Italian Jews were not subjected to mass executions as Croatian and Eastern European Jews were. Mussolini believed Fascism had to be ruthless in dealing with leftist opponents, including Communists, trade unionists and democrats, but he did not identify Jews as specific enemies. Despite the fact that anti-Jewish laws had been passed in Italy in 1938, one could live a relatively normal life as an Italian Jew provided one professed loyalty to the state.

On June 23, Vittorio Castellani, the Italian Foreign Ministry's liaison officer with Supersloda, dispatched a telegram to the Foreign Ministry in Rome in which he reported the conversation that had occurred in Mostar. He had been informed that at that meal the Germans had also let slip the destination of the Jews; they were going to be shipped to areas in Russia occupied by German forces. He further stated that the senior officers were of the opinion that this policy should not be allowed to take effect in the areas under Italian control.[30] Five days later Lanza d'Ajeta responded, "For reasons of a general nature this Ministry agrees that the said agreement between the governments of Germany and Croatia should not be carried out in the areas under our occupation."[31] This marked the beginning of a cooperative effort on the part of senior soldiers and Foreign Ministry officials to obstruct the implementation of the German plan and thereby save the lives of the Jewish refugees.

The officers of Supersloda believed that the German-Croatian agreement would surely do damage to Italian prestige in the region. Setting aside the humanitarian aspects of such a pact, the agreement infringed upon Italian sovereignty, as the Italians had not even been informed immediately that such an agreement existed. In addition, it would send the wrong message to their Chetnik allies who might wonder, if today the Jews are handed over to the Germans, tomorrow we may be surrendered to the Ustasha. Soldiers as well as diplomats also dismissed as unfounded the German charge that Jews in the Italian zone posed a significant security risk. On several occasions the Germans had already made their concerns known to Ambassador Casertano. They accused the Jews of committing acts of espionage, and cooperating with the Communists partisans, allegations that the Italians could not substantiate, and therefore did not take seriously.

Over the next month, the Italians took no action against the Jews which frustrated Foreign Minister Ribbentrop enormously. In early August, Ribbentrop decided to act. On the morning of August 18, he sent the Minister of State at the German Embassy in Rome, Prince Otto von Bismarck, to see Blasco Lanza d'Ajeta, Ciano's Chief of Staff. In his hand, the grandson of Germany's famous chancellor carried a telegram from Ribbentrop. The message asked that the Italian government instruct its military not to interfere with the German-Croatian agreement for the transfer *en mass* of Jews from the Italian zone to territories in the East. During their meeting, Bismarck revealed that the Jews were not actually going to be resettled but rather "the purpose of the planned operation was in fact their physical dispersal and elimination."[32]

Why Bismarck made such a statement is still an open question as he was not on especially good terms with Ciano's staff. Bismarck had a low opinion of Italians in general and did not like working with the Italian diplomats. Many viewed him as arrogant and condescending. In October 1944, after the Allies had liberated Rome, an official of the Italian Foreign Ministry described Bismarck as:

> Though a grandson of the great chancellor, he [Otto Christian von Bismarck] was nothing like the founder of the German Empire. He did not inherit [his grandfather's] physical stature, that of a Pomeranian Grenadier (his face was flabby, he wore glasses, his hair was pomaded and curled) nor even a modicum of his intellectual power. It did not prevent him however from imitating, as much as he could, his grandfather's arrogance. The young Bismarck was afflicted with an inferiority complex in regard to the English and the Anglo-Saxon world generally, a frequent manifestation with all Germans which, with the upper class takes the form of a kind of nostalgic snobbism. And this sometimes impelled him—in a quiet voice, and among people of whom he felt sure—to venture a few critical remarks about certain manifestations of Nazi policy. For the rest he carried out the orders he received, no matter how revolting they were, overcoming the disgust he may have felt, with the aid of a deliberately unpleasant harshness.[33]

Bismarck was told that the German request would be sent on to Ciano and Mussolini for a decision within a few days. Perhaps it was Bismarck's conscience that made him speak out, but whatever the reason, for the first time members of the Italian diplomatic corps were made aware of the grim fate that awaited these people.

Over the next few months, the true nature of the Holocaust would be revealed to Italian government officials through a variety of sources. While Hitler used the cover of war to commit his acts of genocide, he never directly informed any of his Axis partners of his plans to murder the Jews of Europe. Rumors, of course, were widespread all over Europe about what was happening to the Jews, but it would not be until 1945, with the liberation of the concentration camps, that the sheer magnitude of what had occurred would be revealed. During the war itself, the use of such euphemisms as "resettlement" and "relocation to the East" were very effective at concealing the Nazi's true intentions. Nevertheless, in 1942 and 1943, reports began to trickle in to the various Italian ministries from Italian military units fighting in Russia and businessmen traveling in Eastern Europe about mass murders and the existence of death camps. Some diplomats turned a blind eye to this information, or dismissed it as wildly exaggerated, while others took it seriously and were prepared to do whatever they could to help the persecuted.

On August 21, Ciano met with Mussolini. The foreign minister was apparently unwilling to take a stand on the Nazi policy of slaughtering Jews without first knowing where the dictator stood on the matter. Mussolini was handed a summarized version of Lanza d'Ajeta's memorandum that contained Ribbentrop's request, as well as Bismarck's warning. If Ciano was afraid to commit to a position the same could not be said of Mussolini. On the question of consigning the Jews to the Germans in a bold hand across the top of the memo he wrote *"Nulla osta"* (No objection) and signed it "M."[34] With these two words Italy's leader had for all intents and purposes condemned to death over 3,000 people. At the time it appears Mussolini did not think twice about his action. After all these people were not even Italians and he was cooperating with the wishes of the German Foreign Ministry and by extension those of Adolf Hitler.

At the end of August, Lanza d'Ajeta, following instructions from Mussolini informed the Supreme Command of the Armed Forces *(Comando Supremo)* of the German request and of Mussolini's decision and asked that they provide him with the exact number of Jews currently residing within the Italian zone. At the same time, two important pieces of news arrived at the Foreign Ministry from Croatia. The first came from Supersloda stating that the Germans had begun to deport those Jews still in the German sphere of influence, including those interned at the Stara Gradiska concentration camp. The second came in the form of a dispatch from Ambassador Casertano on August 22, 1942 stating specifcally that the Jews were being sent to Poland in special trains, as opposed to the vague language used by the Germans of "territories in the East." He also mentioned the fact that the Papal envoy, Monsignor Ramiro Marcone, had attempted to stop the deportations but had failed.[35]

To his credit, Marcone did try to put a halt to the deportation of Jews. One month earlier, he had informed his superior Luigi Maglione, the Secretary of State to Pope Pius XII, of the German plans concerning the Jews. On July 17, 1942, Marcone reported:

> The German government has ruled that within a period of six months all the Jews residing in the Croat State must be transferred to Germany, where according to what [Eugene] Kvaternik [Chief of the Croat police] himself told me, two million Jews have been recently killed. It appears that the same fate awaits the Croat Jews particularly if old and incapable of work.
>
> Since this news has also spread among the Jews, I am continually beseeched to do something for their salvation. Also the Chief Rabbi himself of Zagreb comes to see me and to inform me of new misfortunes.[36]

The Vatican took no action at that time.

Kvaternik listened to Marcone's pleas and then patiently told him that he would be pleased if the Germans, rather than deporting the Jews, would instead leave them in Croatian territory to live in peace. This rings hollow coming from a high ranking official of the Ustasha government. On October 6, 1942, Maglione instructed Marcone to intercede with the Ustasha on behalf of the Jews. While the Papal envoy was allowed to meet with Pavelic, his efforts to have the transports suspended ended in failure. In a report sent to the Vatican on December 1, Marcone explained that the position of the Ustasha government had not changed; the Jews would be forced to leave Croatian territory. Marcone next tried to save the lives of a few dozen people. Miroslav Freiberger, the Chief Rabbi of Zagreb, had conceived of a plan to send fifty Jewish children to neutral Turkey and from there to Palestine. Although the Turkish government agreed, of the three countries through which the young people would have to travel, Hungary, Romania, and Bulgaria, only the last would allow them to cross its territory. Marcone relayed the Rabbi's request for assistance to Maglione who instructed the Papal nuncios in the two countries to pressure the Hungarian and Romanian governments. A second obstacle emerged as the Croatian police at first refused to issue exit visas. After several months of delay the police relented, as did the governments of Hungary and Romania, and transit visas were issued. In the end, the small group was allowed to leave Croatia for Turkey, eventually arriving in Palestine in early 1943. Among the children saved was the Rabbi's own son.

Freiberger, while grateful for the Vatican's help, wrote directly to the Pope begging him to intervene to stop further deportations. While the Pope publicly remained silent on the issue, on October 6, 1942, Maglione directed Marcone to appeal to the Croatian government on behalf of the Jews. Marcone met with only limited success. In a letter to the Rabbi, Marcone wrote, "Unfortunately, we have not been able to bring about any change in the course of events. Nevertheless, many exceptions proposed by us in the deportation of the Jews have been granted and the families, on the basis of mixed marriages between Jews, even though not baptized and Catholics, have been spared."[37]

For the rest of the year and into 1943, the trains, packed to the point of bursting with terrified people, continued to roll out of Croatia. The direction was northeast. After several days travel, with no food, water, or sanitation facilities, the victims arrived at their destination: the Nazi death camp at Auschwitz in German occupied Poland. Almost all were sent to the gas chambers upon their arrival.

The reasons why Pope Pius XII did not publicly and forcefully denounce the Nazis and their crimes during the war has been debated by historians ever since. The Pope was undoubtedly aware that acts of genocide were occurring. In late 1942 the Geneva office of the World Jewish Congress made public its findings on the status of Jews in Europe. With regard to Croatia it was determined that some 4,000 Jews had escaped into the Italian occupied zone and "Nearly all the others have either been killed or imprisoned in labor camps where they are starving."[38] Regardless of whether or not the Pope read this report, over the course of the war, information was gathered from all over the continent and sent to the Vatican. He was informed numerous times by Catholic priests, bishops, his own Papal envoys, as well as non-Catholics that Jews by the millions were being slaughtered throughout Nazi controlled Europe. In August 1942, the Orthodox Archbishop of Lwow, Andrea Szeptyckyj, sent word to the Pope from Poland describing conditions there. He wrote:

> For at least a year, there is not a day when there are not committed the most horrible crimes, murders, robberies and rapes, confiscations and injuries. The Jews are the first victims. The number of Jews killed in this small region has certainly passed two hundred thousand. As the [German] army moves east, the number of victims increases.[39]

Allied governments, through their intelligence organizations, had begun receiving reports that detailed elements of the catastrophe as early as the closing months of 1941. On December 17, 1942, at the insistence of the British, the United States, Great Britain, and the Soviet Union jointly issued the Allied Declaration. The document accused the Reich of:

> carrying into effect Hitler's oft-repeated intention to exterminate the Jewish people in Europe. From all the occupied countries, Jews are being transported, in conditions of appalling horror and brutality, to Eastern Europe. In Poland, which has been made the principal slaughterhouse, the ghettos established by the German invaders are being systematically emptied of all Jews except a few highly skilled workers required for war industries. None of those taken away are ever heard from again. . . . this policy of cold blooded extermination . . . can only strengthen the resolve of all freedom-loving peoples to overthrow the barbarous Hitlerite tyranny. . . . those responsible for these crimes shall not escape retribution.[42]

While the pontiff was aware of the declaration, he did not support it publicly. At the time he believed sections of it had been "exaggerated" for propaganda purposes. Unfortunately, it would eventually be revealed that the charges contained within this document were all too real. Unlike the Pope, some of Mussolini's government and military leaders had no trouble believing the worst about the Nazis. As history would show, when it came to achieving their *weltanschauung* (world view), Hitler and his henchmen were completely ruthless.

The Vatican's responses to such reports were weak. One example may be found in Pius XII's statement of December 24 in which, clearly referring to Jews, he regretted the fact that "hundreds of thousands who through no fault of their own, and sometimes only because of their nation or race, have been consigned to death or slow decline."[40]

The Pope's defenders point to the fact that his primary responsibility was to protect and care for members of the Roman Catholic Church along with its assets. While it is possible that had he openly criticized Nazi policies Hitler may have seized church property, it is unclear whether the dictator would have made such a move as this would surely have offended millions of German and Austrian Catholics.

Yet in predominately Catholic countries such as Slovakia, Lithuania, and Croatia, the Pope's pronouncements against harming minorities, including Jews, would have been taken seriously and would surely have saved lives. In addition to influencing laypeople, strong Vatican leadership would have bolstered the position of the numerous priests and nuns throughout Europe who took it upon themselves, without direction from their hierarchy, to aid those being persecuted.

It appears that the main reason Pius XII did not openly criticize Hitler's regime was the fact that he viewed it as a bulwark against Communism. The Pope's greatest fear was that this ideology, within which there was no place for God, would sweep across Europe. He became obsessed with stopping the spread of Communism, which is one reason why he tried to strengthen ties between the Church and Fascist governments, including those of Germany, Italy, and Spain. [41]

Italian Red Tape

The fact that Mussolini had issued no timetable for, or further directives concerning, his decision to surrender the Jews of Croatia gave the Italian diplomats time to create a plan to save the Jews. Count Luca Pietromarchi, Head of the Occupied Territories Department in the Italian Foreign Ministry, was the first official to take action. As he wrote in his diary, "I sent for Castellani, who serves as liason with the Second Army, and agreed with him on ways to avoid surrendering to the Germans those Jews who have placed themselves under the protection of our flag."[43] On September 11, 1942, Castellani, after having returned to Second Army Headquarters, wrote a long letter to Pietromarchi ascertaining that the Italian Army would support them in attempting to save the Jews. He informed his superior, "As soon as I got back from Rome, I went to see General Roatta about the question of the Jews. He shares completely our point of view."[44] The diplomat also sent along a copy of a summary written by staff officers of Supersloda that detailed a delaying tactic that would be used over the next few months. The Italians would play to the German perception of their army as being inefficient and encumbered by a large military bureaucracy. In this way it was hoped that the Jews could be kept out of German hands, and thereby avoid deportation.

One must remember that in 1942, the Axis nations were far from being defeated. Although Hitler had not taken Moscow or Leningrad, German armies were deep inside the Soviet Union and Field Marshal Erwin Rommel's *Afrika Corps* still posed a threat in North Africa. The Nazis were still a force to be reckoned with, to challenge them (even surreptitiously) at this point in the war took courage.

German arrogance was another reason as to why the Italian army did not want to give the Jews over to the Germans. Throughout the war, the various Italian military commands were well aware of the Germans' low opinion of the ability of Italian soldiers. Italian commanders bristled at German criticisms and were defensive of the importance of the Italian military in the war. The Germans' demand that the Jews be turned over to them (even though it was couched in the form of a request) was seen as infringing upon Italian sovereignty.

The Italian diplomats decided to buy time for the Jews by drowning the German request in a sea of bureaucratic red tape. In order to accomplish this, the army would have to appear to be following the wishes of Mussolini without actually doing so. To that end, the *Comando Supremo* was informed by Count Luca Pietromarchi, the diplomat responsible for the occupied territories, that there were several obstacles to be overcome before the Jews could be expelled. First, it was explained, the Jews were scattered all over Zones II and III (the instructions to surrender the Jews did not apply to those in Italian annexed Zone I, although after the Italian surrender to the Allies in September 1943 German troops did sweep through this area rounding up Jews). Secondly, the refugees were mixed in with Jews from Zone I, as well as the local population. Thirdly, it was reiterated that handing over these people would not sit well with the local Serb population and would diminish Italian prestige in their eyes (especially the Chetniks).

The communiqué specified that the first steps should include determining where the Jews were located, taking a census of their exact numbers, and classifying them so as to know which should be given to the Germans. Lastly, even though the Jews posed no real security threat, the idea was put forward by the Italian diplomats that they be interned on one of the islands off the Dalmatian coast. Although not stated in so many words, this last measure was intended to make it appear as though the army was taking action against the Jews, while the army was actually working to keep them out of German hands. General Roatta wholeheartedly supported this strategy.

Mario Roatta was not the kind of general who followed orders blindly. Like most men of his military rank, he had a large ego. He also knew that Mussolini, as well as his fellow officers, respected his judgment in military affairs. On September 22, 1942, he sent a dispatch to the *Comando Supremo* entitled "Jews in Zone II" in which he reiterated his belief that the Jews should not be handed over:

The number of Jewish refugees in the territories occupied

by our troops is approximately 3,000, and they are mostly
located along the coast. This number includes all Jews without distinction of nationality. It is presumed that most of
them are coming from the annexed territories since the others have not escaped [Croatian] persecution. I have given
instructions to find out the Italian or Croatian status of each
one of them. They believe that they will not be bothered or
moved from this area and they are behaving correctly, awaiting the end of the war. My opinion is that turning the Jews
over to the Germans or Croatians would compromise our
prestige and integrity because we took them under our protection and because such an action would scare the rest of
the population and could make them think that we could do
the same to them, leaving them to the Ustasha. . . . I await
further orders regarding the Jewish situation.[45]

Clearly Roatta could easily cite several reasons why it was not in
the interest of the Italian army to comply with the German request.

The man who could have issued orders and demanded that
Roatta comply immediately with Mussolini's instructions was the
Chief of the General Staff of the Armed Forces, Marshall Ugo
Cavallero. Cavellero was a cultured and very well educated man who
had studied mathematics at the University of Turin. Before the war,
he had been an industrialist and head of the Italian forces in East
Africa. Fluent in German, Cavellero worked closely and coopera-
tively with Field Marshall Kesselring, the commander of German
troops in Italy. Although Cavellero was seen as part of the "pro-
German" wing of the Fascist Party, there is no evidence that he was
an anti-Semite. According to SS *Obersturmbannfuerer* (Lieutenant
Colonel) Eugene Dollman, the police attaché at the German
embassy, Kesselring actually regarded Cavellero as "absolutely sub-
missive" and Roatta as "the true chief among Italian senior commanders whose acute intelligence, if without scruples, made a great
impression."[46]

Cavellero was certainly aware of Roatta's feelings on protecting
the Jews, as well as the Germans' demands to have them turned over.
He decided to issue no instructions for the time being to the Second

Army. By 1943 as the war began to go badly he felt that it would not be in Italy's interest to help the Germans murder Jews.

Cavellero's term as Chief of staff would not last long however. Due primarily to Italian setbacks in North Africa, Mussolini replaced him with General Ambrosio in February 1943. Later that year, immediately following Italy's surrender to the Allies, Cavellero's close ties to the Germans would prove pivotal. Although he was briefly jailed after Mussolini's downfall, he was soon freed by his longtime friends and offered the command of the pro-Nazi Italian forces that were being organized to fight in the North of the country. For whatever reasons, he informed his wife that he intended not to accept the position. On September 14, 1943, in a bizarre twist, his body was found in the garden of Kesselring's villa in Rome. He had been shot in the head. Whether he was murdered or committed suicide is still a matter of conjecture.

One man who never wavered in loyalty to his German partner was Ante Pavelic. In late September, Pavelic traveled north to meet Hitler at German Staff Headquarters. During the course of their discussions, the Croatian leader raised the topic of the Jews in his country. Hitler, in a typically paranoid response, stated that the Jews were all an integral part of the resistance movement and had to be dealt with. Pavelic then pointed out that the Italians were not cooperating in the effort to rid Croatia of these people. The German dictator placed the blame squarely at the feet of the Italian commanders in Croatia. Singling out Roatta for particular scorn, he contemptuously referred to him as a "half politician"[47] not to be trusted.

Ribbentrop, who also attended the meeting, decided to have his representatives in Rome press the Italian Foreign Ministry to find out why the military was not adhering to Mussolini's instructions. Johann Von Plessen, a German diplomat, met with Lanza d'Ajeta on 3 October and informed him that according to reports received by the Germans, no orders had yet been issued by the *Commando Supremo* to Supersloda concerning the "consignment" (this term was used throughout the war) of the Jews. This information was based upon a report sent to Berlin on the state of conditions in Croatia signed jointly by Ambassador Kasche, General Glaise, and the Supreme Commander South East, General Alexander Loehr. In reference to the Jews they stated:

> The implementation of the Jewish laws of the Croatian state are being hindered by Italian officials to such an extent that in the coastal zones, especially in Mostar, Dubrovnik and Crkvenica, many Jews stand under Italian protection and many others are being helped over the border into Italian Dalmatia or Italy. Thus the Jews gain help and can continue their treasonable activities and especially those directed against our war aims. To be sure, according to a report of our Embassy in Rome of the beginning of September the Duce has decided that the Jews are to be treated according to the Croatian laws. Up to today neither the Italian Minister Casertano nor the Supreme Commander of the 2nd Army General Roatta has received direct instructions.[48]

The German generals in Croatia had believed that this dispatch would clarify the situation to their superiors in Berlin. In their view, this Italian "non-cooperation" would have to stop.

Ciano, bowing to German pressure, sent a message to the *Comando Supremo* reminding them of Mussolini's decision. On October 12, they in turn cabled Supersloda relaying the German concerns and requesting a report on the census that was being conducted. Additionally, they demanded to know what steps Roatta's command was taking to facilitate the handing over of Jews. The next day Supersloda responded, claiming that they had received no orders requiring them to surrender these people to the "German authorities." Although merely a matter of semantics the officers stationed in Dalmatia were correct since technically the Jews were to be handed over to the Croatians. As for the census, the tally came to 2,025 in Zones II and III, although in his letter to the Foreign Ministry of October 15, 1942 Castellani reported an additional 1,626 refugees that would also have to be included. These people had been overlooked as they were in transit between Spalato and Ragusa (Split and Dubrovnik).[49]

The next step for Supersloda concerned how to classify the Jewish refugees. Although on the surface this seemed like a simple task, the "conspirators" in the army and Foreign Ministry would use it to buy time. The officers argued that there were numerous questions to be answered including: Who was a Croatian Jew? Should a complicated formula be employed, such as that used by the Germans, to determine who is a "full" Jew as opposed to a "half" or "quarter" Jew? What should be the cutoff date, after which Jews arriving should be considered refugees? What should become of those Jews that had moved into Italian territory from other parts of Croatia but who were originally from nations such as Poland, Austria, or Slovakia? And who among these people were entitled to apply for Italian citizenship? As to the last point, the Foreign Ministry responded on October 16 with a list of criteria to be met by those who wished to claim Italian citizenship. People who would be considered included Jews born in the area, those who had lived there for a substantial amount of time, property owners, Jews with relatives within the two zones, and Jews who had provided outstanding service to the Italian army.

In Rome, German pressure to relinquish the Jews intensified. Five days prior to the Foreign Ministry dispatch establishing which Jews were eligible for citizenship, Heinrich Himmler, the head of the SS and Gestapo, had made an appearance in the Italian capital. The *Reichsfuehrer* SS met with Mussolini at the dictator's ornate office within the Palazzo Venezia. The two men discussed a number of issues, including the status of the Croatian Jews. Himmler asked that Mussolini enforce his earlier decision which allowed the Germans to deport the Jews. Nothing was said, however, about plans to send these people to their deaths. Curiously, the second most powerful man in Germany did admit that it was true that Jews were being killed in Eastern Europe, but claimed this was only because they were working with Communist partisans. Mussolini was skeptical but did not debate the point.

Shortly thereafter, another point of contention arose between the two nations. In the last months of 1942, German officials not only lobbied to take possession of the Croatian Jews, but also sought to get their hands on Italian Jews living outside of Italy. From the Nazi point of view, it made no sense that as hundreds of thousands of Jews were being sent to death camps from all over occupied Europe Italian Jews residing in occupied countries were exempt from arrest and deportation. The German ambassador Hans-Georg von Mackensen took the matter up with Foreign Minister Ciano's Chief of Staff Lanza D'Ajeta. The chief German diplomat was informed that Italy would not allow any actions against its Jews living abroad as they were "regarded as Italian citizens, who had rights to the same protection as any other citizens."[50] This, of course was not entirely accurate since the anti- Jewish laws of 1938 had stripped Jews of certain political and social rights. Nevertheless, Italy would not hand over its Jewish citizens as other collaborationist governments had. As tensions between Italy and Germany mounted, the Head of the Occupied Territories desk Pietromarchi comment-ed in his diary on October 14, "The Germans behave with their usual arrogance towards us. They have renewed several times their request to consign the Jews of Croatia to them, stating that they have learned that the command of the Second Army has not yet received instructions in that sense."[51]

Over the next few months, Hitler suspected that the Italian mil-itary establishment, which he held in low regard anyway, was inten-tionally sabotaging his and Mussolini's plan by failing to act decisive-ly on the Jews. Yet Hitler still had every confidence in Mussolini himself. A few months earlier Joseph Goebbels, Hitler's Propaganda Minister, noted in his diary the thoughts of his leader on Mussolini and the Italian people:

> The Fuehrer is very much attached to Mussolini and regards him as the only guarantor of German-Italian collaboration. The Italian people and Fascism will stick to our side as long as Mussolini is there . . . The Fuehrer spoke about Mussolini only in terms of greatest respect. He has made of the Italian people whatever it was possible to make of them. If here and there German-Italian collaboration doesn't function, that isn't Mussolini's fault, but is rather because of the lack of mil-itary qualities in the Italian people themselves.[52]

Hitler had always admired Mussolini and he was right in assuming that if the Italian dictator was ever removed from power, the Italian people would not continue the war by Germany's side.

In an interesting diplomatic twist, on October 20, 1942, Roberto Ducci, the desk officer responsible for Croatia at the Italian Foreign Ministry, met with the Croatian Ambassador to Italy, Stj. Peric. The ambassador suggested that the Croatian government might be agreeable to a deal in which the Jews in the Italian zones would be allowed to move to Italy proper in exchange for the transfer of all Jewish property to the Croatian state. The ambassador also hinted at the fate that awaited those slated for deportation.

Unfortunately this proposal was doomed from the beginning. Unbeknownst to the two men, that same day Croatian Foreign Minister Lorkovic, who stridently opposed such an arrangement, contacted German Ambassador Kasche and announced that no deal would be implemented without German approval. Needless to say the Germans were unwilling to give their stamp of approval to such an enterprise.

The following day, the Minister of State at the German embassy, Otto von Bismarck, again made an appearance at the Italian Foreign Ministry in Rome. Once more he requested the surrender of the Jews at once "not to the German armed forces, but to the Croatian authorities who were working in close cooperation with special units of the German police."[55] (It was apparent what role the German police were to play in this case). In all areas under German military control, the various branches of police, including the Gestapo, moved in to the area in the wake of the army. The Germans had been busy assisting the Croatian government in building, training and supplying the newly formed police units of the NDH. The Ustasha leaders were eager to model their own police force on that of the Germans. One example of this desire can be seen in a telegram marked "secret" dated October 5, 1942 that was sent from the German embassy in Zagreb to the Foreign Ministry in Berlin. It contained a request from the Ustasha that Germany help train a cadre of Croatian policemen. The new recruits would include 150 men that would work with the *Ordnungspolizei* (order police), with the *Kriminalpolizei* (criminal police), and 30 with the Gendarmerie who would thereafter serve as instructors at a soon to be established police academy. On a more sinister note, the Croatians also asked that two representatives from the *Sicherheitspolizei* (security police) be sent to Zagreb to instruct officials on the operating of concentration camps.[56] The German government was more than willing to provide technical and material supplies to the various police forces in an effort to assist their ally in establishing and maintaining a totalitarian state.[57]

In the autumn of 1942, two of the most forceful individuals involved with the plan to deport the Jews from Croatia were Ambassador Kasche and his friend in the German Foreign Ministry, Undersecretary Martin Luther. The two men had similar motives. Aside from being rabid anti-Semites in their personal lives, both hoped to advance their careers by steadfastly adhering to Nazi policy when it came to the Jews. In addition, Luther became locked in a power struggle with his superior Foreign Minister Ribbentrop, and hoped that by appearing to be even more fanatical than his boss on the "Jewish question" he could undermine the Foreign Minister's power, while increasing his own. In telegrams sent between Kasche and Luther throughout 1942, they decided, in cooperation with Croatian Foreign Minister Lorkovic, that constant pressure must be applied through the German embassy in Rome in order to force the Italian government to cooperate.[58] Each man realized the delicate position he was in. For the feuding German officials the question was how to obtain their objective, which would please Hitler, while at the same time not provoking a crisis by constantly badgering the Italians on the matter. As diplomats, they knew the value of appearing to respect Italian sovereignty, even if privately they had little regard for Italian policies. As the pressure mounted from both Luther and Ribbentrop, who did not want to be seen as "soft" when it came to the Jews, the small group of Italian conspirators decided that something dramatic had to be done.

Italian Internment of Jews

In order to stall the Germans and Croatians, the Italian diplomats prepared a detailed memo that was sent to Ciano and

Mussolini for their signatures. The document proposed that all Jews living in Zone II immediately be interned in one of several camps that would be created specifically for that purpose. This action should be taken, it was argued, to better facilitate the evaluation process that was designed to divide the refugees into two categories: those eligible for Italian citizenship and those to be handed over for deportation. Privately, this calculated move was designed to allow the army to better protect the Jews by concentrating them in a few places rather than having them scattered over such a wide area. Publicly, it would demonstrate to the Germans that concrete steps were being taken to comply with their requests.

On October 23, Mussolini approved the plan. He apparently viewed this as the next logical step following his decision of August 21, in which he had written "No objection" to expelling the Jews. At this point, there was no evidence to suggest that Mussolini knew the real motives of his diplomatic corps. However, he may have suspected, as he was aware of their feelings toward the Germans and Croatians. Although Kasche and Lorkovic were still very suspicious of Italian motives, most German and Croatian government officials were satisfied for the moment that the Italians were finally cooperating. After all, in other countries in which the deportation of Jews was taking place, the first step had always been to assemble the victims in confined areas. It was then a simple process to deport the Jews from these "transit camps" to the east.

One move in particular on the part of the Croatians further motivated the Italians to assist the Jews. In a telegram dispatched to Berlin on October 16, Ambassador Kasche relayed a proposition that was wretched even by Ustasha standards. Kasche stated that on October 9, the Croatian Finance Minister, Vladimir Kosak, had offered to pay the German government thirty Reichsmarks for every Jew deported. Apparently this despicable offer was designed to help cover part of the transportation costs. Foreign Minister Lorkovic would handle the actual payment.[59] The figure reminded many of the biblical account of Judas receiving thirty pieces of silver for betraying Jesus. It is not known whether this number had been arrived at with this in mind or whether it was merely a coincidence.

In any case, the sum, in the words of one Italian official amounted to "thirty devalued pieces of silver."[60]

On October 28, Ciano's Chief of Staff Lanza d'Ajeta met with German Ambassador Mackensen and informed him of Croatian Ambassador Peric's earlier idea of transferring the Jews to Italy. Knowing that this initiative was now dead, Lanza d'Ajeta pretended to be the staunch German ally declaring that the Italian government had refused the offer since "Italy is not Palestine."[61] The ambassador was also informed that the Italian army would immediately begin interning Jews as a prelude to their deportation. Mackensen left the meeting well satisfied with the new information. That same day, Marshal Ugo Cavallero issued orders to Supersloda to begin rounding up Jews in Zone II. The order did not apply to Zone III since following the signing of the Italian-Croatian agreement of June 19, 1942, most Italian military units had been withdrawn and the civil administration of this area had been assumed by the Croatians. Fortunately at this point, very few Jews remained within this jurisdiction since most had moved toward the Dalmatian coast in an effort to get as far away from both the Ustasha and the Germans as possible.

From the Italian military's viewpoint, the internment of the Jews was completed in an efficient and timely manner over the next two months. Those from southern Dalmatia were placed in camps, and in some cases hotels that had been requisitioned by the army, near Dubrovnik. Jews from Split and its surrounding area were sent to camps on the islands of Brac and Hvar, while those taken in the north were driven to a camp at Kraljevica (Porto Re) near the city of Rijeka. On March 1, 1943, the Italian army circulated a document that listed the numbers of internees under its control throughout Croatia. The report detailed where and for what reasons various groups were being held. It also classified people based on their religious beliefs. According to this summary, 822 Jews had been interned near Dubrovnik, 554 on the islands of Brac and Hvar, 1,170 in Kraljevica, and 3 in other areas of Dalmatia for a total of 2,549.[62]

However the noted historian Jasa Romano, writing after the war, placed the number of internees higher than the official figure listed by the army. According to Romano, a recognized authority on the Jews of Yugoslavia, the actual number was 3,565.[63] Assuming this higher number is accurate, there is the possibility that the Italians purposefully underreported the number of Jews taken into custody. If this was the case, it would put them in a position to argue the point with the Germans that it was not worth creating friction between the Axis partners over such a small number of Jews. Of course these figures do not represent the additional numbers of Jews who found sanctuary in Zone I or inside Italy itself.

Reactions to the new policy of internment varied widely among the local Croatian population, the Italian soldiers, and the Jews themselves. Although anti-Semitism in Dalmatia was less pronounced than in other parts of the country, it existed nonetheless. Many Croatians were pleased with the idea of ridding the area of Jews. They were further excited by the rumors that Italy had been forced to take such a step by the Germans and had been reduced to a vassal state of Germany. This is not surprising since the vast majority of the coastal population opposed Italian rule and longed for the day when Italian soldiers would withdraw back across the Adriatic.

The order from Rome to intern the Jews had come so rapidly and without prior warning that officers of the Second Army had been taken completely by surprise; even General Roatta had not been informed. Not understanding at first that this was part of the Foreign Ministry's delaying tactic, many soldiers, including Roatta were outraged. Again they voiced their objections to handing the Jews over to the Germans based on political as well as humanitarian grounds. Military Police (*Carabinieri*) General Giuseppe Pieche, in a letter to the Foreign Ministry dated November 14, 1942, stated that the decision to deliver the Jews to the Ustasha was equivalent to a death sentence and that it had provoked numerous negative comments from the troops. The general also forwarded a copy of a letter he had received from an Italian living in Zone I that read:

Almost three thousand Jewish refugees have been living for more than a year along the Croatian coast occupied by Italian troops. These people have lost their houses, their country, their belongings, their civil rights, and everything that makes life beautiful. They found protection and shelter in these areas. Nobody bothered them as long as they were not politically active. Recently they were locked up in concentration camps near Porto Re. The ones that cannot prove that they have relatives or property inside the Kingdom [Italy] risk consignment to the Ustasha and this means slavery and death. As an Italian patriot, I beg you to cancel the new steps taken against the Jews. We have a moral duty to save those people. They sought protection under the Italian flag, and we are obliged to save them and give them freedom at the end of the war. . . . Italy must obey the moral law. . . . What a tragedy if our proud tradition shall be trodden upon.[64]

In another letter sent to Foreign Minister Ciano, a colonel made his views on the subject very clear, "We refuse to be pimps to such an ignoble enterprise . . . Even standing by and allowing such things to happen would soil the honor of the Italian Army."[65]

General Pieche was no stranger to the Balkans. In addition to his position within the *Carabinieri*, he was also charged with gathering intelligence in order to help form Italian policy in the region. In late October, Pieche had voiced no objection to the *consegna*, as the consignment of the Jews was known. His position shifted dramatically however, as he discovered the fate that awaited them. On November 4, 1942, he dispatched a telegram to the Foreign Ministry that stated, "The Croatian Jews who had been deported from the area of the German occupation to territories of the East had been 'liquidated' by poison gas which had been introduced into the train carriages into which they had been sealed."[66]   While Pieche's information as to the use of poison gas in sealed trains was inaccurate, he was correct in his overall assessment of what awaited the unfortunate deportees. Many did perish on the overcrowded and tightly packed trains through exhaustion and lack of food and water. As for those who reached Auschwitz, the vast majority were sent directly to the gas chambers.

The message was quickly sent to Mussolini who undoubtedly

saw it since "VISTO DAL DUCE" (seen by the Duce) is stamped across the top of the page. This information about the fate of the deported Jews along with other factors would influence the Italian leader in the months to come and help save the lives of many Croatian Jews. While the general may have been mistaken about the specifics, he was correct in his assessment that the Nazis were using poison gas as a means to murder people.[B]

Although the Italians may not have had all the facts, after November 4, Mussolini could not deny knowing about the Holocaust. He even made a bad joke on the subject two days later. While meeting with his friend the industrialist Alberto Pirelli, the businessman began talking about German treatment of Jews to which Mussolini replied: "they are letting them emigrate . . . to another world."[67]

As the internments began, Jews were confused as to what exactly was happening. Reactions ranged from surprise to outright panic. Sadly, there were even a few cases of suicide. Hearing rumors about what was taking place in other parts of Europe, the internees feared they would be handed over to the Germans. They knew nothing about the diplomatic maneuvers that were taking place behind the scenes. One Jewish internee, Imre Rochlitz, remembered the Jews being taken by Italian soldiers and placed onto trucks to be driven to an unknown destination. Everyone knew there was a fork in the road: to the right led inland, toward Croatian controlled territory, while to the left the road continued toward the Dalmatian coast. For hours the tension continued to build until it became almost unbearable. Finally a palpable sigh of relief was heard as the convoy veered to the left. The trucks stopped at Kraljevica where the Jews were

---

[B]Although gas was not introduced into the boxcars that transported victims to the death camps, Zyklon B was used extensively at the larger camps such as Auschwitz and Treblinka. In addition, within Serbia, specially designed vans were used to kill Jews. The vehicles were modified to allow the tail pipe to feed directly into the rear compartment thus suffocating the victims with exhaust fumes from the engine. A van was also used at the Zemun holding camp that was located across the Sava River from Belgrade and therefore technically on Croatian soil.

housed in a former army camp surrounded by barbed wire. Once at the camp, Rochlitz recalled:

> Life in the camp was like an oasis. We were completely free within the camp. We were permitted by the Italian authorities to elect a board of five people who really organized life in the camp and who had contact with the Italian military authorities. Whenever we asked the authorities we got; for instance, they built a gangway from the barracks to the latrine so during the winter when it was cold we wouldn't catch cold. They supplied us with food and during the winter they even supplied us with military clothing ... whatever was needed. They even permitted us and assisted us in setting up a grade school and a high school within the camp, the teachers of course were also inmates who had been teachers and professors before. We had musical evenings in the camp in which officers came, Italian officers and soldiers from the entire area. It was a very pleasant life in the camp. Food was not plentiful but healthy and a number of people who were overweight before and had ...health problems became well in the camp."[68]

Another former internee, Lucy S., also has fond memories of this camp and of Italian soldiers in general. This stands in sharp contrast to the way she viewed her fellow Croatians at the time. A young girl of sixteen when the war began, she was amazed by how ecstatic the population was to see the Germans march into Zagreb. Her family quickly realized that they would have to flee if they were to survive. Along with her father, mother, and brother she traveled by train to the city of Karlovac (in Zone III). She recalled, "Although this was still administratively Croatia, the military administration was Italian and the Croatians did not have jurisdiction to eliminate the Jews. They wanted us to wear the Jewish sign but many people didn't and they couldn't do much about it."[69] After the family was arrested they were also sent to the camp at Kraljevica. At first the camp was divided into two sections, one that housed the men, and one for women and children. The two areas were separated by barbed wire, but eventually the wire was taken down. According to Lucy in the beginning the quality of the food was poor, but it improved over time. What impressed her most was the fact that within the camp the Italians established a hospital and issued special rations to the pregnant women as well as to the children.

While prisoners were not forced to perform hard labor or tortured at the camp, there was great uncertainty among the internees as to their future. One day in late November the camp received an unexpected visitor. General Roatta, who had been informed of the real reason for the internments, arrived to reassure the inmates that no harm would come to them. The general chose his words carefully since he obviously could not announce publicly that this was all part of a secret plan to keep them out of German hands. Lucy remembered that he proclaimed, "I'm terribly sad that this had to happen, we are doing this for your own good." She also recalled that no one believed him at the time.[70]

Boris N. was one of a number of Jews interned on the Italian occupied island of Korcula. There, "civil confinement" meant that the prisoners could move about freely. They were allowed to rent rooms from the locals and even receive money from the Italian Jewish community. The newcomers were also allowed to interact with the local Croatian peasants. Some Jews chopped wood for the natives or caught fish that they would then sell or trade. The internees did not know much about the Holocaust or concentration camps at that time, but they did know that under German rule the Jews suffered terribly. As to his own fate, Boris recalled, "We heard on the radio sometimes that there is [sic] Jews living in Italian islands and that Germany wants them; to be extradited, we heard stories about that."[71] Long after the war, a grateful Boris expressed his feelings that "wherever the Italians occupied, the Jews were not molested, if they did nothing against the Italian authorities."[72]

Paul A., another internee on Korcula, shared his own story involving the Italians, "The role of Italians in saving Jewish lives has been very much forgotten."[73] A boy of 13 when the war began, he had been very impressed like so many others as the Germans rolled into his home city of Zagreb. "They exuded such overpowering frightful might . . . the German war machine flowing through the city. The worst thing of all was all these Croatians lined up cheering them along. ... From then on I never thought we would survive because of what I had heard of German treatment of Jews."[74] During those first few days, Paul's father had tried to reassure the family by saying that the German occupation would not last long. However, the situation for Jews was deteriorating rapidly. News filtered through that the Italians were less harsh in their rule than the Germans and Ustasha. The family therefore boarded a train bound for Split. After being arrested and confined on Korcula, Paul described his feelings at being so close to the Croatian mainland, "throughout this stay this fear of being turned over stayed with us . . . we just had to trust the Italians."[75]

Life for the internees on the island, though far from ideal, was pleasant enough. Most had arrived with some currency and unlike the systematic looting that accompanied arrests by the Germans, the Italians allowed the Jews to keep their money. This simple act made life much easier. Food and goods were purchased from the natives, and while their children were not allowed to attend the local schools, permission was given for parents to hire tutors.

Yet the war was never far away. Even on Korcula, Tito's partisans were active. In such a guerrilla war, quarter was rarely given. The partisans routinely executed German, Italian, and Ustasha soldiers if captured, and the Axis troops did the same to any of Tito's men unfortunate enough to be taken by their troops. Paul remembered a curious dichotomy among the Italians. While "Italian troops were extremely vicious toward combatants if they caught them," they were also relaxed in their mannerisms; even though they held military parades, and sang fascist songs "somehow their hearts were never in it."[76] What the young teenager had observed was an army that did not believe in this war and like the Italian population as a whole, was rapidly losing confidence in the man that had led them for the past twenty years.

In early December 1942, General Roatta journeyed to Rome to meet with Mussolini. Urgent military matters had to be addressed. In addition to talks about countering Communist movements in the

Balkans, of paramount importance was the fact that Axis forces were dangerously overextended on all fronts. Military setbacks were beginning to plague the Axis powers. On November 4, the British had won a vital battle near a small railroad station sixty miles west of Alexandria, Egypt named El Alamein. Four days later, on the other side of the African continent, American and British troops had landed in Morocco and Algeria. At the same time, some 2000 miles to the northeast in Russia, the decisive battle of Stalingrad was raging.

Far down the list of topics to be discussed was again the issue of the Croatian Jews. Roatta suggested that the Italian government revisit the plan, first proposed by Croatian Ambassador Peric, to transfer Croatian Jews *en mass* to Italy in exchange for their agreeing to forfeit all property and valuables to the Croatian government and to renounce their Croatian citizenship. Since Croatian law had already stripped Jews of their fixed assets, and as Jews obviously received no protection as citizens of Croatia, persuading the refugees to accept these two conditions would hardly be difficult. Mussolini was less than thrilled with the idea, however, so no further action was taken. Instead Mussolini gave instructions that basically kept the status quo, the refugees were to remain in the camps, and the authorities would continue the process of ascertaining who was entitled to Italian citizenship. Although no one could have known it at the time, it was fortunate for the Jews that Peric's plan never came to fruition. In less than a year, Mussolini would be out of power and much of northern Italy would be under direct German control. If the Jews had been sent to the north of the country, many would surely have been seized by the Nazis and sent to the death camps.

The diplomatic maneuvering continued on the part of the Italians, Croatians, and Germans. While the Italians stalled, the Croatians urged the Germans to be more forceful. The Nazi officials in turn sought a new avenue that would allow them to achieve their goal. On December 9, 1942, German Minister of State Bismarck once again called upon the Italian Foreign Ministry the surrender of the Jews, but this time he added a new twist. He said his government was aware of the difficulties involved in transporting a large number of people through hostile territory (i.e. areas in which partisan units were active). He therefore proposed that the Jews be sent by ship to the city of Trieste and from there to Germany. This new idea took the Italian diplomats completely by surprise. After some quick thinking they managed to avoid this proposal by stating that such a plan would be impossible to implement immediately due to a lack of available ships. This response apparently placated Bismarck for the moment.

Mussolini of course was far more concerned with larger military issues than the fate of a few thousand Jews. The Allied landings in North Africa had deeply shaken his confidence. Apparently, the Allies' strategy was to drive out the Axis forces by launching a two-pronged attack with the Americans moving east and the British army advancing from the west. As 1942 turned into 1943, this plan appeared to be succeeding. On January 22, 1943 Tripoli fell to the British. The Axis partners were keenly aware that once North Africa was controlled by the Allies, it could be used as a springboard from which to launch an invasion of mainland Europe, by way of either Sicily or Greece.

In that same month, in the far off Soviet Union, the colossal battle of Stalingrad was coming to a conclusion. The previous November had seen the arrival of desperately needed Soviet reinforcements. After months of some of the most brutal fighting of the war, some 250,000 German, Romanian and Italian troops had finally been surrounded and cut off by the Red Army. On February 2, 1943, German Field Marshal Friedrich von Paulus surrendered his army along with what remained of the city to the Soviets. The Russians took 91,545 Axis soldiers as prisoners of war.[78] The German Sixth, Rumanian Third and Fourth, and Italian Eighth armies were completely destroyed. The exact number of Soviet casualties is not known, estimates range from 500,000 to as high as 1,000,000. This battle marked a turning point in the war on the Eastern Front; after Stalingrad it would be Russian troops that would be advancing, as they drove the invaders back toward Western Europe.

In the wake of such dramatic events, the Italian dictator decided to make some changes within his government. GeneraVittorio Ambrosio replaced Marshal Ugo Cavallero as Army Chief of Staff. Count Ciano was replaced by Mussolini himself as Foreign Minister with the day-to-day operation of the ministry assumed by Giuseppe Bastianini. The former Governor of Dalmatia now found himself in the more influential position of Deputy Foreign Minister. The valuable General Roatta was assigned to a command in Italy proper. In his place, the Chief of Staff appointed General Mario Robotti as commander of the Italian Second Army. Of utmost significance to the Croatian Jews, these changes would allow the Italians to continue to obstruct German and Croatian plans. As German pressure mounted, the Italian diplomats and soldiers knew that they were putting their careers and futures in jeopardy. All of the newly promoted men were familiar with the situation in Croatia and, whether for humanitarian or political reasons, each in his own way was committed to saving the lives of people who had no where else to turn.

1 Tomasevich, p.249.
2 West, Tito, p.102.
3 Jonathan Steinberg, <u>All or Nothing: The Axis and the Holocaust 1941-43</u> (London: Routledge, 1990), p.38.
4 Ibid.
5 Leon Poliakov and Jacques Sabille, <u>Jews Under the Italian Occupation</u> (New York: Howard Fertig, 1983), p.133.
6 Ibid.
7 Milton Meltzer, <u>Rescue: The Story of How Gentiles Saved Jews in the Holocaust</u> (New York: Harper Trophy, 1988), pp.126-127.
8 Susan Zucotti, <u>The Italians and the Holocaust: Persecution, Rescue, and Survival</u> (Lincoln, Nebraska: University of Nebraska Press, 1987), p.77.
9 Desiree E., 1995, "Interview by Survivors of the Shoah Visual History Foundation," Fullerton, California., U.S.A., 20 December, interview code 10450-1, tapes 1, 2.
10 Ibid.
11 Susan Zucotti, <u>Under His Very Windows: The Vatican and the Holocaust in Italy</u> (New Haven, Connecticut: Yale University Press,

2000), p.115.

12 Daniel Carpi, "Rescue of Jews in Italian Occupied Croatia," in <u>Rescue Attempts during the Holocaust: Proceedings of the Second Yad Vashem International Historical Conference, Jerusalem, April 8-11, 1974</u>, ed. Yisrael Gutman and Efaim Zuroff (Jerusalem: "Ahva" Cooperative Press, 1977), p.471.

13 Steinberg, p.53.

14 Ibid., p.45.

15 National Archives and Records Administration (NARA), Collection of Foreign Records Seized Record Group 242, Micr. No. T586, Roll 424, Fr. 12304.

16 Ibid., Micr. No. T586, Roll 424, Fr. 12278.

17 Steinberg, p.47.

18 Zvi Loker, "The Testimony of Dr. Edo Neufeld: The Italians and the Jews of Croatia," *Holocaust and Genocide Studies* volume 7, number 1 (Spring 1993): p.74.

19 Ibid., p.73.

20 Dr. Alex R., 1997, "Interview by Survivors of the Shoah Visual History Foundation," Atlanta, Georgia, U.S.A., 30 September, interview code 34338, tapes 1, 2, 3.

21 Ibid.

22 Ibid.

23 Ibid.

24 Tomasevich, p.592.

25 Zucotti, <u>Under His Very Windows,</u> p.113.

27 Ibid., p.41.

26 Steinberg, p.42.

28 Tomasevich, p.595.

29 Menachem Shelah, "Italian Rescue of Yugoslav Jews," in <u>The Italian Refuge: Rescue of Jews During the Holocaust</u> ed. Ivo Herzer (Washington, D.C.: Catholic University Press, 1989), p.209.

30 Carpi, p.511.

31 Ibid., p.473.

32 Ibid.,p.475.

33 Verax, "Italiani ed ebrei in Jugoslavia," *Politica Estera*, (1944): p.23.

34 Steinberg, p.57.

35 Ibid.

36 John F. Morley, <u>Vatican Diplomacy And The Jews During The Holocaust 1939-1943</u> (New York: KTAV Publishing House, Inc.,

1980), p.153.

37 Ibid., p.154.

38 Ibid., p.157.

39 Ibid., p.136.

42 Jon Meacham, <u>Franklin And Winston: An Intimate Portrait Of An Epic Friendship</u> (New York: Random House, 2003), p.192.

40 Publications International Ltd., <u>The Holocaust Chronicle: A History In Words And Pictures</u> (Lincolnwood, Illinois: Publications International Ltd., 2003), p.403.

41 Avro Manhattan, <u>The Vatican's Holocaust,</u> p.29.

43 Steinberg, p.59.

44 Ibid.

45 Micr. No. T-821, Roll 405, Fr. 749.

46 Steinberg, p.65.

47 Hertzer, p.211.

48 Steinberg, p.69.

49 Carpi, p.481.

50 Steinberg, p.70.

51 Ibid.

52 Louis P. Lochner, ed., <u>The Goebbels Diaries 1942-1943</u> (Garden City, N.Y.: Doubleday and Company, 1948), p.135.

55 Carpi, p.484

56 Micr. No. T-120, Roll 5785, Fr. H300888.

57 Micr. No. T-120, Roll 5785, Fr. H300887.

58 Micr. No. T-120, Roll 5784, Frs. H299623, and 299624.

59 Micr. No. T-120, Roll 5784, Fr. H299660.

60 Shelah, p.209.

61 Carpi, p.487.

62 Micr. No. T-821, Roll 405, Fr. 860.

63 Tomasevich, p.600.

64 Micr. No. T-821, Roll 405, Frs. 829, and 830.

65 Shelah, p.213.

66 Carpi, p.490.

67 Steinberg, p.3.

68 *The Righteous Enemy*, produced and directed by Joseph Rochlitz, 84 min., Parstel Ltd. Films, 1987, video.

69 Lucy S., 1996, "Interview by Survivors of the Shoah Visual History Foundation," Nantucket, Massachusetts, U.S.A., 7 September, interview code 19228-3, tapes 1,2,3.

70 Ibid.

71 Boris N., 1996, "Interview by Survivors of the Shoah Visual History Foundation," Durban, South Africa, 30 January, interview code 08682, tapes 1,2.

72 Ibid.

73 Paul A., 1997, "Interview by Survivors of the Shoah Visual History Foundation," Walnut Creek, California, U.S.A., 14 March, interview code 27046, tapes 1,2,3,4.

74 Ibid.

75 Ibid.

76 Ibid.

77 Steinberg, p.84.

78 Catherine Merridale, Ivan's War: Life and Death in the Red Army, 1939-1945 (New York: Metropolitan Books Henry Holt and Company, 2006), p.186.

3

MUSSOLINI'S TREATMENT OF JEWS AT HOME AND ABROAD

DURING THE SECOND WORLD WAR, THE ITALIANS CREATED TWO distinct types of concentration, or internment, camps. The first category included compounds that were used *per scopi repressivi* (for the purpose of repression). These camps contained people who were opposed to or actively fighting against Italian occupation forces and were employed in such diverse lands as Greece, Slovenia, Albania, Montenegro, and Croatia, as well as in Italy itself. They had also been used extensively in the previous two decades during Mussolini's wars of conquest in Libya and Ethiopia. In all, the Italians set up about 200 camps, large and small, to house foreign enemies of the regime including Montenegrins and Slovenes who fought against Italian occupation. In some cases Italy's opponents were placed under house arrest or confined to towns.

By contrast, the camps to which the Jews and Serbs in Dalmatia were consigned were designated *a scopo protettivo* (for the purposes of protection).[1] The Nazis were doubtlessly displeased with such a designation. The Jews and Serbs that had found haven in the occupied zones were held in what amounted to "protective custody" by the Italian state.

The use of "repressive" camps was intended to control hostile populations. Some prisoners were family members of Communist partisans and some were taken strictly as hostages, as leverage to be used in retaliation for partisan attacks. Sometimes Communist partisans themselves were taken as prisoners and sometimes they were executed at the end of a battle.

Arguably, the people of Italian-occupied Slovenia (Slovenia was divided such that the eastern half was annexed by Italy and part of Zone I and the western half was annexed by Germany) suffered the most under the "repressive" concentration camp system. General Roatta himself was not immune to taking draconian measures against a civilian population when he deemed it necessary. In his circular "3C," directed specifically at Slovenia, he stated, "All those families should be interned (sending them to another locality or putting them in an enclosed area and guarding them) whose male members between the ages of 16 and 60 capable of bearing arms, are or shall be absent without clear and justifiable reasons."[2] The camps were also used to contain whole segments of the Slovene population. The official policy was to deport to Italy or islands in the Adriatic all those who opposed Italian authority in the annexed portion of that land. By one estimate, out of a population of 360,000 Slovenes, some 67,230 were deported.[3]

Approximately 200 "repressive" concentration camps were created, located both within and outside of Italy. As one might imagine, the living conditions in the "repressive" camps were far worse than those in the "protective" category. The food was generally insufficient, medical care was limited, and housing and clothing were inadequate for the cold weather. The situation even drew the attention of the Vatican. In late 1942, based on reports from its representatives in Slovenia, the Holy See registered its protest of the treatment of the internees. In December, Roatta responded to the criticism by acknowledging that while problems existed, military necessity called for this course of action. It has been estimated that approximately 7,000 men, women and children died in Italian camps during the war.[4] While this figure pales in comparison to the number of deaths that occurred in Nazi concentration camps, it shows the cold determination of the Italian Fascist regime in dealing with those that opposed Italian expansionism.

The nature of warfare in the former Yugoslavia does much to explain, although it does not excuse, Italian treatment of the Slovene population. In this region, as in the lands further south, the only serious military threat to the Italian occupation forces came from the Communists. As the Communists were not strong enough to fight pitched battles against the Fascists, they used guerrilla tactics. From the Italian viewpoint, the Communists were an elusive force that enjoyed the support of most civilians. The Italians hoped that by taking hostages and relocating segments of the population, the locals would be discouraged from helping the resistance movement.

Unfortunately, many civilians were caught in the middle and often bore the brunt of Italy's retaliation against the Communists. Throughout the war, the Italian authorities posted instructions to the civilian population warning them as to the consequences if they should be caught aiding partisans. One such decree stated:

FROM THIS DAY ON, IN THE ENTIRE TERRITORY OF THE PROVINCIA LUBIANA [that portion of Slovenia formally annexed by Italy] THE FOLLOWING SHALL BE SHOT WITHOUT WARNING:

> . . . All those in whose possession arms, ammunition, or explosives shall be found;
> All those who in any way shall aid the rebels;
> All those who shall be detected in possession of forged passports, transit permits, or identity cards;
> All qualified male persons who, without an approved reason, shall be found within the military zone, behaving suspiciously.

IN THE ENTIRE PROVINCIA LUBIANA FROM THIS DAY ON THE FOLLOWING SHALL BE COMPLETELY DEMOLISHED:

> . . . All buildings in which arms, ammunition, or explosives as well as any material of military character shall be found;

All dwellings whose inhabitants, of their free will, give shelter or render hospitality to the rebels.[5]

This decree, like dozens of others issued during the war, failed to have the desired effect. Slovenia, like most regions occupied by Italy during the war, saw the formation of a resistance movement determined to expel the foreign Fascists.

These measures, although harsh, met with the approval of most Italian soldiers who found themselves surrounded by a hostile population and fighting an elusive and cunning enemy. If captured by the Communist partisans, Italian soldiers, along with German soldiers, could expect to be shot and have their bodies mutilated. After a decree on the shooting of hostages was made public on April 21, 1942, members of the National Liberation Front (partisans) responded with a policy of their own: for every hostage executed by the Italians, someone involved with or supporting the occupation would also die. There was no shortage of targets including soldiers, policemen, Italian officials, and those civilians deemed to be "collaborators."

While the Italian army never destroyed towns and murdered civilians on the same scale as the Nazis, they did nevertheless carry out reprisals. Slovene villages were burned and hostages executed. The military did not hesitate to make these incidents known to the public. A notice of May 16, 1942 declared:

> In the morning of May 14 certain Communists kidnapped two men and two women. In the morning of May 14 certain terrorists fired on the train Novo Mesto-Lubiana. The given period of time having passed without the perpetrators being found and in accordance with the decree of April 24, 1942, in retaliation for these terrorist acts, 6 persons were shot, all of them reliably guilty of Communist activities. They were shot this morning at 6:30 A.M.[6]

While this tactic undoubtedly intimidated some, the unintended consequence was to drive many into the ranks of the partisans and strengthen their resolve to drive the invaders out of Slovenia.[A]

Clearly, the Italians were not saints in this war. Mussolini's government created concentration camps in Italy and throughout their zones of occupation in Europe. This was, at the time, an all too common first step Fascist states took in dealing with enemies, both real and imagined. It is both tragic and unforgivable that thousands of Slovenes died at the hands of the Italians.

The difference between the Italian internment of Slovene civilians and Croatian Jews is the fact that the former were seen as posing a direct threat to Italian military interests while the latter were looked upon as harmless individuals. This explains to some degree why General Roatta and the Italian diplomats took the steps they did to save Croatian Jews while giving little regard to the welfare of those in the Slovene camps.

The Italian army defends Jews in Greece and southern France

Croatian Jews were not the only people to benefit from an Italian, rather than a German, occupation of their country. Their co-religionists in Greece and France were similarly fortunate to fall under the control of the more humane of the two Axis nations. Greeks had witnessed the invasion and dismemberment of its nation by the Germans and Italians. By April 1941, the Greek army was destroyed (although resistance movements soon emerged and would continue to fight the Fascists throughout the war). In the north of Greece, Germany occupied Macedonia, eastern Thrace, and the strategically vital port of Salonika (Thessaloniki). Bulgaria, which had played a minor role in the invasion, was allowed to take western Thrace, while Italy occupied the majority of the country, including Athens and the islands of the south. The Greek King George II and his government were forced to flee to Great Britain. As in Serbia, the German military ruled with an iron fist.

The vast majority of Greek Jews were trapped in the German

[A]As in other parts of Yugoslavia, the Communists were not the only resistance fighters, but they were by far the most effective. This was the case in large part because, like the Chetniks in Serbia and Croatia, non-Communist groups such as the Slovene Legion spent more time fighting the Communists than they did combating the Fascist occupation.

controlled zone. Of the nation's 76,000 Jews, some 55,000 lived in and around Salonika.7 This city was unique in that it contained the oldest Sephardic (those whose forefathers had come from Spain) Jewish community in the country dating back to 1492. In that year, King Ferdinand and Queen Isabella, having finally conquered the Moors, expelled all Muslims and Jews from their new Catholic kingdom. Some Spanish Jews, forced to abandon their homes and driven into exile, moved east and found refuge in Greece. Four hundred and fifty years later, that community would come to a sudden and violent end.

Between 1941 and 1943 the Nazis were determined to systematically wipe out the Jewish communities of Greece. In July 1942, the Jews in Greece's German zone were declared subject to forced labor. In February of the next year, the SS moved ahead with its plans for deportation. Jews were forced to wear the Star of David and move into ghettos. It was apparent to many Italian officials what the next step would be: deportation to the Nazi death camps in Poland. On February 2, 1943, writing in the wake of Germany's defeat at the battle of Stalingrad, Count Pietromarchi, the Italian Head of the Occupied Territories department in the Foreign Ministry noted in his diary, "In spite of all the disasters that have struck the Germans they continue to insist that all the Jews of the territories occupied by us be consigned to them. They confirm that by the end of 1943 there will not be a single Jew left alive in Europe. Evidently they want to involve us in the brutality of their policies." 8

The German "brutality" against the Jews that Pietromarchi spoke of began in Greece in 1942. In Salonika, the Germans expelled diplomats and closed the foreign missions as part of their preparation to deport the city's Jews. They wanted no foreign interference with their plans and wished to avoid the spectacle of desperate Jews seeking asylum from diplomatic missions.

Only the Italian consulate remained untouched. The decision to allow the Italian diplomats to remain was made so as not to offend Hitler's partner, Mussolini.

Nevertheless, friction quickly arose between the two occupiers. The tension stemmed from the fact that two Italian officials were determined to aid Jewish victims within the German sphere of influence. They were Guelfo Zamboni, the consul general in Salonika, and Captain Lucillo Merci, the consulate's military liaison officer. Everyday, scores of people arrived pleading for help from the consulate staff and Zamboni was determined to do what he could. At first he demanded that Italian Jews living in Greece be exempt from the increasingly harsh anti-Jewish decrees. It was not long before the consul insisted that this form of protection be granted to the Greek spouses and children of Italian Jews as well. Zamboni, much to the consternation of the German authorities, then began issuing naturalization papers to anyone who could show even the remotest ties of kinship to an Italian citizen. The forceful consul general went even further, issuing the precious documents to those Jews who had no claim to Italian citizenship, but who were fortunate enough to have Italian sounding names. In total Zamboni was able to send some 350 of Italy's newest citizens across the border to safety in Athens which lay within the Italian zone.

Consulate officials were not the only people who attempted to save the lives of Jews in Salonika. In mid 1942, Jews seized by the Nazis were moved to temporary holding camps in preparation for deportation. Each day dozens of Italian soldiers, acting of their own volition and not under military orders, would appear at these facilities. Their goal was simple: to obtain the release of Jews. One favorite tactic was for a soldier to find a single woman among the prisoners. He would then brazenly walk up to the guards and claim that the detainee was his wife and demand that she be released immediately.[9] The Germans more often than not complied. While this activity undoubtedly became a kind of game to the soldiers involved, the stakes were all too real: the Jews' lives were in imminent danger. Although the Italians were motivated to some extent by resentment toward their Germans partners, they were also clearly moved to action by thier sympathy for the Jews.

Although General Alexander Loehr was in command of German forces in Greece, it was the SS that had jurisdiction over the Jews within the occupation zone. It was well known that these elite troops were a law unto themselves. As consul Zamboni noted, when the SS appeared, officers, including General Loehr, "trembled from head to foot."[10] These fanatical Nazis made no secret of the fact that they resented Italian interference in their particular province, namely "Jewish affairs." In February 1943, the infamous SS leader Adolf Eichmann wrote to the German Foreign Ministry to complain that the Italian practice of naturalizing Greek Jews was contrary to Germany's stated policy regarding Jews in Greece.

Italian efforts notwithstanding, by early spring, the SS had arranged for the first Jews to be deported from Greece. In order to transport their Jewish victims with ease, the SS led the Jews to believe that they were to be "resettled" in the east. The German authorities exchanged the Jews' Greek drachmas for checks drawn on a Polish bank. Between March 15 and August 7, trains transported thousands of terrified Jews from Salonika directly to Auschwitz. Of the 48,974 Jews deported to the massive death camp 37,386 were sent directly to the gas chambers upon arrival.[11]

The Germans attempted to persuade the Italian military command to follow their example in dealing with the Jews in their sphere of influence. As was the case in Croatia, the Italians refused. When General Loehr attempted to make General Carlo Geloso, commander of the Italian Eleventh Army then occupying southern Greece, follow suit on the Jewish question, Geloso coldly responded that since he had received no specific instructions from his government ordering him to do so, he would not.

In Rome, the Germans increased diplomatic pressure. On February 25, German Foreign Minister Ribbentrop delivered a letter to Mussolini from Hitler in which the latter detailed the dangers posed by the Jews of Europe. In an effort to placate the Germans, Mussolini responded on March 13, 1943 by informing the German ambassador that the Italian government pledged to intern Greek Jews on the Ionian Islands and expel those Jews of neutral countries living in Greece.

Yet as Mussolini's heart was not in the pledge, neither provision was carried out. No orders were issued to the Italian military in Greece. So long as Italy retained a separate administrative area in Greece, those few Greek Jews who could escape to the south found a safe haven. Unfortunately, this situation was not to last.

Following Italy's withdrawal from the war in the summer of 1943, after American and British forces took Sicily and landed on the Italian mainland, the German army rapidly moved into southern Greece to fill the vacuum left by the departing Italians. This move was to have disastrous consequences for the Jews who had until that point been shielded from the horrors encountered by Jews elsewhere. In 1939, the Jewish population of Athens was small, numbering only about 3,500. By mid 1943, due to the arrival of Jewish refugees, that number had increased to approximately 5,000. A sense of dread settled over the Jewish community, as it did over the entire city, when it was learned that the German commander of the area was to be SS General Jurgen Stroop. Stroop had proven to be utterly ruthless in his suppression of Jews in the Warsaw ghetto uprising that had occurred earlier that year. After nearly a month of fighting, the lightly armed Jews had been finally forced to surrender as the ghetto burned to the ground and some 60,000 people were either dead or on their way to concentration camps.

As General Stroop began compiling lists of Jews who were to be arrested, Archbishop of Athens Papandreou Damaskinos and the Greek Orthodox clergy refused to sit idly by and do nothing. The elderly cleric secretly set about issuing false certificates of baptism and identity papers for Jews allowing them to slip though the German lines and join Communist partisan groups in the mountains. The Archbishop instructed monasteries and convents to hide Jews and priests to aid those fleeing in every way possible. All over southern Greece, clergymen complied with the directive. Unfortunately, many of them paid with their lives. By the end of the war, the Germans had deported over 600 Greek Orthodox priests for assisting Jews.

Archbishop Damaskinos was not afraid to make his views clear to the German authorities. He dispatched a letter detailing his position, knowing full well that it would fall upon deaf ears. The document, which was written by the poet Angelos Sikelianos and signed by several prominent citizens, stated in part:

. . . The Greek people were… deeply grieved to learn that

the German Occupation Authorities have already started to put into effect a program of gradual deportation of the Greek Jewish community . . . and that the first groups of deportees are already on their way to Poland . . .

According to the terms of the armistice, all Greek citizens, without distinction of race or religion, were to be treated equally by the Occupation Authorities. The Greek Jews have proven themselves . . . valuable contributors to the economic growth of the country [and] law-abiding citizens who fully understand their duties as Greeks. They have made sacrifices for the Greek country, and were always on the front lines of the struggle of the Greek nation to defend its inalienable historical rights . . .

Today we are ...deeply concerned with the fate of 60,000 of our fellow citizens who are Jews . . . we have lived together in both slavery and freedom, and we have come to appreciate their feelings, their brotherly attitude...and most important, their . . . patriotism . . .[12]

The Archbishop took a public stance against the Germans at a time when leaders of religious communities all over Europe remained silent on Nazi crimes. He was a man of remarkable fortitude.

General Stroop was furious with the Archbishop for siding with Jews and threatened to have him shot. Undeterred, Damaskinos bravely sent word back that "Greek religious leaders are not shot, they are hanged. I request that you respect this custom."[13] The strength of this response so impressed the SS general that he decided not to have Damaskinos executed.

Despite the best efforts by men like Damaskinos, the German plans for the liquidation of the remaining Jews of Greece moved forward. As long as the Italians had been in the region it had not been possible, for the sake of Axis unity, to move against the Jews in the south. However once Italy's soldiers had withdrawn, there was nothing to impede the SS from carrying out its murderous mission.

In early 1944, trains began moving north carrying the Jews of Athens. At the same time, their co-religionists who lived on the islands of Crete and Rhodes were arrested and prepared for deportation. By 1945, over 60,000 Greek Jews, or 87% of the country's Jewish population, had been murdered. Approximately 10,000 people survived.[14]

Archbishop Damaskinos continued to serve as regent, and also briefly as prime minister, until the king's return in 1946. As for his nemesis Jurgen Stroop, following the war, the SS general was brought to justice for his actions. He was tried and convicted of war crimes by a Polish court and executed in 1951.

The third segment of European territory to fall under Italian control and see resident Jews protected during the war was a region of southern France. Like their comrades stationed in Croatia and Greece, the officers and soldiers of the Italian Fourth Army shielded Jews who were desperately trying to elude capture by the Nazis and their collaborators.

On November 11, 1942, following the Allied landings in North Africa, German troops moved into Vichy, or unoccupied, France. Hitler made this decision for several reasons. Firstly it was now necessary to reinforce the southern flank of his "fortress Europe" against the Allies. Secondly, such a move would facilitate the transfer of German troops to North Africa to oppose the Allied advance. Thirdly, it had become clear that the French collaborationist government of Marshal Henri Philippe Petain, which established its capital in the southern town of Vichy, could no longer be trusted and might switch sides should the U.S. and British land in France.

At the same time that German forces were moving into Vichy territory from the north, Benito Mussolini, seeing an opportunity to seize land from France, ordered his army to occupy eight French departments in the southeast of Vichy France. The Italian military quickly overran territory that included the cities of Nice, Toulon, and Marseilles. (Eventually the border was readjusted leaving Marseilles in the Vichy controlled zone.)

This invasion marked the second time in two years that Italian soldiers found themselves on French soil. In June 1940, one month after Germany launched a devastating attack against its western neighbor, Mussolini had declared war on both France and Britain to show his loyalty to Hitler. The Italian leader revealed his plans to to his army chief of staff Marshal Pietro Badoglio, "I need only a few thousand dead to ensure that I have the right to sit at the peace table in the capacity of a belligerent."[15] By the time Mussolini gave the order to deploy Italian divisions, the French army was already on the verge of collapse from fighting the Germans. This fact notwithstanding, the invasion was less than popular with the common soldiers. They soon found themselves crowded into narrow, mountain passes that made ideal terrain for the few stubborn defenders. President Franklin D. Roosevelt, who had tried to persuade Mussolini to remain neutral, angrily declared, "The hand that held the dagger has stuck it in the back of its neighbor."[16] It was a cowardly act on Italy's part to attack a country that was on the verge of being defeated by the Nazis.

By the time France formally agreed to an armistice with Italy on June 24, 1940, two days after surrendering to Germany, Mussolini had the "few thousand dead" he needed. With the German establishment of a French puppet government at Vichy to administer the southern part of the country, Mussolini ordered his Italian forces to withdraw. He had shown his loyalty to Hitler, although Hitler was less than impressed by the Italian military.

Italy's second entry into France would prove to be far easier than the first and would greatly benefit one segment of the French population—the Jews.

In the German-occupied north of France, shortly after that country's capitulation, ordinances were passed that defined Jews in racial terms, setting them apart from the rest of society, and allowed for the confiscation of their property. The first mass arrest took place in May 1941. The Germans began with Jews who had come to France as refugees, but soon included those of French birth as well. In August, 4,300 Jews, including 1,300 French citizens were sent to the compound at Drancy, which throughout the war served as a transit camp for Auschwitz. Over the next few months, Jews were ordered to register with the police, abide by a curfew, and wear the Yellow Star of David on their outer clothing for easy identification. On March 28, 1942, the first train departed Drancy for Auschwitz.[17]

By the war's end some 90,000 French Jews had been murdered.

While the plight of Jews in the north was desperate, the situation facing those in the unoccupied zone appeared to be uncertain. On July 2, 1942, Petain and his Council of Ministers drew a distinction between French Jews and those of foreign origin. Those holding French citizenship were safe for the time being, while the foreigners were to be rounded up and interned. Under pressure from Germany to hand over all foreign Jews, the officially anti-Semitic Vichy government willingly complied. Under the Vichy regime, French Jews were not permitted to hold public office, serve in the military, or engage in the teaching or banking professions. In August, some fifteen thousand foreign Jews, the majority refugees from Germany, Austria, and Eastern Europe, were turned over to the Nazis for deportation.

Following the dramatic events of November, although Vichy officials technically remained in charge of the southern third of France, the real power lay with the German and Italian militaries. As in Croatia, the Axis partners implemented very different policies toward Jews in their respective zones of influence. In the Italian zone, Jews were left unmolested. By contrast, in the German controlled area, the French police were encouraged to continue rounding up foreign Jews and keeping those of French birth under close surveillance. The Germans felt it would be easier to pressure the Vichy government into handing over foreign Jews, who were not even French citizens, for deportation first, before persecuting French Jews.

As in other occupied lands, including Croatia, the Germans depended on the cooperation of the local authorities to help them carry out their "final solution to the Jewish question." The amount of assistance given by puppet regimes varied greatly from country to country, and largely depended upon the degree to which anti-Semitism had permeated the local population. In the case of France, while Jews had been granted full citizenship since the time of the French revolution, a stubborn streak of anti-Semitism continued to run through French society. The Christian Church called Jews Christ killers so they were rejected by God and from time to time pogroms occurred especially in Eastern Europe. Even many secular Frenchmen thought of Jews as outsiders who could not be trusted to be loyal to the state. In 1894 the notorious Dreyfus affair occurred in which a French officer Alfred Dreyfus was wrongly convicted of spying for the Germans. Some French men and women were never quite able to live up to the Revolution's ideals of *liberte egalite fraternite*.

In December 1942, the first instance of conflict over Jews between the Vichy/ German authorities and the Italian administrators took place. The French prefect Marcel Ribiere ordered all foreign Jews to register at the nearest police office. The prefect then planned to send the Jews to internment camps across the Rhone River in the German occupied sector. Upon hearing the news and perceiving it as a direct challenge to Italian authority in the region, the Italian Foreign Ministry quickly cancelled the French order. Foreign Minister Ciano declared in no uncertain terms that, "measures ...with regard to said Jews must pertain solely to Italian authorities without exception...the disposition regarding the Jews must be suspended."[18]

A month later, the French attempted to force Jews within the Italian zone to wear the Star of David on their clothing. As in the previous instance, the Italian military cancelled the edict. *The Times* reported the incident on January 21, 1943. The article stated:

> Last week in the Italian-occupied departments of Savoie, Haute Savoie, Basses Alpes, Hautes Alpes, Alpes Maritimes and Var, the Italian commanding generals notified the Prefects that it was irreconcilable with the dignity of the Italian army that in territories occupied by Italians, Jews should be compelled to appear in public with this stigmatizing badge, and consequently notified the prefects that Vichy's orders were to be cancelled.[19]

It was clear that as far as the Italians were concerned, military law would henceforth supersede French civil law in the areas under their control.

This decision not only infuriated Vichy officials, but caught the attention of the SS in France as well. Over the next few months, from his office in Paris, SS *Standartenfuehrer* (Colonel) Helmut Knochen sent a stream of messages to Heinrich Mueller, head of the Gestapo section of the *Reichssicherheitshauptamt* (Main Office of Reich Security), in Berlin complaining about the actions taken by the Italian military on behalf of Jews. "Gestapo" Mueller, as he was known, was one of the most efficient and feared members of the Nazi leadership. Content to keep a low profile, Mueller focused on hunting down those considered to be disloyal to the Reich. He had long been involved with the "Jewish question." During *Krystallnacht* (November 9-10, 1938), he had issued orders forbidding the police to interfere as Nazi gangs burned and looted Jewish homes and Synagogues. The next year Mueller had arranged for the deportation of Austria's Jews. Following that assignment he had been a participant at the Wannsee Conference and therefore had been directly responsible for helping formulate the policy of genocide.

On January 13, 1943, Knochen sent a message to Mueller entitled "Treatment of the Jews in the Newly Occupied French Territories" which detailed Vichy's Prime Minister Pierre Laval's complaints of the Italian's interference with his plans for the Jews. Knochen suggested that *Reichsfuehrer* SS Heinrich Himmler be made aware of the situation as soon as possible. He continued, ". . . the Italians are acting as the champions of the foreign Jews, if this continues the political Jewish agenda as we understand it will be rendered impossible, and we cannot count on obtaining the French Jews in the next few months so as to deport them."[20]

Over the next few months, the Italian military continued to frustrate the Germans as well as their French collaborationist partners. The Italian military authorities refused to allow the Vichy government to establish detention camps for foreign Jews within its territory or to stamp the word "Jew" on official identification papers and in ration books.

Following an incident in which members of the French resistance shot two German officers, the Germans arrested and deported some 2,000 Jews between the ages of 16 and 65 to Auschwitz in retaliation.[21] By 1943, it had become common practice in lands occupied by Germany to take hostages, often Jews, and deport them whenever partisan attacks occurred. This tactic not only provided an excuse to send Jews to the East, but also served as a warning to the local population against aiding local resistance movements. Vichy policemen were charged with carrying out the assignment of taking and deporting Jewish hostages and soon began detaining Jews within both the German and Italian occupied areas. In his report to Mueller of February 22, Knochen described how the chief police administrator of Lyon had ordered his officers to arrest some 200 to 300 people, all ex-German and ex-Polish Jews, as per the instructions of his government. Once again the Italians objected to the arrests that were taking place within their jurisdiction.

One dramatic example of Italian action occurred when approximately 100 Jews were taken to the town of Grenoble to be placed on trains to Auschwitz. SS *Standartenfuehrer* Knochen's communiqué described how, "The Italian General stationed at Grenoble demanded that the French retract the arrest orders of the Jews. The chief police administrator was obliged to retract the arrest orders." He further lamented, "the Italians...again have stopped the implementation of measures against the Jews prescribed by the French government."[22] In the case of those imprisoned at Grenoble, the local commander actually had Italian troops block the railroad tracks and ordered his men to surround the prison to insure that the Jews were released.[23] Needless to say the Germans were furious. In Knochen's lengthy message he blamed not only the Italians but, the Jews themselves. He charged that, "the Jews are trying to establish good relations between Italian soldiers and the French population stressing that the French and Italians are of the same race and are much more compatible than Germans and French or Germans and Italians... I plead with you to intervene so that Italian civil and military authorities receive instructions from the Italian government so as not to create difficulties for the French in dealing with the Jewish question in the French areas occupied by the Italians."[24] Standartenfuehrer Knochen ended his report by relating rumors that he had heard whereby Italians were

Inmates working in a sewing factory in Jasenovac Concentration Camp.
Courtesy of The Croatian History Museum.

Inmates at Jasenovac Concentration Camp.
Courtesy of The Croatian History Museum.

Croatian leader Ante Pavelic reviewing officers at Zagreb airfield.
Courtesy of The Croatian History Museum.

Civilians on forced march to Jasenovac Concentration Camp.
Courtesy of The Croatian History Museum.

Josip Broz (Tito) 1943.
Courtesy of The Croatian History Museum.

German soldiers kicking a man to death, the man on the far left is an
Ustasha officer.
Courtesy of the USHMM.

The Jewish battalion formed on Rab—it lasted only three weeks until
Tito assigned its members to other units.
Courtesy of the USHMM.

Communist partisans in a forest including Jewish fighters.
Courtesy of the USHMM.

Bulgarians deporting the Jews of Macedonia March 1943.
Courtesy of the USHMM.

Iinmates at hard labor
Jasenovac
Concentration Camp.
Courtesy of the USHMM.

Maks Luburic
Commandant of
Jasenovac
Concentration Camp.
Courtesy of the USHMM.

Ante Pavelic and Adolf Hitler.
Courtesy of the USHMM.

Italian Ambassador to Croatia Raffaele Casertano (back left) and Luca
Pietromarchi (front left) in Venice June 1941.
Courtesy of the USHMM.

Croatian leader Ante Pavelic (third from left), Italian Foreign Minister Galeazzo Ciano, Luca Pietromarchi, Head of the Occupied Territories Department of the Italian Foreign Ministry (seated behind Ciano), and German Foreign Minister Joachim Ribbentrop at the signing ceremony that made Croatia a partner in the Tripartite Pact, June 15, 1941.
Courtesy of the USHMM.

Andrija Artukovic Croatian Minister of the Interior.
Courtesy of the USHMM.

General Paride Negri, commander of the "Murge" division.

General Giuseppe Amico, commander of the "Marche" division, murdered by the Germans in 1943.

General Mario Roatta.
Courtesy of the Italian Ministry of Defense.

Ustasha members pose as they
murder a Serb.
Courtesy of the USHMM.

Ruins of the main synagogue in Zagreb. *Courtesy of the USHMM.*

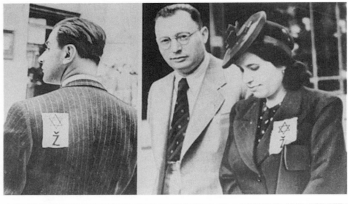

Jewish man and woman forced to wear the Star of David. *courtesy of the USHMM.*

Marshal Tito (left).

Italian dictator Benito Mussolini

Italian soldiers fighting in Croatia, April 1941. *courtesy of the Italian Ministry of Defense.*

secretly allowing Jews to escape across the border into Switzerland and even Italy itself.

Knochen's complaints did not fall upon deaf ears. His superiors in Berlin, including Mueller, Himmler, and Ribbentrop, were determined to apply maximum pressure to convince the Italians to cooperate with the Vichy government. Himmler, who was convinced that the Italian military was obstructing his plans, strongly suggested that Mussolini place the matter in the hands of the Italian police rather than the military. The SS leader knew that the police were technically part of the Ministry of the Interior which was headed by the notorious anti- Semite Guido Buffarini Guidi. Himmler reasoned therefore that the police would be more likely to cooperate with the French in their quest to deport Jews.

In a meeting with Mussolini in late February 1943, Foreign Minister Ribbentrop raised the issue of the French Jews. He bluntly stated that he believed the Italian army was protecting Jews in France as well as those in Croatia. Soon thereafter *Il Duce* also met with Germany's ambassador to Italy, George Mackensen. The Italian dictator knew what was happening in France, but evaded any personal responsibility by placing the blame squarely upon the shoulders of his generals. In his dispatch to Berlin of March 18, Mackensen wrote that Mussolini had stated, "This is a question with which the [Italian] Generals must not meddle. Their attitude is the result not only of lack of understanding, but also of sentimental humanitarianism, which is not in accord with our harsh epoch. The necessary instructions will therefore be issued this very day to General Ambrosio, giving a completely free hand to the French police in this matter."[25]

Fortunately, Italy's leader never issued the promised explicit orders commanding his generals to cooperate with the French authorities. Despite his promise to the Germans, Mussolini seems to have had reservations about involving his country in genocide. Whether his hesitation was based on humanitarianism, a defense of Italian sovereignty, or a combination of the two is a matter of conjecture.

The immediate action taken by Mussolini was to confer with his newly promoted Foreign Minister Giuseppe Bastianini, the former governor of Dalmatia, and General Ambrosio. Bastianini later shared details of the meeting with his subordinate Luca Pietromarchi who recorded the information in his diary. According to Pietromarchi, General Ambrosio denied the army was protecting Jews and *Il Duce* stated he did not believe him. Bastianini then asked to speak candidly to Mussolini. As an early member of the Fascist Party, he had known the Italian dictator for many years and felt secure enough to express what was on his mind. He stated:

> The real reason for the attitudes of our officers was not said by Ambrosio, but I am going to say it to you, Duce. Our people know what fate awaits the Jews consigned to the Germans. They will all be gassed without distinction, the old women, babies. And that's why our people will never permit such atrocities to take place with their connivance. And you, Duce, may not give your consent. Why do you want to assume responsibility which will fall on you entirely?[26]

Mussolini responded that he had already promised Mackensen that he would issue orders calling for an end to the Italian military's obstructionist activities. In order to save Mussolini from giving such orders, Bastianini asked for permission to handle the situation by speaking to Mackensen. Mussolini eagerly granted the request.

Throughout the month of March, the battle between the Vichy government and the Italians over who had legal jurisdiction over both foreign and French Jews continued. The Vichy government continued to assert its authority only to be rebuffed by the Italian military. One such clash occurred on March 3, 1943. The Italian Supreme Command's liaison officer to Vichy, General Carlo Avarna Di Gualtieri, wrote to Admiral Charles Platon, the Vichy official hand-picked by the Germans to handle Jewish affairs, that it had come to his attention that the prefects of Valence, Chambery, and Annecy had detained numerous Jews and subsequently transferred eight to the Pyrenees. When Italian soldiers questioned the policemen they responded by saying they were following orders from Vichy. He went on to say, "With these facts the Italian Supreme

Command cannot give it's consent and support these measures—arrests, internments etc. independent of the fact that they are Italian, French, or foreign Jews. These measures are solely the responsibility of the Italian occupation authorities. For this reason, the Italian Supreme Command requests that the Vichy government annul the arrest orders, and orders the prefects of the territories to abstain from these measures against Jews of Italian, French, or foreign nationality." [27]

The Italians found it much easier to refuse to cooperate with the French than with the Germans. Nevertheless, they were determined to stand up to their powerful northern neighbor. In spite of Germany's position as the dominant member of the Axis alliance, General Mario Vercellino, commander of the Fourth Army, stationed in southern France, like his counterparts, Generals Geloso in Greece and Roatta in Croatia, would not tolerate German interference in his zone of occupation.

Fortunately, a showdown never occurred between Vercellino and his German superior Field Marshall Karl Gert von Rundstedt. This was likely because deporting Jews was not a priority for Rundstedt. The German Field Marshall had more pressing military issues to deal with such as ascertaining where the Allies would strike next and how to defend against such an attack.

Mussolini was constantly walking a tight rope between satisfying the Germans and listening to the wishes of his Generals. He attempted to placate the Germans by heeding Himmler's advice and placing the Jews under the jurisdiction of the Italian police. Mussolini sent former police inspector Guido Lospinoso to France to act as his personal representative. Lospinoso's immediate assignment was to establish a Commissariat for Jewish Affairs. The Germans were delighted that the police, rather than the army, would now determine the future of the Jews. This was not surprising considering the fact that General Vercellino had actually requested permission from Rome to be allowed to arrest French policemen who refused to acknowledge his authority and continued to harass Jews.

Both Gestapo Chief Mueller and SS Colonel Knochen were pleased to hear of Lospinoso's appointment, believing he would be sympathetic to their goals. They soon found that they were mistaken. From the time of his arrival in Nice, the new official was determined not to assist the Nazis in any way. Lospinoso believed that Mussolini had told the Germans what they wanted to hear and that his leader had not been serious about cooperating with either the SS or the French police. He therefore decided to avoid meeting with top German officials for as long as possible.[28]

During all this diplomatic maneuvering throughout the spring of 1943, Jews who were able to travel continued to move into the Italian zone of France where they were allowed to live normal lives, free from harassment and persecution. This situation was, of course, similar to that which had existed in the early days of the Italian occupation of Croatia. Most refugees made their way to the city of Nice, where the local Jewish Committee supplied them with ration cards and identity papers. One such man was Albert Sharon. One day Sharon had a frightening encounter on the street with two French policemen. The gendarmes had stopped him during a routine document check and, not satisfied that his papers were legitimate (papers bearing the stamp of the Jewish Committee were not official documents), they threatened to take him to the nearest police station. Fortunately, Sharon spotted two Italian policemen walking nearby. Summoning all his courage, the frightened man called out, "If you don't stop pestering me I'll call the Italian police."[29] The move so startled the Frenchmen that they let him go with the warning to stay off the streets.

As the number of Jews arriving in the Italian sphere increased, German pressure for their deportation mounted. Heinz Roethke, head of the Jewish Department of the Gestapo based in Paris, submitted a report to Berlin entitled "Present Situation of the Jewish Question in France." According to the Gestapo's statistics, it was estimated that there were some 50,000 Jews in the Italian zone as of July 21, 1943.[30] As a way to motivate the Italians to action, the Germans used the argument that Jews were loyal to the Allied cause and therefore a security risk.

Finally, after months of delays, during the spring of 1943, the Italian authorities agreed to act and move all the Jews who were living along the Cote d'Azure to towns inland from the coast. Yet following this forced transfer to the interior, the Jews were able to live comfortably. Since the war had disrupted so many lives, there were numerous vacant hotel rooms and vacation homes available for their use. Albert Sharon found his new surroundings quite pleasant, "It was like a respite after being so long under the German occupation and being afraid of every little thing; a rumor ... a knock at the door, you felt completely at ease. You knew that you were safe, but for how long we didn't know."[31] Another Jewish refugee, Alfred Feldman, whose mother and sister had been deported, recalled being amazed by what he saw upon reaching the town of Saint-Martin-Vesubie:

> I arrived at Saint-Martin toward evening and I saw something that I had not been accustomed to seeing for a long time; Jews were passing peacefully through the streets, sitting in the cafes, speaking in French, German, some even in Yiddish. I also saw some carabinieri [Italian military police] who passed through the narrow streets of the town with their characteristic Napoleonic hats, and even a group of bersaglieri [Italian elite light infantry] with their black plumes. Everything seemed to be happening freely, there were no particular regulations concerning relations between refugees. Discussion flourished with the greatest liberty.[32]

As one might expect, the assigning of refugees to enforced residences in small towns did not satisfy the Germans, who continued to complain that this move accomplished very little. Nevertheless, as in Croatia and Greece, the Germans respected Italian sovereignty in their areas. Pressure could be brought to bear, however sending the German army or the SS in to seize Jews was simply out of the question.

Nazi officials often expressed their feelings of frustration in reports to their superiors. A clear example may be seen in Roethke's dispatch of July 21. Under the subheading "Attitudes of the Italians in the Face of the Jewish Problem," he wrote, "The attitude of the Italians as always is incomprehensible. The Italian army and police protect the Jews with all means and power available to them. The Italian zone of Influence, particularly the Cote d'Azure, has become a veritable sacred ground for the Jews of France." Roethke concluded with an appeal to make known to the SD (security service) that, "The Italians have transferred 1,000 poor Jews from the Cote d'Azure to the departments of l'Isere and Savoie. The Jews are living under no restrictions and are lodged in the best hotels."[33] SS Colonel Knochen of course, shared his colleague's perspective:

> The best of harmony prevails between the Italian troops and the Jewish population. The Italians live in the homes of the Jews. The Jews invite them out and pay for them. The German and Italian conceptions seem here to be completely at variance. We are informed on the French side that Jewish influence has already given birth to pacifist and Communist rot in the minds of Italian soldiers, and even creating a pro-American tendency. These Jewish intermediaries also see to it that good relations are established between Italian soldiers and the French population. They say that the French and the Italians, both Latin peoples, understand each other much better than the French and the Germans or the Germans and the Italians. They work according to a system—strong criticism of the German-Italian relationship on the one hand, preparation for a Franco-Italian understanding on the other. They endeavor at the same time to distort the way of thinking of the entire population, on the pretext that in the event of an American attack the Italians will not defend themselves because . . . the Americans will at last bring them peace . . . If the anti-Jewish measures throughout France are to succeed, they must also be applied in the Italian zone.[34]

This impasse continued until September 8, 1943 when news of the Italian armistice became public. Over the weeks that followed, as the Italian army withdrew across the border, the Germans moved in to seize the now vulnerable Jews. Some were captured and deported, including approximately 5,000 from the city of Nice.[35] Most went into hiding or made contact with the resistance and those that could followed the retreating Italians into northern Italy. Of course this move was no guarantee of finding safety, as the Germans soon occupied that region as well.

The Position of Jews in Mussolini's Italy

Many Italians in Mussolini's Italy both admired and respected Jews. The status of Jews in Italian society had vastly improved following the *Risorgimento* (the process of unifying the nation). Jews were integrated socially and economically into Italian society. After 1870, ghettos (areas of cities in which Jews were forced to live apart from the Christian population) that dated from the Middle Ages were closed and Jews were granted the same rights under the law as their fellow countrymen. Modern Italy was founded by men whose philosophies included both liberalism and anti-clericalism which assured major benefits for Italy's Jews. They were allowed to move into mainstream society and, as education and the professions were opened to them, most prospered.

As they became integrated into society, Jews aligned themselves with various political ideologies according to their individual values. Over time, as more Jews entered the middle class, they, like their neighbors, became more conservative. By the early 1920s, some had even moved to the far right and become active in the Fascist movement. When Mussolini staged his March on Rome in 1922, close to 250 Jews were among his black shirted supporters. By the mid 1930's, approximately one in four adult Jews in Italy was a member of the *Partito Nationale Fascista* (National Fascist Party). This number is surprising in that only ten per cent of Italian population held membership in the Party.

There were of course those Jews on the left of the political spectrum that sought to keep the spirit of liberalism alive and vehemently opposed the rise of Fascism. The Rosselli brothers, Carlo and Nello, became the most well known of these activists. The two men loathed Fascism and all it stood for and together founded the opposition movement *Giustizia e Liberta* (Justice and Liberty). They eventually became such an irritant that they were murdered by

Mussolini's regime in 1937. It was thought by many that both Count Ciano and General Roatta had a hand in the killings.

A German Diplomatic Offensive to Seize the Croatian Jews

In his marathon meeting with German Foreign Minister Ribbentrop of February 1943, Mussolini was able to avoid giving in to German pressure to deport French Jews, but faltered when it came to the Jews of Croatia. According to Colonel Vincenzo Carla, a Supersloda officer under General Robotti, Mussolini had admitted, "Minister von Ribbentrop was in Rome for three days and employed all kinds of pressure to ensure that the Yugoslavian Jews will be extradited. I tried to put him off with excuses, but he persisted, so in order to rid myself of him I was forced to agree. The Jews should be transferred to Trieste and given over to the Germans."[36]

General Robotti immediately objected, citing as his reasons the same arguments that had been made previously by others. He made it clear that the deportation of Jews would surely lead to their deaths. Secondly, and of equal importance, the prestige of the Italian army would suffer, as it would appear to be weak and subservient to the will of the Germans. In response, a frustrated Mussolini declared, "O.K, O.K., I was forced to give my consent to the extradition, but you can produce all the excuses that you want so that not even one Jew will be extradited. Say that we simply have no boats available to transport them by sea and that by land there is no possibility of doing so."[37] This pivotal statement marked a turning point in the struggle to save the lives of Croatian Jews. From here on, the soldiers and diplomats would be supported in their efforts by the head of state.

Mussolini's Attitudes toward Jews

Benito Mussolini had never been an anti-Semite. However, he had been a political opportunist. He praised Jews in the 1920s when he was at odds with Hitler and encouraged anti-Semitism in the 1930's as he grew closer to Germany's dictator. On a personal level, Mussolini had several friends who were Jewish and there were even a few Italian Jews in the forefront of Italy's Fascist movement. One of his early and highly esteemed mistresses, the intelligent and sophisticated Margherita Safatti, was Jewish. Safatti, who was older than her lover, is credited with teaching him a great deal about art and culture.

The only Jews that Mussolini routinely criticized were those who described themselves as Zionists (Jews who sought to establish a Jewish state in what had been their ancient homeland in Palestine). Throughout his life, Mussolini stated that Zionists could not be trusted as they possessed divided loyalties (to their home country of Italy and to the country of Israel, should it come into being). As Mussolini hoped to see Italy dominate the Middle East he therefore had no disire to see an independent Jewish state emerge in that part of the world.

Mussolini explained the violently anti-Semitic position of the Nazis by stating that Hitler needed some group to blame for Germany's defeat in the Great War and had chosen the Jews as scapegoats. Hitler believed that Germany had been betrayed by a conspiracy of Liberals and Jews within Germany and had lost WWI as a result. The Jews could also be blamed for Germany's problems of unemployment and a poor economy, especially after the Great Depression struck.

As to Mussolini's own country he stated, "Anti-Semitism does not exist in Italy . . . the Italian Jews have always shown themselves good citizens, and they fought bravely in the war. They occupy leading positions in the universities, in the army, in the banks. Quite a few are generals."[38] In a1932 treatise, *Il Duce* rejected Hitler's idea of Fascism in which race was the central factor in creating a nation. He wrote that a nation is, "not a race, or geographically defined region, but a people, historically perpetuating itself; a multitude unified by an idea and imbued with a will to live, the will to power, self-consciousness, personality."[39] Accordingly, Jews were welcomed to participate in his vision of Fascism.

Yet Jews did not lead a worry-free existence in Mussolini's Italy. In February 1929, Mussolini signed a concordat with the Vatican in which Catholicism was declared the state religion. Although he disliked Catholicism and had been raised in an anti-Catholic socialist household, Mussolini saw the political benefits of making peace with the Church. The Vatican agreed not to interfere in state matters and Mussolini agreed not to interfere with religious affairs (for example, marriages were deemed legitimate even without state involvement). Many Jews worried they might be persecuted by a newly strengthened Church. Although the Church had consistently been losing power since 1870 when Italy was finally unified and a spirit of secularism and liberalism prevailed, it was still a powerful entity. Jews were reassured by Mussolini in a speech on May 13 that "The Jews have been in Rome ever since the time of the kings. . . . There were fifty thousand at the time of Augustus, and they asked to weep on the corpse of Julius Caesar. They will stay here undisturbed."[40]

Naturally, there were some anti-Semites within the Fascist Party who lobbied for measures against Jews, but they were for the most part ignored. Between 1922 when Mussolini came to power and 1938, the Jews of Italy were left alone to live their lives. This situation began to change when Adolf Hitler assumed the office of Chancellor of Germany on January 30, 1933.

While the Italian dictator had been gratified to see a fellow Fascist in power he viewed the relationship between Hitler and Mussolini, Mussolini was gratified to see a fellow Fascist in power, but he viewed Hitler less as an equal and more as a successful protégé. After all, it had been Hitler who, nine years earlier, had written to Mussolini declaring his admiration and asking for Italian support of his movement.[B]

Mussolini first met Hitler face to face at a meeting especially arranged for that purpose in Venice in 1934. The Italian dictator was less than impressed with Germany's new leader. He found Hitler's longwinded speeches tedious and was annoyed that he insisted that pressure should be brought to bear on Austrian Prime Minister Engelbert Dollfuss to include Austrian Nazis in his cabinet.

[B]The letter, which was delivered by Hermann Goering to Giuseppe Bastianini, had been written from Lansberg prison. Hitler at the time was behind bars for the 1923 *putsch* in which he had attempted to overthrow the Bavarian government.

While Mussolini may have initially underestimated Hitler's ruthless political nature, his perception soon changed. In July, when Austrian Nazis assassinated Dollfuss, many assumed that Hitler had a hand in the murder. Over the next few years, Europe witnessed Hitler's power grow. Germany was rapidly rearming, in direct violation of the Treaty of Versailles, and making territorial demands. German troops marched triumphantly into the Rhineland in 1936 and absorbed Austria in 1938. In spite of misgivings Mussolini had about Hitler personally, he felt that the time had come to form an alliance with the new rising power.

As Italy moved closer to Germany, Mussolini knew an expression of solidarity was in order. To that end, in November 1938, were laws was passed that set Jews apart from other Italians. There is no evidence to suggest that Hitler demanded such laws be implemented in Italy; they seem to have been entirely Mussolini's idea. These laws, like those that would be enacted in Croatia three years later, were based on the Nuremberg laws of 1935.C   Following the German model, Jews were prohibited from joining the military, civil service or the Fascist Party. They were not allowed to marry Aryans, as the Italians now called themselves, or employ them as servants. They were barred from owning large tracts of land or controlling companies that employed large numbers of people. Those Jews that had become naturalized Italian citizens after January 1, 1919 (the beginning of the first full year after the end of WWI) had their citizenship revoked and were forced to emigrate.   (In 1938, Italy's Jewish population numbered approximately 57,000, less than one percent of the total population. Of these, some 10,000 were foreign-

---

CThe Nuremberg laws went into effect on September 15,1935 with the intent of excluding Jews from German society. The first law, known as the Reich Citizenship Law, stripped Jews of German citizenship since they were not "Aryans." They were now considered "subjects" of the German Reich." A second piece of legislation entitled the "Law for the Protection of German Blood and Honor" prohibited marriage between Aryans and Jews as well as sexual relations between members of these two groups. It also forbade German women under the age of 45 to be employed as servants in Jewish households. Over the next eight years an additional thirteen ordinances were added to the first law depriving Jews of other rights within Germany.

ers, mainly refugees from Germany and Austria.) Foreign Jews, like their denaturalized brethren, were also ordered to leave the country by March 1939.

There were notable differences between Italy's new laws and those of Germany. One variation concerned the treatment of veterans. While the Nazis ignored the contributions made by Jews who had served in the military (12,000 had given their lives for Germany in the First World War),[41] in Italy, a distinguished war record could exempt a man from the new legislation. Prior service to Fascism was also recognized as grounds for exemption. While Jews in Italy could be pressed into forced labor for the benefit of the state, as they could be in Germany, they were not treated as badly. The prisoners were neither physically abused nor worked to death in Italy as they were in German-occupied lands.

A further distinction may be seen in how the two states actually applied the anti-Jewish laws. Unlike the government of Nazi Germany that prided itself on its superior organization and capacity to implement assignments (despite the fact that departments and ministries often squabbled over jurisdictional matters), the Italian government in the 1930's was hardly a model of efficiency. Mussolini never achieved the degree of central control over the country that Fascist theory called for. This lack of tight management combined with some sympathetic party officials in the provinces meant that the anti-Jewish measures were applied unevenly.

The Italian Camp System

The camp system that the Italians had established throughout the Balkans was also employed in Italy proper. In 1940 officials began to intern those foreign Jews that had not left the country. Jews were arrested and sent to half a dozen camps, the largest of which was Ferramonti Tarsia in Calabria. At first only Jewish men were sent to the camp, but by September women and children began to arrive as well. Even though this facility was technically designated as a "repressive" camp, it soon took on the semblance of those of the "protective" variety. The inmates were given a great deal of latitude in organizing their own affairs. To that end, a school, three synagogues and a library were established. Sports teams soon appeared and even a theatre troupe was formed for the entertainment of those interned. While living behind wire and sleeping in barracks with thirty other prisoners was far from comfortable, the food was sufficient and unlike the camps run by the Germans no inmates were ever tortured or murdered in Farramonti Tarsia. While the majority of inmates were Jews, political prisoners and "enemies of the regime," some from Slovenia and Greece, were also sent to the camp. Eventually the population reached 3,900.

The internees were allowed to receive Red Cross parcels, letters and money from relatives, and amazingly even a small stipend from the Italian government.[42] It was not long before the inmates and the local townspeople began to trade with one another. The Jews sought fruit, vegetables, and eggs, while the locals were only too happy to accept cash or items from the Red Cross packages.

The first camp commander, Paolo Salvatore, did nothing to stop such actions. In January 1943, he was replaced for being too lenient with the prisoners. His successor was Mario Fraticelli. Although the new commander announced that strict standards of discipline would be established, for the most part, he followed the example set by his predecessor. After initiating roll call for all prisoners three times a day, at which prisoners were required to give the Fascist salute, it was back to business as usual in the camp.

Although life in the camp was tolerable, the inmates were concerned about their future. By 1943 rumors were rampant about gas chambers and mass executions in the east. That same year, two men who had escaped from death camps arrived at Ferrimonti and informed the prisoners of the ghastly events they had witnessed in Poland and Czechoslovakia.[43] As a result, the internees became extremely concerned when a truck arrived one summer evening and Fraticelli ordered that all one hundred children in the camp be loaded on board. After the vehicle's departure, the apprehension of mothers and fathers soon turned to panic when a rumor spread that the young people were being sent north. After enduring several agonizing hours of waiting, parents were relieved beyond measure to see the truck bearing their children return. It turned out that

Fraticelli and his wife had taken the youngsters to town for *gelato*. In the words of author Paul Paolicelli, "If there were ever a symbol for the extraordinary differences between the German and Italian camps, the night of the gelato run stands out as the most profound example."[44]

Following Mussolini's fall, there was a distinct possibility that the Germans, who were quickly assuming control of Italy, would deport the entire population of Ferrimonti. Unsure of who was in command, Fraticelli traveled to Rome to seek instructions. During the commandant's absence, a harrowing moment occurred that could have led to the deportation of the inmates. A German general moving through the area by rail decided to inspect the camp. Word spread quickly of the presence of this unexpected and unwanted visitor. In a moment of inspiration, the internees lowered the Italian flag and in its place raised a quarantine banner. The local priest arrived and told the German that a cholera epidemic had broken out, but that he was welcome to enter the compound at his own risk. The General refused the invitation and continued on his way.[45]

On September 14, 1943, British troops liberated the camp at Ferrimonti. Two months later, an official of the British Foreign Office, A. W.G. Randall reported that the mortality rate among inmates at the camp had been 12 per 2,000 due mainly to heart conditions and tuberculosis. He further added that, "Professor Mirski, a Yugoslav Jew and head of the Camp Committee, did not attribute any death in the camp to treatment received from the Italian authorities, who appear to have behaved humanely."

Mussolini's Attitudes toward Hitler and the Nazis

The relationship between Mussolini and Hitler was complicated and moved through several stages between 1922 and 1945. At first Mussolini was seen as the master and Hitler the student. In the early 1920s Hitler saw Mussolini as a role model and sought to emulate the older leader in his political skills and style of public speaking. After Hitler came to power in 1933, however, the situation began to change. As the 1930s wore on, Hitler's power increased, he became more confident on the international stage, and he began to see himself as Mussolini's equal. By the middle of WWII, *Il Duce* had become entirely dependent upon his one-time admirer not only for power, but for his very survival as well.

In the early 1930s, the two nations were actually rivals for power and influence on mainland Europe. By 1934 Mussolini was well aware that Hitler sought to destroy Austria as an independent state and absorb it into the German Reich (which he did four years later) and feared the shift of power in Germany's favor that would follow. Mussolini weighed the risks and benefits of war with Germany. Had Mussolini decided to attack the Nazis in 1934 in order to defend the independence of Austria, rather than chosen to seek an alliance with the Nazis in 1939, Europe could have been spared a devastating war. On July 25, 1934 Austrian Nazis, who favored unification with Germany, assassinated the Austrian Chancellor, Engelbert Dollfus.[D] Whether or not Hitler had a direct hand in the murder is uncertain, but the destabilization of Austria surely benefited the Germans. *Il Duce*, wary of German intensions toward Austria, actually moved troops to the Brenner Pass to prepare for action should Germany invade its weaker neighbor and discussions were held between the Italian and French militaries concerning possible joint action should an attack upon Austria take place. Following the Dollfuss murder Mussolini referred to Hitler as a "horrible sexual degenerate, a dangerous fool."

On the personal side, between 1933 and 1945 the two dictators met several times and despite their public pleasantries, Mussolini privately showed his contempt for Hitler early. In the 1920s, Hitler had written to Mussolini asking for an autographed picture, but Mussolini did not respond. At their first meeting in Venice on June 14, 1934, Hitler dressed in civilian clothes and a wrinkled raincoat felt insecure standing next to Mussolini in his smartly tailored Fascist militia uniform. Hitler learned about appearances. In their next meeting in Germany in 1937, Hitler spared no expense to impress Mussolini with parades, receptions and his own uniform.

[D]Dollfus had been a personal friend of Mussolini, and in fact the chancellor's wife had been visiting Rome when news arrived of her husband's assassination.

Mussolini was not alone in his negative opinion of *Der Fuehrer*. While on a state visit to Rome in May 1938, Hitler received a lukewarm reception from the Italian King Victor Emmanuel III. The king, somewhat comically, expressed the view that Hitler was a psychopath with very poor table manners. Mussolini thought Hitler was mentally unbalanced, but by the late 1930s he had come to admire the way Hitler had turned the German economy around and was now respected and feared in the international community.

As for Nazi philosophy, in the mid 1930s *Il Duce* did not try to conceal his contempt for "certain doctrines from the other side of the Alps which are espoused by the descendants of people who were illiterate at a time when Rome had Caesar, Virgil and Augustus." Mussolini at first had nothing but contempt for the Nazi's racial philosophy and the idea of the superiority of the Aryan race (but by the early 1940s, after the alliance with Germany, he began calling Italians "Aryans").

Unfortunately, by the middle of 1938, with the Spanish civil war ending in Fascist triumph and Hitler annexing Austria, Mussolini had become convinced that an alliance with Germany would ensure Italian power and prestige. Italy's leader was mesmerized by the emerging German war machine, the development of which seemed to be wholeheartedly supported by that country's public. He hoped to instill the same type of militarism among his own population, although despite his best efforts he was never able to achieve this feat.

Once he decided to side with the Nazis, Mussolini jumped in with both feet. In March 1938, Hitler moved to annex Austria, the country of his birth. Had that same act been attempted only four years earlier, it would have led to war with Italy; now it was accomplished without a word of protest from Italian officials. Mussolini then invaded Albania in 1939, hoping to emulate his fellow dictator's accomplishments. Mussolini was no stranger to foreign military adventures, having already enjoyed some limited success in waging a brutal war against poorly armed Ethiopian tribesmen and having sent some 50,000 soldiers to assist Fascist forces in Spain.

On May 22, 1939, a military accord with Germany was agreed upon. With this so called "Pact of Steel," Italy drew even closer to the Third Reich. In September of that same year, at a conference in Munich (the Munich Pact), Mussolini went so far as to assist *Der Fuehrer* in seizing the Sudetenland from Czechoslovakia. In a shameful display, Great Britain and France attempted to appease Hitler by surrendering land (that conveniently belonged to another country) in an effort to avoid war. This only reinforced Mussolini's view that the western democracies were weak and indecisive when confronted by the growing power of Fascism.

Despite the outward appearance of close cooperation between the two Fascist states during the war, tensions simmered and occasionally came to the surface. Mussolini was annoyed by Hitler's constant talk of German racial superiority. In the early years of the war, he was also well aware of Italy's junior status vis-a-vis Germany. On a trip to the Russian front in late 1941, a story got back to him that as he drove by, a German soldier supposedly said about him, "There goes our *Gauleiter* [district administrator] for Italy." According to Foreign Minister Count Ciano, Mussolini kept a file on German slights and insults directed at Italians. One document contained a transcript of a telephone call during which one of General Albert Kesselring's aides referred to the Italians as "macaroni" and expressed his hope that Italy, too, would become an occupied country.

Mussolini often complained about the arrogant manner with which many German soldiers stationed in Italy treated the native population. Except for die-hard Fascists, most Italians had little regard for Germans, especially, as the war ground on and life grew increasingly difficult. In his diary entry of April 21, 1942, Foreign Minister Ciano recorded:

> Bismarck tells d'Ajeta that the German Consul General in Milan receives many offensive letters. The last one ran like this: 'We hear that you are looking for a new residence. We offer you one which is very beautiful, and worthy of you and your people and of your leader. The address is so and so.' The Consul went solemnly to the address indicated, and found himself at the doors of the jail.[50]

Throughout the war, Mussolini was well aware of the fact that

Hitler, like his generals, regarded Italian forces with distain. In March 1943, German Propaganda Minister Joseph Goebbels noted:

> The Fuehrer is very angry at the Italians because they are actually doing nothing. They aren't any good on the Eastern Front; they aren't any good for North Africa; they aren't any good for submarine warfare; they aren't any good even for anti-aircraft at home. The Fuehrer is right in asking why they are in the war anyway.[51]

Italy's unreliability was a theme that ran throughout the Propaganda Minister's diary. On March 9, he wrote that only as long as Mussolini was in power would Italy remain loyal to the Axis alliance and that, "you just can't play ball with the Italians. They are undependable, both militarily and politically."[52] While German and Italian armed forces fought together in operational theatres such as North Africa and the Soviet Union, Italian troops never gained the respect of their German comrades. German officers continually derided the Italians' lack of fighting spirit, pointing out that during joint operations in the Balkans, Italian forces either allowed partisans to escape or, worse yet, attempted to avoid military engagement altogether. The Germans' low opinion of the Italians' ability was summed up in a joke that was making the rounds in Germany in April 1942: "In two months we shall win the war against Russia, in four months against England, and in four days against Italy."[53]

In reality, Mussolini's soldiers fought bravely in numerous actions. The lack of military success can most often be attributed to the fact that, throughout the war, the Italian army was poorly led and inadequately supplied. Italian industry lagged far behind that of Germany and was the least productive of the major wartime combatants.

As the Allies brought more pressure to bear upon the overstretched German and Italian troops, cracks began to appear in their partnership. On November 12, 1942, Ciano noted, "[General Erwin] Rommel continues to withdraw from Libya at breakneck speed. There is a great deal of friction between Italian and German troops. At Halfaia they even fired on one another, because the Germans took all our trucks in order to withdraw more rapidly, leaving our divisions in the middle of the desert, where masses of men are literally dying of hunger and thirst."[54]

Unlike the Fascists, the Western Allies constantly shared information and their commanding generals and admirals worked closely together throughout the war years. President Roosevelt and Prime Minister Churchill considered this cooperation so vital that they created the Combined Chiefs of Staff immediately following America's entry into the war. The primary role of this organization was to coordinate military operations against their common enemies. As for the average soldiers, a level of mutual respect was reached between American GIs and British Tommies that was never equaled by Axis troops.

While the admiration between the British and Americans was genuine, naturally there was no lack of healthy competition between men of the two major Western powers. Like the jokes made by the Germans at the expense of the Italians, the Allied camp also saw its share of jibes between the two friendly nations. The most popular of which among the British stated that the problem with the Americans was that they were, "over paid, over sexed, and over here." The equally amusing American retort to this barb was that the problem with the British was that they were "under paid, under sexed, and under Eisenhower."

The Transfer of the Croatian Jews to the Island of Rab

By March 1943, at about the same time Mussolini was endorsing his officers' refusal to hand over the Croatian Jews to the Germans, the military authorities completed their census and questioning of the refugees. It had taken months to interview them and determine their status-which had been the Italian plan all along. The number of interned Jews was officially documented as 2,662.[55] Of these, 893 had qualified for Italian citizenship (in order to be included in this category a Jew had to have been a permanent resident before the war in one of the areas now under Italian occupation, had owned property there, or had rendered valuable service to the Italian military). Also included in the official tally were 1,485 Croatian Jews, even though they had already technically been stripped of their Croatian citizenship, and 283 Jews of various nationalities. According to Jewish sources, however, including Dr. Jasa Romano, an inmate, the number of people under Italian military custody within the camps was actually between 3,500 and 3,600.[56] It seems quite probable that the discrepancy is due to the fact that the military authorities purposefully minimized the number of internees.

During the same month, across the Mediterranean in North Africa, the war had decisively turned in favor of the Allies. As Mussolini's attention was focused on the fighting in Tunisia, a telegram arrived from Ambassador Casertano in Zagreb. The message, which was addressed to "AL CAPO DEL GOVERNO E MINISTRO DEGLI ESTERI, MUSSOLINI "(the head of the government and Minister of Foreign Affairs, Mussolini), communicated the fact to *Il Duce* that, to no one's surprise, the Germans and Croatians had grown even closer. The diplomat informed his superior that the Croatians were following German interests at the expense of those of Italy.[57]

As Italian military fortunes waned, the question of what to do with the interned Jews took on a new urgency. The Italians were afraid the Nazis might try to kill as many Jews as possible before their final defeat. As the Italians grew militarily weaker, the Ustasha might try to exercise greater control over the Dalmatian coast. As the war went on, every military defeat of the Axis by the Allies seemed to spur the Nazis to redouble their efforts to murder every Jew in Europe. In 1944 and 1945, there are numerous examples of German trains carrying desperately needed supplies and ammunition to troops on the eastern front being delayed as priority was given to those carrying Jews to the death camps. Of no less danger to the Jews was the fact that once North Africa fell to the Allies, which was now only a matter of time, Italian troops would have to be recalled from overseas to defend Italy proper. After such events occurred, should the refugees in Croatia fall into the hands of the Ustasha, there would be little doubt as to their fate.

Italian officials now had two options to consider. They could evacuate the Jewish detainees along with the army to Italy and place them in camps such as Ferrimonti already functioning on the Italian mainland. The army favored this approach as it would place the Jews in a more secure location, far away from the Ustasha, and it would relieve the army of the responsibility of having to care for the interned Jews. The second plan, which the Foreign Ministry advocated, involved transferring all inmates from the various facilities to one central camp located within the annexed area (Zone I). The site selected would have to be as near to the pre-war Italian border as possible, thus making it easier for units of the army to return should they be needed to defend the Jews. The main reason the diplomats lobbied the army to accept this plan rather than the first option was because they knew they would encounter opposition from the Ministry of the Interior. It was feared that this arm of government, which had little sympathy for the plight of the Croatian Jews, would oppose, and/ or, through bureaucratic red-tape, hinder, the movement of the internees to Italy. After three weeks of debate as to the merits of both proposals, it was decided by members of Supersloda and the Foreign Ministry that the Jews should be sent to the island of Rab (called Arba by the Italians) in the Adriatic. Mussolini gave his consent to the operation on March 31, 1943.[58]

The island itself is separated from the Croatian mainland by a little over a mile of water at its closest point. Rab is one of a group of islands in Kvarner Bay in the northern Adriatic. While Croatians have always claimed it theirs, it has changed hands many times over its long and colorful history. This strategic bit of land, which is approximately 55 square miles, had been occupied by numerous peoples throughout the ages including the ancient Greeks, Romans, Byzantines, Croatians, Venetians, French, Austrians, and Italians. The Italian name Arba came from the ancient Romans. The island was first colonized by Rome in 155 B.C. and in the year 10 B.C. it was given the title Felix Arba (municipality Arba) by Emperor Augustus. Some twenty centuries later, it would again be occupied by men from Italy as they attempted to save what was left of Croatian Jewry.

The Foreign Ministry, now under the direction of Giuseppe

Bastianini, along with Supersloda, commanded by General Mario Robotti, set about making plans for the transfer of the refugees to Rab. The two organizations agreed that the operation should be carried out in two phases. Jews from camps nearer the demarcation line (the German controlled zone in which the Ustasha was still active) would be transported to the island first as these people stood a greater chance of being seized by the Nazis or by Pavelic's men. This part of the plan was implemented, after several delays, in late May. Phase Two involved the transfer of the Jews from the Kraljevica (Porto Re) camp. The army began moving these people to the island on July 5, 1943. By July 20, the last of the Jews had arrived on Rab.

A large internment camp already existed on the island and it was determined that the Jews should be sent to this facility. The compound had been built in December 1942 to hold Slovene partisans and Slovene civilians who had been taken as hostages from Italian occupied and annexed southern Slovenia. Civilians taken captive were indeed shot in reprisal for partisan attacks, according to Slovene historians such as Franc Potocnik. While such barbaric incidents undoubtedly occurred, the majority of inmates that died while in Italian custody did so due to disease caused by the lack of sanitary conditions.

Unsanitary conditions were a fact of life in Italian run internment camps in the Balkans. While Italian camps were never designed to be mass killing centers such as those erected by the Germans in Central and Eastern Europe, thousands of people suffered and died in these camps between 1941 and 1943. Even the Jews interned at the Kraljevica facility, who were treated better than other groups, suffered as the camp population increased. Major points of concern included the fact that the camp turned into a sea of mud when it rained, the lack of a sufficient number of toilets, and an inadequate sewage disposal system.

Fortunately, though unbeknownst to the Jews at the time, their situation was about to improve. Following their transfer to Rab, they found that the accommodations and living conditions were far better than those they had left behind on the mainland. As they were being ferried across the narrow strait to their new place of residence, many people must surely have wondered whether the Italian state would, or even could, continue to keep them safe from the Germans. For the time being, however, all they could do was wait and hope.

The camp, known officially as *Campo de concentramento per internati civili di guerra*—Arbe (concentration camp for the internment of civilians of war), was a large complex by Italian standards and held approximately 20,000 inmates by 1943.[59] A separate wing was established to house the Jews separately from the Slovenes, although contact was made surreptitiously and maintained by members of both groups. Since the Croatian Jews were viewed by the authorities as people being held under "protective custody," it is not surprising that they were treated better than their fellow inmates who were being held under "restrictive custody". The unfortunate Slovene civilians who had been taken either as hostages, or captured as partisans, were seen as enemies to be dealt with harshly. The Jews on the other hand posed no military threat to Italian forces in the field, nor did they seek to thwart Italy's ambition to dominate the Balkans. Potocnik, as an inmate in the Rab camp, witnessed the superior accommodations and more lenient treatment from the guards enjoyed by the Jews:

> The internees in camp I [Slovenes] could watch through the double barriers of barbed wire what took place in the Jewish camp. The Jewish internees were living under conditions of true internment for their 'protection', whereas the Slovenes and Croatians were in a regime of 'repression'. . . They brought a lot of baggage with them. Italian soldiers carried their luggage into little houses of brick destined for them. Almost every family had its own little house . . .They were reasonably well dressed; in comparison, of course, to the other internees.[60]

While the Italian's treatment of the Slovene civilians at the Rab camp was inexcusable, their treatment of the Jews was quite decent, a situation rather remarkable in Nazi dominated Europe.

During this same period, the situation had become dire for those Jews still living within German occupied Croatia. The Germans had deported no Jews since August 1942, mainly due to the fact that Croatian Jewry by this point had largely been annihilated. In April and May, as the Italian army was preparing to transport the first contingent of Jews to Rab, the Germans were conducting their own operations. Working in conjunction with the Ustasha, they rounded up some 2,000 Jewish men, women, and children whom they deported in groups of between 20 and 150 by train to the death camps. After May 1943, German Ambassador to Croatia Kasche considered the "Jewish question" in Croatia, for the most part, solved.

Yugoslav Jews in lands occupied by Bulgaria and Hungary

Those Yugoslav Jews who could not reach the Italian zone of occupation had a different fate indeed. As noted earlier, the Nazis were much more successful in implementing their murderous plans for Jews in countries in which the ruling regimes shared their world view. The collaborationist regime of Ante Pavelic and the Ustasha worked all too efficiently with the Nazis to destroy Croatian Jewry. Unfortunately, such an alliance was hardly unique. Jews in those areas of the former Yugoslavia annexed by Hungary and Bulgaria were also turned over to the Nazis as there was no equivalent to the group of Italian conspirators in either country. No soldiers or government officials in the ministries of these German allies were prepared to risk their lives or careers in order to save foreign Jews.

In early 1941, Germany needed to use Bulgaria as a transit point through which to move troops to assist the Italians in Greece. Bulgarian officials, seeing a chance to regain territories lost following World War I, joined the Tripartite Pact (the agreement that formalized the alliance between Germany, Italy, and Japan and later Hungary and Romania) on March 1. Bulgaria was soon allowed to seize and annex western Thrace from Greece and Serbian Macedonia from Yugoslavia. Almost 8,000 Yugoslav Jews were now subject to a new authority. From the capital of Sofia, the Bulgarian government enacted numerous anti-Jewish laws in 1942, most following German examples. While the Yugoslavs were not granted Bulgarian citizenship, they were subject to the same punitive statues as Bulgarian Jews.

In January 1943, SS *Standartenfuehrer* (Colonel) Adolf Eichmann dispatched SS *Obersturmfuehrer* (First Lieutenant) Theodore Dannecker to Sofia to begin negotiations on the deportation of all Jews, including the former Yugoslav Jews, from Bulgaria to Auschwitz. Eichmann, head of Section IV B4 of the *Reichssicherheitshauptamt* (this section of the Reich Security Main Office was charged with organizing the Holocaust), was a fanatic when it came to completing assignments. By 1945, he would be responsible for the deaths of hundreds of thousands of Jews. Dannecker, ever eager to please his superior, coordinated efforts with local representatives of the Commissariat for Jewish Affairs, a division of the Bulgarian Ministry of the Interior. Soon lists began to be compiled as to the age, sex, occupation, and address of Jews living within the country. Dannecker's meetings went well and on February 22, 1943, the Bulgarian state agreed to deport its Jews, including those in the new territories. In late March, some 7,300 Jews from Macedonia were sent by rail to Treblinka. Only 166 survived to be liberated.[61]

While the Bulgarians were not willing to help non-Bulgarian Jews, the story of the 50,000 native Bulgarian Jews had a much happier ending.[E] While the government had given its consent to the deportation of Yugoslav Jews, opposition to the idea was voiced by many including King Boris; Exarch Stefan, leader of the Bulgarian Orthodox Church; and by some members of the *Sobranie* (parliament), led by Dimiter Peshev. Peshev's fervent protests succeeded in stopping the implementation of the agreement so far as it applied to the Jews of Bulgaria proper.

In May 1943, King Boris ordered all Jews residing in Sofia to be resettled in provincial towns. Apparently in his eyes, this course of action was seen as an alternative to the German demand that the Jews be handed over to them. Boris was not anti-Semitic and was influenced by the faction led by Peshev that did not want to see Jews slaughtered. King Boris died on August 28, but by that time, the war was slowly turning in the Allies' favor. A new Cabinet was

---

[E]The Bulgarian government and the majority of the population viewed non-Bulgarian Jews as foreigners who were not worthy of protection.

installed, led by Prime Minister Dobri Boshilov and over the next year, Bulgaria attempted to distance itself from Germany as the tide had turned against Hitler's army. On August 29, 1944, the government decided to rescind all anti-Jewish laws. On September 8, the Soviet army entered Bulgaria, thereby ensuring that the Jews of that country would survive the Holocaust.

Although the Yugoslav Jews were consigned to the Germans, credit must be given to those Bulgarians who struggled against cooperating with the Nazis. Their efforts shielded the whole of native born Jewry from the Nazi death camps. The only other countries that could lay claim to saving the vast majority of their Jewish citizens were Denmark and Italy.

The other German ally to occupy Yugoslav territory with a substantial number of Yugoslav Jews was Hungary. In March 1941, the Hungarian state assumed control of the areas of Backa, Baranja, Medjimurje, and Prekmurje. The Jewish inhabitants of these regions were hopeful that the Hungarians would treat them fairly. In fact, some Croatian Jews fleeing Ustasha attacks hurried across the new borders into the newly annexed territories or on to Hungary itself.

On June 22, Hungary joined Germany in the invasion of the Soviet Union. From the beginning Hungary proved to be a reluctant ally. The Regent, Nicholas Horthy, refused to order full military mobilization and in March 1942, he replaced the pro-German Prime Minister Laszlo Bardossy with Miklos Kallay. As Hungarian losses in Russia mounted, Kallay attempted to break the ties his nation had established with the Third Reich and gradually withdraw from the war.

In a defiant move, Kallay openly rejected German demands that Jews be made to wear a yellow badge as a preliminary step to deportation. Although the government refused to send native born Jews to Poland, they did subject Jews to restrictions on employment, property expropriation, and forced labor. As bad as the situation was becoming for Hungarian Jews, it was worse for the people in Backa. Throughout the war they were subjected to attacks by the Hungarian army in retaliation for partisan operations. Over 1,000 Jews, and perhaps twice that many Serbs, were killed in early 1942 alone.

As the war progressed, the Germans increasingly viewed Hungary as an undependable ally. In March 1944, they decided to act. The German occupation of Hungary, coupled with the installation of a new pro-German government, spelled disaster for the Jewish community. SS Colonel Eichmann arrived in Budapest on March 19 to take charge of organizing the transport of Jews out of Hungary. The SS and Hungarian police quickly set about arresting and detaining the Jewish population. Those Jews captured in the annexed territories were first held in Backa, then sent to transit camps in Hungary, and finally transported along with Hungarian Jews to the death camps. The total number of Jewish victims from Backa and Baranja stood at roughly 13,500. A further 1,300 people from Medjimurje and Prekmurje were also murdered. In all, some 14,800 Jews, or 85% of those living in these regions, were killed either by the Nazis or their Hungarian collaborators.[62]

As for the Jews of Hungary proper, the trains continued to depart with their human cargo throughout 1944. Even when the transports were interrupted due to the war, the SS and Arrow Cross (Hungarian Fascists) found alternative methods to keep the process moving forward. The prisoners were simply marched north on foot in long columns in which hundreds died. By October 29, 1944, the Soviet army had reached the outskirts of Budapest and had begun to lay siege to the city. There were still some 160,000 Jews left in the capital. Trapped between the two armies, they, along with the rest of the civilian population, suffered from wartime shortages of all kinds. Worse yet was the ever present threat of death either intentionally at the hands of Fascists, or accidentally from the barrages of Soviet shells. Approximately 20,000 died that winter as a result of the murderous actions of the Arrow Cross, or from cold, hunger, or disease.

The death rate for Hungarian Jews would have been much higher had it not been for the heroic actions of the Swedish diplomat Raoul Wallenberg. This extraordinary man had arrived in the capital the previous July and soon realized that he could not stand idly by and allow innocents to be slaughtered. Making the most of his diplomatic status, he immediately set about issuing Swedish visas to Jews and establishing safe houses in which inhabitants were under the protection of the government of Sweden. In the end, Wallenberg managed to save the lives of tens of thousands of people. In January 1945, as it became evident that the city would soon be taken by the Red Army, Wallenberg attempted to make contact with the advancing Russians. Before he departed, well aware of his own contribution to thwarting Nazi designs, he remarked to a friend, "I'm pleased to see that my mission has not been in vain."[63] Unfortunately, this courageous man would have very little time to savor his success. On January 17, he drove east to meet the Soviet commander Marshal Malinovsky; this was his last day as a free man. He was arrested by the Russians who, for whatever reason, believed him to be a spy. What became of Wallenberg has been a mystery ever since. The Russians have changed their story several times, first stating that the Swede had been killed by Germans before he reached Soviet lines, then that they had no knowledge of his fate whatsoever, and finally that he died in their custody in 1947 from a heart attack.[64] These explanations do not appear to be credible since fellow prisoners, who were subsequently released, claimed to have had contact with him long after war ended. A few witnesses are said to have seen him alive in prison as late as the 1970s.

The Italians and the Jews of Kosovo

The first test of how the Italians would react to German demands for Jews to be handed over to them came not in Croatia, but in Serbia's southern province of Kosovo. Following the collapse of Yugoslavia, this area had become part of Italian controlled "Greater Albania." This region, unlike the rest of Serbia, was not homogeneous. Long before the war, there had been ethnic strife dating as far back as the twelfth century. The Fascists would, of course, use these divisions to their advantage. By the time of the Italian occupation, over sixty percent of the population consisted of ethnic Albanians, the majority being Muslims, while Orthodox Serbs were actually in the minority. The Jewish population was tiny, numbering only some 400 people living mainly in the town of Pristina. Between 1939 and 1941 an additional 100 central European Jews seeking refuge from the Nazis arrived in the area.

They were followed by another 300 to 400 Jews who arrived following the German conquest of Serbia.[65] Most of the newcomers had come from Belgrade when it became obvious that the capital could not hold out long against the German onslaught.

In March 1942, as plans were being formulated in Rome to save the Jews of Croatia, the Italian authorities in Kosovo handed the two groups of refugees over to the Germans who sent them to the concentration camp at Zemun where they were all murdered. Two months later, however, as it became apparent to officials what had become of the Jews, the Italians transferred the original inhabitants of Kosovo to the Albanian towns of Berat and Elbasan. Following Italy's surrender in 1943, some of the refugees attempted to return to Pristina and were seized by the Germans, but of those who remained in Albania, the vast majority survived the war.[66]

1   James Walston, "History and Memory of the Italian Concentration Camps," *The Historical Journal*, 40, 1 (1997): p.170.
2   Ibid. p.175.
3   Ibid.
4   Ibid. p.177.
5   Franklin Linsay, Beacons in the Night: With the OSS and Tito's Partisans in Wartime Yugoslavia (Stanford, California.: Stanford University Press, 1993), p.37.
6   Ibid. p.38.
7   Dawidowicz, p.393.
8   Steinberg, p.93.
9   Zucotti, The Italians and the Holocaust, p.81.
10 Steinberg, p.99.
11 Ibid., p.100.
12 "Archbishop Damaskinos," The International Raoul Wallenberg Foundation [home page on-line]; available from http://www.raoulwallenberg.net; Internet; accessed October 13, 2006.
13 Ibid.
14 Ibid.
15 William Fowler, "Battle of France 1940," *War Monthly*, Issue 36, March 1977, p.8.
16 Ibid.

17 Dawidowicz, p.362.

18 Steinberg, p.108.

19 Ibid. p.112.

20 "Relations concerning operations of the Ministry of Foreign Affairs to help the Jewish community (1938-1943)", (Rome) p.64, Trans. [from French] Jean-Yves Widmeyer, Italian Ministry of Foreign Affairs Library.

21 Rochlitz, *The Righteous Enemy*.

22 "Relations concerning operations of the Ministry of Foreign Affairs," p.69.

23 Zucotti, The Italians and the Holocaust, p.84.

24 "Relations concerning operations of the Ministry of Foreign Affairs," p.70.

25 Zucotti, The Italians and the Holocaust, p.85.

26 Steinberg, p.126.

27 "Relations concerning operations of the Ministry of Foreign Affairs," p.71.

28 Steinberg, p. 129.

29 Rochlitz, *The Righteous Enemy*.

30 "Relations concerning operations of the Ministry of Foreign Affairs," p.81.

31 Rochlitz, *The Righteous Enemy*.

32 Zucotti, *The Italians and the Holocaust*, p.85.

33 "Relations concerning operations of the Ministry of Foreign Affairs," p.82.

34 Meir Michaelis, Mussolini and the Jews: German-Italian relations and the Jewish Question in Italy 1922-1945 (Oxford: The Claredon Press, 1978), p.306.

35 Dawidowicz, p.362.

36 Carpi, p.495.

37 Ibid., p.496.

38 Michaelis, p.29.

39 Ibid.

40 Ibid., p.53.

41 Peter Neville, Mussolini (London: Routledge, 2004), p.117.

42 Paul Paolicelli, Under The Southern Sun: Stories of the Real Italy and the Americans It Created (New York: Thomas Dunne Books, 2003), p.100.

43 Ibid., p.104.
44 Ibid.
45 Ibid., p.109.
46 Walston, p.173.
47 Neville, p.124.
48 Ibid.
49 Gibson, p.391.
50 Ibid., p.474.
51 Steinberg, p.122.
52 Lochner, p.287.
53 Gibson, p.467.
54 Ibid., p.543.
55 Verax, p.27.
56 Loker, p.75.
57 Document 173, Ministero Degli Affari Esteri, Documenti Diplomatici Italiani, serie 1939-1943 volume X (7 Febbraio—8 Settembre 1943), Libreria Dello Stato Roma MCMXC.
58 Zucotti, Under His Very Windows. P.125.
59 Carpi, p. 499.
60 Steinberg, p.131.
61 Tomasevich, p.589.
62 Ibid., p.591.
63 Danny Smith, Wallenberg: Lost Hero (Springfield, Illinois: Templegate Publishers, 1987), p.122.
64 Ibid., p.148.
65 Tomasevich, p.589.
66 Ibid.

4

THE ITALIAN WITHDRAWAL

IN MAY 1943, WHILE THE JEWS ALONG THE DALMATIAN COAST were being relocated to Rab, Jews still unable or unwilling to flee Zagreb were deported. The arrests of the last Jews in the city were timed to coincide with the visit that month of SS *Reichsführer* Heinrich Himmler. As usual, raids were carried out strategically in the predawn hours when victims would most likely be at home, asleep, and unable to mount much resistance. Papal Nuncio Marcone estimated that some 600 people were taken by the Croatian authorities in such manner and turned over to the Germans (though many others had gone into hiding). On May 24 he reported to the Vatican:

> . . . I am extremely saddened to inform you that, except for now, at least, mixed marriages, all the Jews, including those who had already been baptized for years, have been arrested and transported to Germany...The scene of arrest of these unfortunate people was truly pitiful: During the night, while they were peacefully asleep, agents of the police came to their homes, and without any regard for their age, social condition, or baptism, arrested them. Several of the more elderly ones died of fright.[1]

Among those sent to their deaths that month was Marcone's friend Miroslav Freiberger, the Chief Rabbi of Zagreb.

According to Slavko Radej, who lived through this dangerous time, the only reason the Zagreb Jewish community survived until 1943 was that it served the interests of the Ustasha. Through extortion Ustasha leaders were able to steal items of value from the Jewish community. He recalled:

> The [Jewish] District continuously collected the clothing and food, for the prisoners in the concentration camps. A very large quantity of food and clothing was shipped to the prisoners. But the prisoners received very little, because the Ustashas stole almost everything for themselves. We knew that, but we kept sending supplies hoping that at least some would reach our people. We even sent medicine, which Ustashas used for themselves when they feared an outbreak [of disease].[2]

Although Redej himself was jailed, he was eventually released because his wife was a Catholic. Many other Zagreb Jews were not so fortunate.

Even before the May deportations, the Ustasha had murdered small groups of Jews from time to time. As in Germany, Jews served as a convenient scapegoat for the nation's ills. Most often the Croatian government accused Jews of supporting the Communist partisans, which they often did, but largely only as a last resort. Redej observed how the Jewish community suffered as a result of their scapegoat status:

> Whenever there were acts of sabotage such as those against the post office, botanical gardens etc. they always arrested several Jews and executed them. In the newspapers it was reported that they were executed after a summary court trial as revenge for the sabotage. There were never any summary court trials. I am sure several hundred Jews in Zagreb died in this manner. Many of them went through the Ustasha prison on Rackoga street No. 9, where they were

severely tortured. I heard from some people who went through this prison and the torture. The Ustasha tortured the arrested Jews by pushing needles under their fingernails, burning their feet, beating and whipping them until their skin became raw, and hanging them in different ways.[3]

The vicious brutality of the Ustasha once again rivaled the Nazis.

The Wider War

Following the successful invasion of North Africa, President Franklin Roosevelt and Prime Minister Winston Churchill decided to meet in Morocco to coordinate their strategy against the Axis nations. The Independent State of Croatia was included among the enemy combatants as it, along with its more powerful Fascist neighbors, had declared war upon the United States and Great Britain in December 1941. Between the fall of France in June of 1940 and Hitler's invasion of the Soviet Union a year later, Britain had stood alone against the power of the Nazi state. Though battered and bruised, Britain had not been defeated.

After Japan's surprise attack of December 7, 1941 upon the U. S. Pacific fleet at Pearl Harbor, the British wholeheartedly welcomed a desperately needed ally to the fight. Upon hearing the news of the events in Hawaii, Churchill called Roosevelt to ask if what he had heard was true. The President responded "Yes" and wryly remarked that they were all in the same boat now. In his massive six volume work entitled *The Second World War*, Churchill described his feelings at the time:

> No American will think it wrong of me if I proclaim that to have the United States at our side was to me the greatest joy. I could not foretell the course of events. I do not pretend to have measured accurately the martial might of Japan, but now at this very moment I knew the United States was in the war, up to the neck and in to the death. So we had won after all! . . . after seventeen months of lonely fighting . . . England would live; Britain would live . . . How long the

war would last or in what fashion it would end no man could tell, nor did I at this moment care. Once again in our long island history we should emerge, however mauled or mutilated, safe and victorious. We should not be wiped out. Our history would not come to an end. . . . Hitler's fate was sealed. Mussolini's fate was sealed. As for the Japanese they would be ground to powder. The British Empire, the Soviet Union, and now the United States, bound together . . . were . . . twice or even thrice the force of their antagonists . . . Many disasters, immeasurable cost and tribulation lay ahead, but there was no more doubt about the end. . . . I thought of a remark that Edward Grey had made to me more than thirty years before-that the United States is like "a gigantic boiler. Once the fire is lighted under it there is no limit to the power it can generate." Being saturated and satiated with emotion and sensation, I went to bed and slept the sleep of the saved and thankful.[4]

On December 8, 1941, Churchill, citing the bombing of Singapore and Hong Kong, notified the Japanese ambassador that a state of war now existed between their two countries. The letter he dispatched was formal, yet eloquent almost to the point of being poetic. He recalled that there were those at the time who objected to his "ceremonial style." Demonstrating the sharp wit he was known for all his life, he responded to these critics by stating, "when you have to kill a man it costs nothing to be polite."[5]

Four days after the Japanese attack on the United States, America entered the war against Hitler. In his message to Congress, Roosevelt was as articulate as he had been in his famous speech asking for a declaration of war against Japan. He stated:

On the morning of December 11 the Government of Germany, pursuing its course of world conquest, declared war against the United States. The long-known and the long-expected has thus taken place. The forces endeavoring to enslave the entire world now are moving toward this hemisphere. Never before has there been a greater challenge to life, liberty and civilization. Delay invites great danger. Rapid and united effort by all of the peoples of the world who are determined to remain free will insure a world victory of the forces of justice and of righteousness over the forces of savagery and of barbarism. Italy has also declared war against the United States. I therefore request the Congress to recognize a state of war between the United States and Germany, and between the United States and Italy.[6]

Historians agree that along with his attack upon the Soviet Union earlier in the year, one of Adolf Hitler's biggest mistakes was his decision to declare war on the United States. The German leader badly misjudged America's ability to simultaneously wage war in Europe and in the Pacific. In addition, he and his ministers underestimated the industrial capacity of the United States as well as the ability of American industry to rapidly shift to a war footing. The huge infusion of manpower and material from the United States would in the coming months not only remove the threat of a Nazi invasion of Great Britain, but would allow the western Allies to take the offensive within a year.

The Casablanca Conference was held January 14-24, 1943. Strategically, the British and American delegations agreed that a cross channel invasion of occupied France was a necessity, but that such a large military operation could not possibly be mounted before mid 1944. In the meantime, Churchill advocated additional action in the Mediterranean. In general terms, he lobbied for some sort of military movement against either Italy or the Balkans. Both sides also agreed that the destruction of Hitler's U-boat fleet and aid to the hard pressed Soviet Union would be assigned top priority. On the political level the two leaders agreed that they would accept nothing less than "unconditional surrender" from the Fascist nations.

In May the two leaders met again, this time in Washington, D.C. for what amounted to a follow up conference in to work out the details of the military operations first put forth at Casablanca. A target date of May 1, 1944 was established for the invasion of France. Twenty nine divisions were to be assembled for this massive assault upon the Nazi held country. In the Mediterranean theatre an invasion of Sicily was agreed upon. Churchill was, however, forced to abandon his idea of a Balkan campaign as troops and material were simply not available since both countries also had to allocate resources to fight the Japanese in the Pacific.

The same month in which Roosevelt and Churchill met in the American capital also marked an end to the Axis presence in North Africa. The Allies had begun to chip away at the Nazi empire. The city of Tunis fell on May 7, and by May 13, 1943 all of Tunisia was in Allied hands. This marked the end of General Erwin Rommel's vaunted *Afrika Corps, a*s well as what was left of the Italian First Army. With the surrender of the last Fascist stronghold in North Africa, some 125,000 German, and 115,000 Italian soldiers were seized as prisoners of war. After taking North Africa, General Dwight Eisenhower, the supreme Allied commander in the Mediterranean, along with his deputy in command of operations, Sir Harold Alexander, next set about planning the invasion of Sicily. Eisenhower created a unified command which allowed him to take advantage of the best minds within both the U.S. and British militaries. He later used this system with great success in Northwest Europe as commander of Supreme Headquarters Allied Expeditionary Forces (SHAEF) in the last two years of the war.

The attack upon Sicily (codenamed Operation *Husky*) was set to take place in the early morning hours of July 10, 1943 and would have dramatic consequences for Benito Mussolini, Italy, and by extension the Jews in the Italian zone in Croatia. For the Allies, the goal was simple: to defeat the Axis forces on the island. Once this task had been accomplished they would not only gain a strategic piece of land but could secure their lines of communication in the Mediterranean as well. At this point there were no plans to invade Italy proper as priority was being given to the buildup for the forthcoming Normandy invasion.

The Allied forces assembled for the operation consisted of the U.S. Seventh Army led by General George Patton and the British

Eighth Army commanded by General Bernard Montgomery. Together the Allied soldiers numbered some 140,000. They were opposed by approximately 240,000 Italian and 40,000 German troops. The fact that so few Germans were present was due in part to Allied efforts to deceive German intelligence as to where the actual attack was to take place. In one particularly clever act, the body of what appeared to be a British officer was allowed to wash up on a beach in Spain complete with his orders (the man had actually died of natural causes and had been dressed in a military uniform). Intelligence operatives knew that German spies would soon report what had been found among the dead man's affects to their superiors. Anticipating this action they had planted information on the body that indicated the real attack would fall elsewhere in the Mediterranean. As a result of this ruse, German reinforcements were sent not to Sicily, but instead to Greece and Sardinia.

The Allied assault met with little resistance, although bad weather and lack of experience among pilots led to the scattering of airborne troops far beyond their intended drop zones. By day's end, eight divisions had been put ashore. The landings took place on the southern coast, with the Americans to the west of the point known as Cape Passero, and the British to the east. Montgomery's troops advanced along the coast toward Messina, while Patton's men moved to the northwest to take the city of Palermo. Both armies faced stiff opposition, mainly from German units, as most Italian soldiers by this point were reluctant to die for Mussolini and offered little resistance to the advancing Allies.

The well known rivalry between Patton and Montgomery that would continue after the Normandy landings first appeared during this campaign. While personally the two men disliked each other intensely, as professional soldiers they knew they had to work together in order to achieve victory. To that end, as the key to the island was the capture of Messina, on July 20, General Alexander ordered Patton to move east to support Montgomery's flank and aid in his advance. On July 25, the *Commando Supremo*, realizing that the battle for Sicily was lost, began to withdraw its troops across the Strait of Messina to the mainland. The Germans soon made the same decision. By August 15 when the U.S. Seventh Army reached the outskirts of Messina, the evacuation of Axis troops was well underway. With the arrival of Montgomery's forces the following day, the campaign came to an end. Approximately 30,000 Allied soldiers had been killed, captured, or wounded. Although they had successfully taken the island, the escape of some 100,000 enemy soldiers troubled the Allied leaders knowing as they did that they would most probably have to confront these same troops at a later date.

At the same time that the western Allies were fighting to take Sicily and the Croatian Jews on Rab anxiously awaited their fate, the Soviets were engaged in the largest tank battle of the war near the Russian city of Kursk. By this point, the Soviets had driven the Germans back to western Russia and where poised to move into Ukraine. The Kursk salient was huge, stretching from the cities of Orel in the north to Kharkov in the south. The Germans hoped to crush the Red Army by attacking from both the north and south simultaneously. Approximately 900,000 German soldiers, 3,155 tanks, and 2,600 aircraft were moved into position to achieve this goal. To oppose this force, the Soviets deployed 1,272,700 men, 3,275 tanks, and 25,000 heavy guns and mortars.[7] The German attack began on July 5, 1943. While the Germans relied on the medium Panther and heavy Tiger tanks, the Russians continued to use the T34 (albeit with an upgraded 85 mm. main gun). After a week of intense fighting, Soviet defenses, although battered, remained in tact. On July 12, they launched a massive counter-offensive.

In terms of weapons, the Soviet strategy was to out-produce the Germans (the United States also adopted this philosophy as it sharply increased its production of the simple yet reliable Sherman tank). In the early months of the war, this idea seemed all but impossible since many of the Soviet production facilities had been overrun by the Germans. Soon, however, entire factories were rebuilt farther to the east. Hitler's tanks were truly awesome pieces of machinery, especially the Tigers with their devastating 88 mm. guns. They were, however, also complicated and time consuming to produce. By contrast, the rugged T34, like its American counterpart, was much more suited to mass production. Throughout the war, due to high production costs and constant interruptions by Allied bombing raids, the Germans were only able to assemble 1,354 Tiger I and 5,976 Panthers. In contrast, by the time of the battle of Kursk, the Soviets were building 1,200 T34s a month.[8]

Throughout the month of August, the battle raged. Although massive numbers of soldiers fell on both sides, Red Army troops led by General Konstantine Rokossovski continued to gain ground. On August 23, the city of Kharkov was liberated. Throughout the war, the Soviets suffered staggering losses in battle. The causes can be traced to the savage ideological nature of the war itself, the sophisticated weapons possessed by the Germans, the fact that Stalin's purges of the 1930's had decapitated the military's leadership, and the incompetence of those officers who survived. This last point would be remedied as the war progressed and officers at every level gained experience in the tactics and strategies of fighting a modern war. One example of the horrific sacrifices made by Russian troops is clearly illustrated by the number of casualties among tank crews. Of the 403,000 soldiers assigned to tank and mechanized units, 310,000 would die.[9]

The soldiers of the Red Army knew that Hitler was waging a war of annihilation against their country and that the Nazis considered them, along with all other Slavic peoples, racially inferior. This, as one might imagine, gave great impetus to resist the invaders. Further incentives included patriotism, and for those true believers in communism, the thought that they were defending the ideals of the 1917 Revolution. Many soldiers actually went into battle shouting the phrase, "For the motherland, For Stalin!" Of course, there was one more stimulus that forced men to fight, namely Stalin's Order No. 227. This decree, which was first issued on July 28, 1942, stated that soldiers who showed cowardice in battle would be shot. Though never actually published, the order, which was spread by word of mouth, was summed up by the slogan, "Not a step back!" The troops that enforced the new policy were the state's NKVD (People's Commissariat for Internal Affairs) men. As they took up their positions in the rear all along the front lines, their mission was clear, to shoot anyone who retreated without orders while fighting the Germans. To this day, no one knows exactly how many soldiers were killed by their fellow countrymen in this way. For lesser offenses such as stealing, or spreading defeatist rumors, men could be sent to "penal battalions" which was also tantamount to a death sentence. These units were sent into battle on suicide missions such as those to clear minefields (by walking straight through them) or to purposely move into the open in order to draw enemy fire. Russian observers could then determine the exact position of the enemy. Throughout the war, approximately 422,700 men were forced into such penal battalions. Most, of course, did not survive to return home.[10]

The Fall of Mussolini

By mid 1943, Italy's Fascist government, along with its leader, was becoming increasingly unpopular with the Italian people. Most Italians disapproved of the German alliance and had come to view the war as a total disaster for their country.

Mussolini had also lost a great deal of support among common soldiers within the military. Throughout the war, supply problems plagued the army and many men blamed their government in general and Mussolini in particular for the fact that they were undersupplied. When comparing their situation with that of their German counterparts in the field, Italian rank and file troops found that the Hitler's soldiers were consistently provided with superior quality uniforms and better food.

In addition, there were splits within the Fascist Party itself. The main points of contention centered on the conduct of the war and the alliance with Germany. Some men, such as Buffarini Guidi, were prepared to fight with the Germans to the bitter end, while others, including Dino Grandi, had been critical of the Nazis from the beginning. Grandi, like Bastianini, was an early Fascist and had served in numerous positions within the government during the 1930s, only to be dismissed for opposing the increasingly close ties being forged with Germany. He and his supporters now believed the time had come for a change in leadership at the top. While it would be the Fascists themselves that would remove Benito Mussolini from power after twenty-one years of rule, it was Italy's deteriorating military situation that forced party members to take such drastic action.

Once Sicily had fallen to American and British troops, the *Commando Supremo* believed it was only a matter of time until the Italian mainland was attacked by Allied forces. Mussolini's generals reported that in the event of such an assault, they could not guarantee that the country's defenses would hold. Evidence that such a move was a distinct possibility was dramatically illustrated on July 19 as Allied bombers struck the city of Rome. Over one thousand people were killed in the raid (unbeknownst to the Italians it was not until after Mussolini's removal that Eisenhower moved forward with a plan for the invasion of Italy, as preparations for the Normandy landing continued to take priority).

The dictator had no choice but to convene the Fascist Grand Council to hear its advice on what should be done next. In theory, this group of twenty eight leading Fascists was the supreme governing body of both the party and the state. In reality, its authority was somewhat unclear as it had not actually convened since the war began. The meeting began late on the afternoon of July 24 and lasted until 3:00 am. Mussolini, in a long and rambling speech, attempted to blame the army for Italy's current situation. The council members remained unconvinced. Grandi, knowing that the Allies would never make peace with Italy as long as Mussolini was in charge, proposed a plan that would in effect remove *Il Duce* from power. The resolution required Mussolini to turn the war effort over to the king. King Victor Emmanuel would formally be named head of the Armed Forces, thus stripping the dictator of much of his power. When it was finally time to decide the issue, Grandi had won over many of the members to his point of view. Nineteen voted for the motion (including Giuseppe Bastianini and Mussolini's son- in- law Count Ciano), seven against, and two men abstained.[11]

Later that afternoon, Mussolini met with the king or, as the dictator disdainfully referred to him, "the Little Sardine." For twenty-two years, the diminutive monarch had meekly submitted to the Fascist leader's will, so it was with shock that Mussolini witnessed

Victor Emmanuel's determination to replace him as head of government. The king boldly asserted, "At this moment you are the most hated man in Italy."[12]   Over the course of their conversation, the king stated that he would assure Mussolini's personal safety, as well as that of his family, but that for Italy's sake, a new government would be formed. The man chosen for this job was to be the victor of the Ethiopian War, Marshal Pietro Badoglio.

As Mussolini left the meeting, he was told that for his own protection he was to travel with a squadron of *carabinieri*. Reports had been received that some people were already beginning to rally in the streets and chanting anti-Fascist slogans. Escorted by the military policemen, Mussolini was driven in an ambulance, rather than his own limousine, to a military hospital. The man who had ruled Italy for more than twenty years now found himself, for all intents and purposes, under arrest.

Over the next month, Benito Mussolini was moved to three different locations. He was first confined to a house on the island of Ponza and then to the naval base on the island of La Maddalena, near Sardinia. On August 26, he was again moved to what was thought to be a more secure location high in the Apennines. The last place in which he was held was not a prison, but a hotel on the Gran Sasso. Although he was guarded by a contingent of 250 men, Mussolini was treated more like a guest than a prisoner. The *carabinieri* were congenial and the entire hotel had been emptied to make room for the new VIP. The hotel's staff catered to his every need. He was allowed to take supervised walks, ate well, and was even permitted to listen to Italian, German, and BBC radio broadcasts.[13]

Italian concerns over a German raid to free the ex-dictator were not unfounded. Hitler issued orders for just such an operation while Mussolini was still confined on La Maddalena. Once he was transferred to the Gran Sasso, however, a new plan was called for. The Colonel Otto Skorzeny, was launched on September 12. At 2:00 P.M., eight gliders loaded with German paratroopers landed near the hotel. To increase their chances of avoiding a violent confrontation with the *carabinieri*, the Germans had thought to bring along an Italian General named Soleti, who was head of the Fascist Public

Security Police. As the first glider skidded to a stop, Soleti jumped out and shouted at the guards not to fire.[14] The Italians offered no resistance and almost immediately surrendered. Within minutes, German troops were in control of the entire area. Mussolini squeezed himself into a small plane for the flight to the airfield at Practica di Mare. The journey was made all the more harrowing since Skorzeny insisted upon accompanying the newly freed prisoner in an aircraft that was designed to hold only two people. From Practica di Mare, Mussolini was flown over the Alps to Vienna. On September 13, the former dictator moved on to Munich where he met his wife and children. After a brief reunion with his family, Mussolini was taken to meet Hitler at the Nazi leader's eastern headquarters near Rastenburg in East Prussia. While humiliated by the fact that he had needed to be saved by Hitler, Mussolini was, nevertheless, grateful for what his friend had done for him.

Although safe enough for the moment in Germany, Mussolini knew that he would never again posses the kind of power he had enjoyed since 1922. Even though Hitler allowed him to control an area of northern Italy for the last two years of the war, he was now, in reality, reduced to nothing more than a German puppet.

Mussolini was eager to return to Rome (with German assistance) primarily to deal with those whom he believed had berated him during the July 25 meeting. Hitler refused to entertain such an idea as Rome was considered too close to the Allied front lines. Instead he allowed his friend to relocate to the town of Gargnano on Lake Garda in the north of Italy. In October, a rump Fascist state, The Italian Social Republic (*Repubblica Sociale Italiano*) was created, although it was better known as the Republic of Salo after the town in which it had been founded. For the last two years of his life, Mussolini was nominally the head of state, while in reality all decisions had to meet with the approval of German officials posted at Salo.

With some form of power, however illusionary, Mussolini immediately sought vengeance upon the men who had refused to support him on July 25. Two of the most important were already within his grasp. The first was the aged Marshall Emilio de Bono. The second man was Mussolini's own son- in- law Galeazzo Ciano.

The Germans had "detained" Ciano and, remembering his opposition to closer ties with their nation, were only too happy to deliver the ex-foreign minister to Mussolini. After receiving a show trial in Verona in January 1944, both men, along with three other Fascists who had opposed the dictator during the vote of July 25, were found guilty and sentenced to death. Ciano accepted the predetermined verdict stoically as he had long since been resigned to his fate. Although Edda begged her father to spare her husband's life, her pleas fell upon deaf ears. On January 11, 1944, the five men were shot to death. Overall, while Mussolini took some comfort in the fact that he had avenged what he saw as the treachery perpetrated by his fellow Fascists, he could not be fully satisfied since the ringleader, Dino Grandi, had escaped to Portugal. As for Edda, although she had always had a close relationship with her father, she never forgave him for failing to stay Ciano's execution, and their relationship was never the same again.

Unfortunately, most Italian Jews lived in northern cities and their fortunes were about to take a change for the worse. Within the Republic of Salo, Mussolini now found himself surrounded by hard line Fascists, unsympathetic to the plight of Jews, and dependent entirely upon the good will of the Germans. Thus when the Republican Fascist Party met in Verona in November 1943, a provision was included in their charter that stripped Jews of their citizenship and declared them to be an "enemy nationality."[15] This cleared the way for the Fascist militia and German troops to begin arresting and deporting Jews. In the coming months, some fled south in an effort to reach the Allied lines, many were hidden by sympathetic Italians, and still others joined the growing Communist partisan movement that emerged to fight both the militia and the Germans.

The Italian Armistice

In choosing Pietro Badoglio to replace *Il Duce*, Italy's king had made a wise decision. Badoglio was both familiar with the workings of government and could command the respect of the army. At the same time, however, a man was needed who was not so closely identified with the Fascist Party that he would be unacceptable to the

Allies. Badoglio had achieved a long record of service to the Italian state. He had risen to the rank of general during the First World War, his reputation cemented by his victory in Ethiopia in 1936. As he was not ideologically a Fascist, privately he opposed his country's involvement in both the Spanish Civil War and the Second World War.16   Persuaded to return to duty, he headed the *Commando Supremo* in 1940, but as the army's advance slowed in Greece, he was forced back into retirement. Now, three years later, he was the man called upon to walk a tightrope between the Germans and the Allies.

Once Mussolini had been removed from office, the first order of business for Badoglio was to begin peace negotiations with the Allies. After a reorganization of government officials, which saw Bastianini replaced by Italy's Ambassador to Turkey, Raffaele Guariglia, the Badoglio government attempted to contact the Allies through diplomatic channels. Blasco Lanza d'Ajeta, Ciano's former Chief of Staff (and one of the first men to attempt to save Croatian Jews) was dispatched to neutral Portugal to seek terms that would allow Italy to detach itself from its German partner and sign a separate peace. Members of the Italian military were also involved in the secret negotiations. On August 10, Badoglio decided to send General Giuseppe Castellano to Lisbon to make contact with Allied representatives. Castellano's mission was successful and he soon moved on to Sicily where he signed the armistice in an olive grove near Syracuse on September 3, 1943. This act allowed Italy to formally withdraw from the war. Under the terms of the document, all Italian air and ground units would surrender to Allied soldiers as the latter advanced upon their positions and the Italian fleet would sail to British held Malta. In addition, all Allied prisoners of war (POW's) would be released and under no circumstances turned over to the Germans. All Italian territory would be relinquished for use by the Allies as operational bases from which to continue the war against Germany. Eisenhower announced the illustrious news to the world on September 8.

Unfortunately, peace did not come to Italy at this time. A German occupation ensued that would last in large areas of the north until the last month of the war. In addition, battles between

Allied and German troops would devastate the country over the next year and a half.

On the day Mussolini was replaced, Marshal Badoglio had addressed the Italian people. In order to placate the Germans, and buy himself time, Badoglio publicly stated that nothing had changed in relation to the German alliance and that, "The struggle continues."[17] Hitler, ever suspicious of the depth of the Italian commitment to the Axis cause, was not taken in by the new prime minister's words. He issued orders to rush German troops south not only to meet a possible Allied attack but also to punish the Italian people for their treachery. As the German army poured across Italy's northern border, Field Marshall Albert Kesselring announced that the entire country would now be considered a "theatre of war" and as such subject to the direct control of the German military.[18] On September 9, knowing that they were certain to be targets of German wrath, the king, Badoglio, and General Roatta, who was now army chief of staff, fled south to the city of Brindisi. As they did so, Hitler's forces quickly moved to occupy Rome. Eventually, the whole of Italy was divided into two zones. The southern part of the country was deemed the "operational" sector in which Kesselring's Army Group South operated, while farther north, Erwin Rommel's Army Group B was in charge of the "occupied" zone.

As the secret talks progressed, General Eisenhower was busy formulating a plan to launch a direct assault upon the Italian mainland. General Montgomery's troops would cross the Strait of Messina and assault the southern coast. Soon thereafter, the main body of the Anglo-American army would come ashore at the Gulf of Salerno. At 4:30 A.M., on the very day the armistice was signed, British soldiers landed on the toe of Italy. They met only light resistance. Six days later, an Allied armada of 450 ships appeared in the Gulf of Salerno, some 30 miles south of Naples. This was the beginning of Operation *Avalanche*. Unlike the British situation to the south, the men of General Mark Clark's Fifth Army faced very stiff opposition. German counterattacks were so fierce that at one point Clark even considered evacuating his men from the beachhead. A major advantage for the Germans was the fact that the *Luftwaffe*, operating from numerous bases around Rome, as well as the large base at Foggia, could attack the landing force at will. Allied fighters, on the other hand, flying from Sicily were forced to operate at the very limit of their range. After days of heavy fighting, Clark's men began to move inland. On September 27, Montgomery's Eighth Army aided the advance by capturing Foggia, which served for the remainder of the war as an important Allied airbase.

In the final days of September, both U.S and British units slowly moved north. On October 1, 1943, Allied troops entered Naples. The city was a mere shell of its former self. Not only had it been damaged by Allied bombers, but the city's basic services, such as water and power systems, had been destroyed by the retreating Germans. More importantly, port facilities had been demolished and ships had been scuttled in the harbor to render it useless to the Allies. Undeterred, Allied engineers worked tirelessly to repair the port, and within a week it was again operational.

In the last three months of the year, the Eighth Army advanced northward along Italy's east coast while the Fifth Army did the same in the west. Both faced stubborn German resistance until their drives were halted at the Gustav line. This formidable defensive barrier cut across Italy from Minturno on the Mediterranean to Pescara on the Adriatic. Due to a combination of fierce fighting, difficult terrain, and the biting winter weather, Clark's men were forced to stop at the Garigliano River while Montgomery's troops faced similar conditions in the Sangro valley. Even though the opposing forces were more or less equally matched (the Allies deployed 18 divisions to the Germans 13), Eisenhower quickly learned that Italy, with it mountains and narrow valleys, worked to the advantage of the defenders. Unfortunately, these conditions would delay the Allied drive on Rome for months.

As American and British forces were slowly moving up the Italian peninsula, the Big Three - Roosevelt, Churchill and Stalin were meeting in Tehran, Persia (Iran). On November 28, the three Allied leaders met together for the first time. Stalin had insisted on being allowed to choose the venue. Both Churchill and Roosevelt acquiesced to this request since they knew, as Stalin was always fond of pointing out, that it was Soviet troops who were still fighting the bulk of the German army. The Soviet dictator had a point. Despite the fact that the western Allies had landed on the European mainland, they had become stalled in Italy and it was the Red Army that was on the move.

The British-American-Russian conference was held from November 28 through December 1 in the capital of Soviet occupied Persia. A wide range of war related issues were discussed, including what should be done with a conquered Germany and which lands should be allocated to Poland and the Soviet Union after the war. The most important agreement to come from the four day summit, however, was that Stalin pledged to enter the war against Japan as soon as Germany was defeated. The president and prime minister again promised that an invasion of France was forthcoming, which would, of course, relieve some of the pressure on the Soviet army. Stalin remained unconvinced, however, since FDR had not even named a military commander for this undertaking, that the British and Americans were serious about mounting such an operation.[19] Instead, he believed that for political reasons his allies were dragging their feet on the issue, all the while leaving his country to do most of the fighting. Roosevelt understood, and in order to ease Stalin's suspicious mind, he stopped in Tunisia on his journey home. There he met with General Eisenhower and informed him that he had been chosen to lead the great invasion.

On December 31, Eisenhower left the Mediterranean, turning command of that theatre over to British General Henry Maitland Wilson (General Alexander assumed command of the fifteenth Army Group composed of Montgomery's Eighth and Clark's Fifth armies). As he prepared for the invasion of northern France, Eisenhower was summoned to Washington, D. C. for further consultation with the president. General Montgomery, who under Eisenhower was set to command all ground forces moving into France, also left Italy bound for England. Alexander was now charged with moving the Italian campaign forward. Unfortunately, struggling north toward the Alps was to become a long, bloody conflict. While it would not lead directly to the downfall of Nazi

Germany, the fighting in Italy did tie down many German divisions that would otherwise have been employed elsewhere, thereby allowing the Allies to win the war on other fronts.

The Disintegration of the Italian Army

General Eisenhower's public announcement that an armistice was in place took Italian officials completely by surprise. The short time span between September 3, when the document was actually signed, and the afternoon of September 8, when it was made public, had not been enough time for the new government to decide on its next move. As they were now caught between the Allies and the Germans, the men of Badoglio's new government scrambled to figure out a way to avoid a showdown with their former partner. While German troops rapidly moved into Rome, the top ministers met with the king, but no one seemed to know what to do next. They found that extricating their country from the war would be no simple task. In an encounter with Badoglio, as they waited to see the king, Foreign Minister Guariglia remembered how the Marshall succinctly summed up their situation: "I ran to him anxious for news. He responded literally: 'we're f----d!'"[20] Knowing that some kind of public statement was now necessary, Badoglio addressed the nation that evening in a radio broadcast:

> The Italian government recognizing the impossibility of continuing the unequal struggle against the overwhelming power of the adversary, with the intention of sparing the country further and much graver disasters, has requested an armistice of General Eisenhower, commander-in-chief of the Anglo-American allied forces. The request has been accepted. Consequently every act of hostility against the Anglo-Americans must cease on the part of Italian forces in every locality. They will react to eventual attacks from whatever other source.[21]

The last line was clearly aimed at the Germans. Unfortunately for Italian soldiers on occupation duty in France and the Balkans, the *Commando Supremo* had no comprehensive plan that would instruct the various commands on how to deal with the now vindictive and still well-armed German army. Italy's senior generals in Rome, unsure of what to do, issued ambiguous and at times contradictory orders. This lack of firm leadership and decisive action would lead to the rapid destruction of the army and the deaths of thousand of soldiers.

The first instructions were issued to the army on September 4, the day after the armistice had been signed (but four days prior to its public announcement). Known as Directive 44, it stated that commanders should be prepared to resist any attack by the Germans, but that they were not to act until they received an additional confirmation order. That order was finally dispatched, but not until September 11, long after the moment for any kind of coordinated action had passed. Directive 44 was never implemented.[22] On September 6, General Ambrosio added to the confusion by issuing an order that declared that army commands should deal with the Germans as they saw fit. This meant that for all intents and purposes, individual division commanders would decide whether to surrender or fight the German troops that would come to disarm them.

In Greece, only five minutes after Badoglio's radio address, the Supreme Command Southeast received orders from Berlin to disarm all Italian military units. Most divisions of the Eleventh Army surrendered without a fight, however, there were those that chose to resist. Against these military formations, the Germans showed no mercy. The most famous incident occurred on the island of Cefalonia. General Antonio Gandin allowed a plebiscite to take place among the men of his Acqui Division in which it was decided that they would not give up their arms. After rejecting a German request to that effect, they prepared for the inevitable response. The assault came a week later following an intense air bombardment. The attack upon the island was made by troops of the XXII Mountain Army Corps led by General Hubert Lanz. The Germans, with their superior numbers and weapons, eventually took the island and then began to systematically massacre the captured "traitors." On September 22, 1943, approximately 4,500 Italian officers and men were executed. Another 400 were put to death over the next few days. The division was wiped out. Counting those that had fallen in battle, the total number of Italians killed on Cefalonia reached some 8,400 men.[23] General Lanz, the man responsible for the executions, was held accountable by the Allies after the war. At Nuremberg he was sentenced to twelve years imprisonment (although he was released in 1951 after having served only six).

As the army collapsed, hundreds of thousands of Italian soldiers were disarmed and imprisoned both within and outside of Italy. The vast majority were subsequently placed aboard trains and sent to labor camps in Germany. Also evacuated north were Allied airmen and soldiers that had been held in prisoner of war (POW) camps in northern Italy. In all some 615,000 Italians were forced to languish in German camps until the end of the war. The combination of poor living conditions, forced labor, and a lack of enough food and proper clothing soon began to take its toll. Approximately 30,000 prisoners did not live to see the end of the war.[24]

Unlike other peoples imprisoned by the Nazis, the Italians were offered an option that would allow them a way out of the camps. If they agreed to enlist in the new army Mussolini was creating at Salo, and fight along side German forces, they would be freed. Very few accepted this offer. In fact over ninety-eight percent chose to stay in the camps rather than fight with the Germans.[25]

Gerda Weissmann Klein, a Jewish survivor of the concentration camps, remembered an encounter with some Italian soldiers turned prisoners following the armistice. In her riveting memoir *All But My Life* she recalled how, while working in a weaving mill in Landshut, Germany, she noticed the new inmates:

> Toward the middle of December we saw something new on the factory grounds: dark-haired, dark-eyed foreign men, in bright green uniforms, with funny green felt hats, elegantly slanted to one side. Such smart uniforms! We caught snatches of their conversation. They were Italian prisoners. We knew now that the war had taken a different turn. Apparently the Italians were no longer gallant Axis partners. . . .

The Italians did not last long. We saw them eating out of garbage cans in the factory, shivering in the frost of the mountain winter. Soon their uniforms were soiled, their gay hats crumpled. The sparkle left their eyes. Their numbers decreased rapidly.

I pictured them under the sunny skies of Italy, at grape harvests, singing in gondolas in Venice, walking through the Forum in Rome. How they must have missed their land.[26]

Those soldiers fortunate enough to have surrendered to the Allies fared infinitely better. As their military fell apart, some 500,000 men became prisoners of the American and British armies.[27] Needless to say they were treated much more humanely than were their comrades who had had the misfortune of being assigned to the north or the occupied lands.

On October 13, 1943 the Badoglio government brought Italy full circle by declaring war upon Germany. Over the next few months, Italian prisoners were slowly released from Allied custody. While many wanted nothing more than to go home, they were encouraged to join the newly formed "Italian Co-Belligerent Forces" also known as "The Army of the South." By late 1944, this new army that fought alongside Allied troops, would grow to include six divisions (*Gruppi di Combattimento*).[28] Generally, the Allied commanders preferred to use the Italians in the role of support units, thereby freeing more British and American troops for combat duty. However this was not always the case. In early 1944, some 5,000 Italians were used in operations along the Gustav line, near Monte Casino. By all accounts, they fought courageously and conducted themselves well. Even Mussolini took notice of their actions. In one exchange with his newly appointed Undersecretary of Foreign Affairs, Serafino Massolini, Mussolini pointed out that a particular *Bersagliere* (light infantry) battalion was advancing rapidly. The Undersecretary forcefully reminded his boss that "they are Badaglio's troops! They are fighting the Germans!" Mussolini, in a calm voice responded "'they are Italians, and they are fighting bravely. That is all that matters."[29]

At the same time these military units in the south were being created, Benito Mussolini was busy forming a new Fascist army in the north called the National Republican Army (*Esercito Nazionale Repubblicano*). The government at Salo would field four regular army divisions, as well as units of the National Republican Guard (*Guardia Nazionale Repubblicana*). The men that now flocked to these units were, as one might expect, Fascist fanatics and Mussolini loyalists. They were prepared to fight the Allies to the bitter end.

The third military force to be raised in the immediate aftermath of the armistice was that of the partisans. The various opponents of Fascism now saw a window of opportunity they had been waiting for since 1922. Groups such as the Socialists, Anarchists, Republicans, and, of course, the Communists wasted no time in forming military units to do battle with troops still loyal to Mussolini as well as with the occupying German army. These military formations received weapons and supplies from the Allies as they carried out missions in the north. In addition to these politically based military organizations, there were also regional or "non-aligned" groups which comprised about 20 per cent of the partisans' total strength.[30]

The Badoglio government hoped to gain the loyalty of the partisans and thereby control and coordinate their activities, but its efforts were doomed from the beginning. The guerrilla fighters, unwilling to take orders from the prime minister, instead created their own organization behind German lines known as the National Liberation Committee for Northern Italy (CLNAI). At times the partisan bands headed the dictates of the committee; at others its instructions were ignored.

With the Communist "Garibaldini" brigades in the forefront, the partisan movement expanded rapidly, especially during the last year of the war. In May 1944, there were some 20,000 guerillas in northern and central Italy. By April 1945, that number had grown to approximately 200,000.[31]   Naturally, the vast ideological differences that divided partisan units made it impossible to form one large coherent army. Nevertheless, their common hatred of the Fascists made these men and women a valuable resource during the last years of the war as the Allies attempted to eject the Germans from Italian soil.

As rapidly as events were unfolding in Italy, in the former

Yugoslavia the situation was changing by the hour. The Italian army's command structure was reduced to shambles. As in other areas, divisional commander were left on their own to deal as best they could with the situation. At the time of the armistice, seventeen divisions were stranded on the eastern shores of the Adriatic.[32] Every single divisional commander refused to continue the alliance with the Germans. Two entire divisions, *Taurinense* and *Venezia*, actually joined the Montenegrin partisans, while *Firenze* aligned itself with the partisans of Albania.[33]

The Second Army had its own problems. On the night of September 9, Mario Robotti and his entire staff abandoned their men and departed for Italy. It was left to General Gamara, commander of the XI Corps, to remain at Sussak and formally surrender the army to the Germans.[34] The Germans moved rapidly to secure what had been the Italian zone of occupation. This had to be achieved quickly for two reasons. Firstly, Italian soldiers had to be disarmed as they now could potentially pose a military threat. Secondly, and more importantly from a strategic viewpoint, the Dalmatian coast had to be secured lest it be used as an invasion site by the Allies.

Pavelic's armed forces, including members of the Ustasha, wasted no time following the Germans into the Italian areas. They were all too happy to accept the surrender of Italian units and seize any stockpiles of arms and supplies. Ustasha leaders Pavelic and Artukovic were thrilled at the prospect of the departure of what they considered to be an army of occupation. In Berlin, Pavelic's position was supported fully by Joseph Goebbels, himself no friend of the Italians. One day after the Italian surrender, he noted in his diary, "The Poglavnik [Pavelic] has issued a sharp declaration against Italy. He stated that at last he was in a position to create a free Croatian state together with Dalmatia; The Fuehrer had already promised him that. He now shook off Italian suzerainty." He went on to pour scorn upon his nation's former ally, "The Italians simply don't want to fight, are happy when they can surrender their arms, and are even happier when they can sell them."[35]

For some Germans and Croatians, it was also a time to settle old scores. One officer in particular, General Giuseppe Amico, appears to have caused both groups endless frustration as a friend and protector of Jews and Serbs and would be forced to pay for this stance with his life.

At the time of his death, Amico was one of the most respected men in the army. As a young artillery officer, he was no stranger to frontline combat, earning two silver and two bronze medals for bravery in battle during the Spanish Civil War and World War I. At age 51 he was given command of a division. From the time he arrived in Croatia, he clashed with Pavelic's representatives and was constantly engaged in jurisdictional disputes with the Croatians. Both the Croatians and Germans accused him of arrogance when he proclaimed that security matters should be left entirely in the hands of the Italian army and scoffed at the idea of handing Jews and Serbs over to the Ustasha. When the Ustasha began to desecrate graves and headstones in the city's Jewish cemetery, the leader of the Jewish community appealed to Amico. The general, already concerned with the behavior of the Ustasha in other areas of the country, immediately responded by posting soldiers at the entrance to the cemetery.

General Amico did not hesitate to defend those in danger of expulsion to concentration camps. The first attempt by the Croatians to deport Jews from the Dubrovnik area came in the autumn of 1941. The prewar Yugoslav government had settled 140 Jewish refugees from Germany and Austria in the small town of Capljina, located between Mostar and Dubrovnik. They were obliged to live under police supervision, a condition they gladly accepted. In mid September, a message was sent from the Interior Ministry ordering local officials to deport the Jews. They were to be sent to a small concentration camp that was in fact a converted Serbian Orthodox monastery. In typical bureaucratic fashion, the official reason given for the order was that these people had to be relocated due to a shortage of food and living space. Once the refugees realized the danger they were in, they appealed to the only group that could save them, the Italian army. General Amico overruled the deportation order, citing the fact that the targeted group included those that were elderly and sick as well as children.[36]

Unwilling to give up, the Croatians compiled a list of 62 men aged 16-60 to be deported. After Amico again refused, the Croatians took their case to another division commander, Angelo Pivano whose response was identical to that of his colleague. When pressed on the issue, General Pivano, supporting Amico's stance thundered, "It is not open to discussion, the Jews stay!"[37] Amico, sensing that the local authorities would not relent, finally moved the entire band of Jews from Capljina to Dubrovnik so as to guarantee their safety.

It was not long before Amico's actions brought him to the attention of German officials in Zagreb. On August 21, 1942, Ambassador Kasche wrote to Foreign Minister Ribbentrop defending Croatian policies, reiterating that the Jews and Serbs were enemies of the German Reich, and complaining that these groups were being protected by the "disloyal" Italians. He explained that Amico told the Croatian police that it went against the honor of the Italian army to deport the Jews because the Italians had promised them protection.[38] This statement by General Amico is remarkably similar to that which was made by General Negri to his German counterpart in Mostar only two months earlier.

Ambassador Kasche was not the only German to voice his criticism of Amico's actions. SS *Obersturmbannfuehrer* (Lieutenant Colonel) Hans Helm reported to Himmler that Amico freed five Jews whom the Croatians had arrested in the town of Konjice. Giuseppi Amico, like other Italian officers, was acting partly out of a sense of moral outrage, but also out of a perceived need to assert his will over the Croatian officials who seemed to challenge his authority at every turn.

The situation in Croatia changed drastically following Badoglio's assumption of power. On the same day that the signing of the armistice was made public, *Standartenfuehrer* (Colonel) August Schmidhuber, commander of the 2nd Regiment of the SS Division "Prince Eugen," received orders to take control of the city of Dubrovnik. This division would also fight the Italians at Split. The SS Colonel requested that Amico surrender the city as well as his division's heavy weapons. If the Italian did not comply, Schmidhuber threatened to call in the *Luftwaffe* and have the city bombed by air. Amico initially refused, but hoping to avoid a bloodbath, he reconsidered and agreed to negotiate. Knowing that other Italian units in the area were surrendering, the general knew he could expect no help and agreed to turn over his heavy weapons. On the afternoon of September 11, as the talks were ongoing, the Germans announced that they had been fired upon by Italian soldiers and therefore negotiations were at an end. The SS was now interested only in unconditional surrender.

That evening, a wave of Stuka dive bombers attacked the Italian divisional headquarters as well as several ships in the harbor. Pitted against the heavily armed Germans and without air cover, the "Marche" division was outmatched. During the night, the SS moved into the city. Shortly after noon the next day, the fighting was over. After signing the document of surrender, Amico was led away by the SS and shot in the back of the neck. His soldiers were disarmed and sent to a prison camp near Sarajevo. With typical SS arrogance, the official report read, "14 brave Germans died a heroic death fighting the traitors. Admittedly over 70 Italians lost their lives. The traitor General Amico, was shot."[39]

Schmidhuber, the man who had ordered Amico's execution, was named military governor of Dubrovnik. His first task was to deport any remaining Jews. Fortunately, by this time the majority of Jews had already been interned on Rab.

Early the next year, as a reward for his actions, he was promoted and given command of a new SS division that was being raised in Kosovo. The 21st SS Volunteer Mountain Division "Skanderbeg" was composed of Germans, as well as ethnic Albanians living in Kosovo. Schmidhuber's primary mission was to engage Tito's partisans in battle. As part of this overall strategy, however, his men were expected to punish, without mercy, all those civilians suspected of giving aid to the Communist guerrillas. In addition, he issued orders for the arrest of those few Jews that had returned to Kosovo from Albania following the Italian surrender. After the war he was brought to trial in Yugoslavia, charged with having committed war crimes. He was found guilty and hanged in February 1947.[40]

The Jews on the Island of Rab

The time period between the successful coup against Mussolini and the public announcement of the armistice, came to be known as "The 45 days." During these turbulent six weeks, a communiqué was received from the Foreign Ministry at Second Army headquarters that would prove pivotal in deciding the question of what to do with the Jewish internees.

On August 19, 1943, the newly appointed Secretary General of the Foreign Ministry Augusto Rosso dispatched a cable, undoubtedly with Foreign Minister Raffaele Guariglia's approval, stating, "Croatian Jews should not be released [from the internment camp] and are not to be abandoned to the hands of strangers [i.e. Germans and Ustasha] without some sort of protection, [they would be] exposed to potential acts of retaliation, unless they themselves prefer to be released and sent out of our area of occupation."[41] A copy of the dispatch was also sent to the Ministry of the Interior, a somewhat less than subtle attempt to warn those officials not to interfere in the matter. The cable went on to insist that the Jews should be prevented from moving to Italy en mass should the army be forced to withdraw, as the diplomats feared the Ministry of the Interior might possibly hand them over to the Germans. It further asserted that the military authorities should feel free to examine individual cases as they saw fit, and that, "We ask you to take this proposal into consideration and to inform us about any decision made in order to continue to protect these Jewish refugees as we have done until now."[42] As no one in Rome had a better idea, the best course of action appeared to be to simply leave the Jews on the island.

Most of the officers of Supersloda believed that the Foreign Ministry was mistaken and that the best idea was to implement the army's earlier proposal of sending the Jews to Italy. On August 29, a letter was sent to Castellani reiterating that position. In fact, the officers believed so strongly in not abandoning the Jews that they sent one of their own, Major Prolo, to Rome to make their views clear. This step, however, was taken too late as the major departed on his mission on September 7 and the armistice was announced the next day.

The day the war ended for Italy was also one of incredible danger for the Jews on Rab. The organization that had protected them for almost two and a half years was now departing and the Germans and Ustasha would surely show them no mercy. Fortunately, as the last soldiers left the island, a force of Tito's partisans arrived. This proved to be the event that saved the Jews from a gruesome death.

Weeks earlier, from his headquarters in western Bosnia, the Communist leader had thrilled to the news of Mussolini's downfall. At the announcement of the armistice, he ordered his irregular troops to seize as much Italian territory as possible. The competition between Germans, Ustasha, and partisan units to fill the power vacuum left by the Italians was fierce. While securing the abandoned positions was important for strategic reasons, it also allowed the various forces access to the Italian army's stockpiles of food, supplies and ammunition.

When the partisans arrived on Rab, the Jews did not hesitate to join their ranks. This day marked the first time in many months that they were free to determine their own destinies. Many of the young people made their intentions perfectly clear as they marched in military formation (or as close to it as untrained civilians could) out the main gate of the camp under the Yugoslav flag. For their part, the partisans were more than happy to absorb this new source of manpower. As partisan strength was not sufficient to hold the island, they evacuated the Jews, along with the Slovene internees to the mainland. Of the 3,500 Jews in the camp, only 204- mainly sick or elderly people- chose to remain behind. Sadly, they were seized by the occupying Germans, moved by ship to Trieste, and from there sent to Auschwitz.[43]

Rab inmate Imra Rochlitz recalled how happy he was to see the arrival of Tito's soldiers. They were very helpful, offering assistance to the older people during the move off the island. He remembered that they "behaved very correctly towards us, of course they expected all the young people to join. They had the attitude that if you're not with us you're against us."[44]

The newly freed Jews and Slovenes were quickly taken by boat across the narrow straight to the city of Crikvenica. There they were given shelter in buildings that had previously been used as boarding schools. The Jews who had been confined to the island of Korcula as part of the "enforced residence" were also freed by the partisans. Although they were all very grateful to the Italian army for its protection, not surprisingly many chose to join the guerrillas.

Boris N. recalled that some Jews went to the Croatian mainland while others followed the Italian soldiers back to their homeland. This was a risky move since they were unsure as to whether certain areas were controlled by the Allies or still held by the Germans. Boris recalled that some 400 Jews went directly to Italy and, "As they arrived Germans were waiting for them, and they collected them all put them in a train and they went straight into the German camps . . . all 400 perished."[45]   Boris was much luckier as, some-time later, he and a few others sailed to the coastal city of Bari in southern Italy. As they approached the harbor, they heard soldiers shouting in Hebrew "Shalom, Shalom!" as he soon found out, they were men of the Jewish Brigade of the British army.

The German army rapidly moved down the coast from the north and by late 1943, along with the Croatian army and Ustasha, had occupied most Dalmatian cities and towns. As the situation was unstable along much of the coast, it became prudent for the parti-sans to withdraw into the interior with tons of supplies left by the Italians. The British estimated that the amount of captured weapons and equipment allowed Tito to double the size of his army. As they moved inland, those too old or too young to fight (there were approximately 500 children that had come from Rab) were placed with civilians sympathetic to the partisans in the liberated areas of Croatia and Bosnia.

As for those Jewish men and women deemed fit for military serv-ice, at first they were organized into a special unit, the Fifth Battalion, that fought alongside four battalions of Slovenes. Together these five units comprised a partisan brigade that was made up of the new recruits from Rab. It did not take long, however, for Tito to real-ize that a Jewish unit would invite undo attention on the part of the Germans and the Ustasha. He therefore ordered it disbanded and the Jews dispersed to other units throughout the partisan army.

These Jews, who had been used as pawns in a diplomatic game

involving the governments of three nations, were now, for the first time, given a chance to strike back at their enemies. They quickly took advantage of this opportunity and, like their brothers in arms, were totally committed to driving the Fascists from their country. They understood that they owed a tremendous debt of gratitude to the Italians for having the courage to shield them from the murderous rage of the Ustasha and Nazis at a time when it would have been easy enough to have looked the other way.

1   Morley, p.161.
2   State Committee, May 21, 1947, p.5.
3   Ibid.
4   Winston S. Churchill, The Second World War, vol.III, The Grand Alliance (Boston: Houghton Mifflin Company, 1950), p.540.
5   Ibid., p.543.
6   The University of Oklahoma College of Law: A Chronology of US Historical Documents [home page on-line]; available from http://www.law.ou.edu/history/germwar.shtml Internet; accessed April 16, 2007.
7   John Erickson and Ljubica Erickson, The Eastern Front in Photographs (London: Carlton Books Ltd., 2001), p.132.
8   Merridale, p.212.
9   Ibid., p.215.
10 Ibid., p.157.
11 R.J.B. Bosworth, Mussolini's Italy: Life Under the Fascist Dictatorship, 1915-1945 (New York: The Penguin Press, 2006), p.495.
12 Neville, p.175.
13 Ibid., p.177.
14 Basil Davidson, Scenes from the Anti-Nazi War (New York: Monthly Review Press, 1980), p.33.
15 Steinberg, p.7.
16 Roy Palmer Domenico, Italian Fascists on Trial, 1943-1948 (Chapel Hill, North Carolina: University of North Carolina Press, 1991), p.18.
17 Steinberg, p.152.
18 Michaelis, p.344.
19 Michael Beschloss, The Conquerors: Roosevelt, Truman and the Destruction of Hitler's Germany, 1941-1945 (New York: Simon and Schuster, 2002), p.29.

20 Steinberg, p.159.
21 Ibid.
22 Davidson, p.21.
23 Ibid., p.23.
24 Ibid., p.24.
25 Ibid.
26 Gerda Weissman Klein, <u>All But My Life</u> (New York: Hill and Wang, 1957), p.162.
27 Bosworth, p.504.
28 Philip Jowett, <u>The Italian Army 1940-45 (3) Italy 1943-45</u> (Oxford: Osprey Publishing Ltd., 2001), p.24.
29 Christopher Hibbert, Mussolini: <u>The Rise and Fall of Il Duce</u> (New York: Palgrave MacMillan, 2008)
30 Jowett, p.36.
31 Ibid.
32 Thomas, p.12.
33 Ibid.
34 Steinberg, p.159.
35 Lochner, p.431.
36 Menachem Shelah, "Kroatische Juden zwischen Deutschland und Italien 1941-1943," Vierteljahrshefte Fuer Zeitgeschichte (April 1993): p.187. Trans. [from German] Heidi Schiefer.
37 Ibid.
38 Ibid., p.191.
39 Ibid., p.194.
40 Ibid., p.195.
41 Document 680, Ministero Degli Affari Esteri, Documenti Diplomatici Italiani, serie 1939-1943 volume X (7 Febbraio- 8 Settembre 1943), Libreria Dello Stato Roma MCMXC.
42 Micr. No. T-821, Roll 405, Frs. 821-822.
43 Carpi, p.502.
44 Joseph Rochlitz, *The Righteous Enemy*.
45 Boris N., 1996, "Interview by Survivors of the Shoah Visual History Foundation

5

FIGHTING WITH
THE PARTISANS

Joining the Partisan Ranks

At the time that the Jews from the Italian zone were being integrated into the Communist partisan army, Tito was busy rebuilding his forces. The Italian surrender had come at a most opportune time as it allowed Tito's troops a chance to gather much needed supplies and recruits.

Tito's army had suffered terrible losses in the first few months of 1943, narrowly surviving two devastating Axis offensives. Operation *Weiss* (White) was launched on January 20 with a combined force of approximately 120,000 German, Italian, Croatian, and even Chetnik soldiers. The Germans and Croatians hoped to sweep into western Bosnia-Hercegovina and push Tito's men toward the Neretva River where the Italians and Chetniks would be waiting. The much smaller partisan force of 40,000 was battered during the campaign but remained in tact.

In March, during the battle at Gornji Vakuf, the partisans succeeded in capturing several German soldiers, including some officers, whom they sought to use as bargaining chips in a plan to exchange prisoners. Tito sent representatives through the lines to negotiate the exchange of German prisoners for partisans captured earlier and for Tito's common-law wife Herta Hass, who was being held in jail in Croatia. Surprisingly, an agreement was reached and the exchange of prisoners actually took place-a rare event in this type of guerrilla war.

Generally in this war, neither side took prisoners. As it was a mobile conflict, those partisans too badly wounded to keep up with the others sometimes had to be killed by their own comrades rather than be left for the Germans. During the battle of Setjeska, a Montenegrin woman who was severely wounded and could not go on was shot by her own husband, who then turned the gun on himself.[1] Those few prisoners taken by Axis troops were usually interrogated and quickly executed. In one particularly gruesome instance, the Germans laid wounded partisan prisoners out in a field and ran them over with their tanks.[2]

In May 1943, Operation *Schwarz* (Black) succeeded Operation Weiss. The German army, along with its allies and backed by planes and artillery, managed to encircle the partisans along the border between Bosnia and Montenegro. The battle took place along the River Setjeska. Although the Germans made an all out effort to destroy their foe once and for all, the guerrillas succeeded in breaking through the lines and retreated in good order. The fight proved costly though, with the partisans suffering some 7,000 killed and at least that many wounded.[3]

Tito himself was wounded in the arm during the battle when a bomb exploded near his position, an incident that served to enhance the partisan leader's reputation. The battle marked a turning point in the war in Yugoslavia, for it demonstrated the resilience of the partisan army. Within weeks, the guerrillas had regrouped and were launching their own offensives in Bosnia.

As the threat from the partisans grew, the Italians and Ustasha were forced by necessity (and ideology) to coordinate their military actions. Although the Ustasha and the Italian army were on the same side, there was friction between the two from the beginning. Members of the Ustasha complained, as did the Germans, that the Italians often arrived late during joint operations which allowed the partisans to escape. The Italians, for their part, criticized the unnecessary brutality of the Ustasha. Nevertheless, they were forced to work together, at times very closely, until Italy surrendered to the Allies in July 1943.

The Italians were not the only people appalled by the policies and tactics of Pavelic and the Ustasha. As the war progressed, the number of average Croatians who joined the ranks of the partisans increased sharply, from 7,000 in 1941 to 150,000 by 1944.[4] As in other parts of Yugoslavia, the numbers of new recruits rose dramatically following the Italian surrender and continued to do so until the end of the war.

Jews were involved in all aspects of partisan life, from fighting on the front lines to serving in support units. Perhaps the area in which Jews made the greatest contribution was in the field of medicine. The 300 Jewish doctors, 100 nurses, and 70 pharmacists were invaluable in forming the partisan's medical corps and saving numerous lives under difficult wartime conditions. In total 4,572 Jews are listed among the ranks of the guerrillas:[5] some 3,000 served in combat units, with the others contributing behind the lines. By war's end, 1,318 had given their lives to defeat the Fascists and 10 had been awarded the partisan's highest medal, that of *Narodni Heroj Jugoslavije* (National Hero of Yugoslavia).[6]

Despite setbacks during the war, Tito was supremely confident in his cause and his troops. He had no doubt that he would eventually emerge victorious over his enemies, be they foreign or, in the case of the Chetniks, domestic.

His adversaries were well aware of his growing popularity and took note of the fact that the partisan movement was expanding rapidly. The Germans considered him to be such a threat that they put a price on his head of 100,000 Reichsmarks. As this did not have the desired effect, on May 25, 1944, Tito's official birthday (although he was actually born on May 7, 1892), they mounted an operation designed to kill or capture him. German intelligence reported that the partisan leader had set up his command center in a cave near the town of Dvar in Bosnia. The man Hitler chose to coordinate this special mission was Otto Skorzeny, the SS officer who had snatched Mussolini from captivity and successfully spirited him north to German territory. Skorzeny, however, clashed with Field Marshal

Maximilian von Weichs, commander-in-chief, southeast. The two men disagreed over tactics; Skorzeny argued for a small surgical strike, while his superior overruled him in favor of a massive attack in force. A frustrated Skorzeny abandoned the project and returned to Berlin. Operation *Roesselsprung* (Knight's Move) opened with German bombers devastating Dvar. A combined attack by paratroopers and glider-born troops ensured that the town was captured within an hour. While the primary mission was to take Tito, it was also important to find and destroy the buildings that contained the partisan radio and telephone communications centers and to round up the members of the Allied liaison missions working with the partisan command. After a brief but fierce firefight, the buildings and the vital equipment within fell to the Germans. As for the Allied delegations, the Americans and British, along with many of the town's civilians, had evacuated a few days earlier. They had been alerted to the fact that something was afoot by the appearance of German reconnaissance aircraft in the area. The Russian representatives were not so fortunate. They were captured and executed.[7]

The Germans wasted no time moving into the countryside. They soon discovered the cave and quickly assaulted the entrance in order to prevent anyone from escaping. Fortunately, Tito's men were able to hold the Germans off long enough for their commander and his staff to escape. As the bodyguards desperately fought to buy time, Tito and his staff officers managed to climb up a rope through a gap in the back of the cave that had been carved by a small stream. They then made their way through a tunnel to the outside where they proceeded up the mountain.

The battle raged for the rest of the day as new partisan forces arrived. In the end, the operation succeeded only in temporarily disrupting the partisans' communication system. As for the man the Germans had set out to kill or capture, he escaped by plane to Bari, Italy and soon reestablished his headquarters off the Dalmatian coast on the island of Vis. The SS troops and paratroopers only managed to "capture" Tito's brand new marshals uniform (which was publicly displayed in Vienna as a war trophy).

One reason for the success of the partisan movement was the

fact that these Communist fighters, unlike the Serbian nationalist Chetniks, saw themselves as part of a larger organization with a well developed command structure. The Croatian Communist leadership, which called itself the "General Staff of the National Liberation Army and Partisan Units of Croatia," began its activities in October 1941. In November 1942, representatives gathered in Bosnia as Tito announced the formation of the Anti-Fascist National Liberation Council of Yugoslavia (AVNOJ). Although the new entity included some non-Communist members, there was no doubt which group was in charge. The AVNOJ became the supreme representative body of the country and soon created the National Liberation Committee of Yugoslavia (NKOJ) which served as the executive arm of government. The organization denied the legitimacy of King Peter's government-in-exile and proclaimed itself to be the sole representative of the people. Tito was formally granted the rank of marshal and the titles of army minister and prime minister. As the partisans took control of more territory over the next two and a half years, the NKOJ would soon come to serve as Yugoslavia's de facto government.

The Allied liaison officers proved crucial to the partisan war effort. Whereas the Germans supplied almost all the weapons used in the NDH, Tito's troops had to rely on a variety of sources to provide their fighting men and women with arms. In late 1941, the British had dispatched the first of the Allied mission to Yugoslavia to make contact with those fighting against the German invaders. At that time, however, the officers had been sent to the Chetnik headquarters in Serbia, rather than to partisan camps, as it appeared the Chetniks had greater support from the Serbian population. It soon became apparent, however, that Mihailovic's forces were unreliable.

The first contact between the British and the partisans occurred in the spring of 1943. While Tito welcomed Allied assistance, for months he remained suspicious of Allied motives, fearing they would side with the Chetniks and restore the young King Peter to the throne. His fears eventually proved to be groundless.

In the autumn, Brigadier Fitzroy Maclean headed a military mission assigned to Tito's headquarters. The general described Yugoslavia as a land of "burning villages, desecrated churches, massacred hostages, and mutilated bodies."[8] He soon theorized, however, that despite the massive amount of suffering the nation was enduring, it would survive. He further contended that the advancing Allied armies coupled with partisan tactics would eventually force the Germans to withdraw and leave the Communists in control of Yugoslavia.

The British general reported that Tito's forces were divided into twenty-six divisions totaling approximately 220,000 soldiers. Of this figure 50,000 were deployed in Bosnia, 30,000 in Serbia and Macedonia, 50,000 in Croatia and the rest operating in other areas of the former Yugoslavia.[9] He estimated that there were fourteen German divisions charged with combating partisan activities. Under the code name "Ultra" the British had already broken the secret German code used to communicate information between military commands. They therefore knew that the number of German and Croatian divisions actively fighting the partisans, and so could not be deployed to other battle fronts, actually stood at thirty.[10]

The Brigadier observed that the bulk of partisan training centered on the handling of small arms, light machine guns, and various forms of explosives. Although they had no tanks or heavy artillery, as the war progressed, Tito's forces were able to acquire some anti-tank weapons and light artillery. What could not be captured from Axis troops had to be supplied by the Allies. While the quality of weapons supplied to troops by both the Axis and Allied powers was excellent, some partisans actually preferred using German weapons in the field so as not to be totally dependent on Allied supply drops. The partisans were in constant need of food, weapons and ammunition. Requests for these items were relayed from the liaison officers to their superiors in Italy. Most provisions and supplies were then sent from Allied controlled Brindisi across the Adriatic in C47 transports or modified bombers such as the Halifax or B24 Liberator. On some occasions, equipment was transported by submarine or small boats which would land on an unguarded stretch of beach. The British, through their Special Operations Executive (SOE), took the lead in maintaining ties with the partisans. While the Americans had liaison missions with both the partisans and Chetniks, William Donovan, head of the Office of Strategic Services (OSS), agreed to place his men under British operational control.

In addition to receiving supplies and advisors from the west, Tito also received help from the Soviets. Not surprisingly, the Russians did all they could to aid their fellow Communists and Stalin's representatives were warmly welcomed at Tito's headquarters. Unlike the Russians, however, mission members from the two "capitalist countries," despite all they were doing for the partisans, continued to be viewed with a certain amount of suspicion. For propaganda purposes, throughout the conflict, the partisans downplayed their dependence on British and American supplied weapons, claiming that the arms were not gifts and would have to be paid for after the war.[11] The Soviets were at least a bit more gracious about the aid supplied to them during WWII.[A]

Tito, like other Allied leaders, had his own agenda. Despite the fact that he was a committed Communist, he was determined not to be Moscow's puppet. When asked point blank by Brigadier Maclean if Yugoslavia would become a satellite of the Soviet Union, Tito replied that the partisans had not fought and endured such tremendous suffering simply to hand the country over to someone else.[12] (Indeed, barely three years after the end of the war Tito would sever his ties with the Soviet Union.) For the time being, however, he needed to stay in the good graces of everyone that could help him achieve victory. Ever the politician, when he met for a two day conference with Winston Churchill in Italy in mid August 1944, he even pledged not to use British supplied weapons against his fellow countrymen (i.e. Chetniks). Undoubtedly, Churchill knew he would

[A]Among the goods shipped by the United States to the Soviet Union under Lend-Lease were some 200,000 Studebaker trucks that greatly aided in the advance of the Red Army. Of equal importance were shipments of desperately needed food. The threat of starvation loomed especially large early in the war as millions of acres of cropland were devastated, while produce and livestock were seized and shipped back to Germany. In the first few months following the invasion, 40% of Russia's farmland had been lost to the enemy. By 1945, the United States had provided some five million tons of food to the Soviet Union. Privately, Stalin was extremely grateful for the outside aid, in fact, the Russian dictator once credited the product Spam with saving millions of Russian lives.

192 • • • DEFYING EVIL

never live up to this promise, but nevertheless agreed to increase the amount of aid being delivered to the partisans.

One group of people who were not easily won over to the partisan cause until late in the war were the Bosnian Muslims. Technically, Bosnia was part of the NDH, and Pavelic encouraged the people of this region to support his government and join Ustasha units. The majority of Muslims in this part of the former Yugoslavia pursued a pragmatic strategy, first siding with the Germans and Italians against the Chetniks and only much later aligning with the partisans as they gained ground in 1944. While their commitment to the Axis nations could never be characterized as wholehearted, thousands of Bosnian Muslims joined two SS divisions that were raised in Bosnia. The first of these, the 13th SS Mountain Division *Handschar* (saber), was created in March 1943. A second force, the 23rd SS Mountain Division *Kama*, existed for only a short time Between June and October 1944, before being disbanded.

As the war progressed, and the Nazis began to exhaust their supply of manpower, Himmler made the decision to begin recruiting men from the occupied countries into SS formations. Naturally, he began with the "Nordic" populations of Northern Europe, as they were seen as being the closest to the "Aryan" people of Germany. Eventually, however, he accepted people from more distant lands into his elite units. Within the NDH, Ante Pavelic was absolutely opposed to the idea of Bosnian Muslim military units and made his views known to the Germans. He believed this would encourage the Muslims to see themselves as a distinct ethnic group and call for an independent Bosnian nation. The Germans ignored the Croatian leader's protests, and the project moved ahead.

To aid in his recruitment efforts, Himmler enlisted the help of the grand mufti of Jerusalem, Mohammad Amin al-Husseini. The

---

[B]A fervent believer in Pan-Arabism, he had been one of the leaders of the 1936 Arab uprising in Palestine. During that rebellion he had railed against Jewish immigration and called for an independent Arab state in Palestine. His followers attacked moderate Arab leaders, British soldiers, and Jewish civilians. It took three years to finally quell the rebellion. Wanted by the authorities, al-Husseini escaped first to Lebanon, then to Iraq. When the British army moved into that country in 1941, he fled to Germany where he was received by Foreign Minister Ribbentrop with open arms.

grand mufti already had a long history of participating in anti-British and anti-Jewish activities.[B] The German foreign minister immediately recognized that the grand mufti could act as an important link to the Arab world. On November 28, the grand mufti met with Hitler. The meeting was cordial as the two men spoke of defeating their common enemies: the Jews, the British, and the Communists. Hitler went on to assure his guest that following the inevitable German victory, Arab lands would be free of foreign control. After proclaiming their mutual admiration, their congenial conference ended. Ever the hypocrite, no sooner had the grand mufti left the room than Hitler turned to an aide and said, "I never want to see that chocolate covered monkey again."

Al Husseini spent the rest of the war in Berlin, broadcasting Nazi propaganda via radio to the Arab countries of North Africa and the Middle East. He was made an honorary general in the *Handschar* division and continued his efforts to sway Bosnian Muslims to fight with the Germans. In addition, before the battle of El Alamein, when it seemed as though German troops might continue their advance all the way to Palestine, he proposed the building of concentration camps there in order to eliminate its Jewish population. Following the war, the crafty Arab leader escaped once again, this time to Egypt, where he would later be active in calling for the destruction of the new state of Israel during its war for independence in 1948.

The Last Year of the War

On June 6, 1944, the western Allies mounted the largest amphibious invasion in world history. This monumental event would come to be known as D-Day. Codenamed Operation *Overlord*, the attack upon Nazi occupied France involved five seaborne and three airborne divisions, along with 5,000 ships, and 12,000 aircraft. Of the five beaches used for the landings on the Normandy coast, the fiercest fighting occurred at Omaha. Despite suffering 10,300 casualties, by the end of the day the Americans, British, and Canadians had breached the coastal fortifications and placed over 150,000 men in France. The liberation of Western Europe had begun.

The success of D-Day overshadowed another important event in the war in the west. On the previous day, June 5, American General Mark Clark's Fifth Army had at last captured Rome. The western Allies were clearly making strides in defeating the Axis enemy.

In that same month, far to the east, the Soviets were preparing their own offensive, which would involve almost a million and a half soldiers. In Byelorussia, Operation *Bagration* (named after a Russian prince killed at the battle of Borodino in 1812) was scheduled to begin on June 22, exactly three years to the day after the German invasion of the Soviet Union. Once again, the Red Army suffered heavy casualties, but by September, it had driven the Germans back to the borders of East Prussia and was nearing the city of Warsaw. Unfortunately, stiff German resistance meant that the Polish capital would not fall until mid January 1945.

Events moved rapidly in Eastern Europe during the last months of 1944. In late August, a coup was staged against the pro-Fascist government of Rumania and King Michael ordered the new officials to surrender unconditionally to the Allies. On August 26, as the Russians drew near their border, officials of another Axis member, Bulgaria, attempted to placate Moscow by declaring neutrality; the tactic failed. On September 5, the Soviet Union formally declared war on that country. Three days later, Russian troops crossed the border. As in Rumania, this action sparked a coup. The new government not only made peace with the Russians but actually declared war on Germany. The Soviets were now in a position to invade the former Yugoslavia.

On September 21, Tito, unbeknownst to the British, secretly boarded a Russian plane and flew from the island of Vis to Moscow to confer with Stalin. When the two Communist leaders met, Tito proposed that following the capture of Belgrade it would be to their mutual advantage to have the Red Army move directly into Hungary and allow the partisans to liberate the rest of their country. In addition, this would also put Tito's forces in a good position to support the Russian left flank as they moved westward. Stalin agreed to the plan.

On October 20, 1944, Belgrade fell to the combined forces of the Soviet army and the partisans. By this point, the partisan ranks had grown large enough that they were often referred to as the People's Army, or the National Liberation Army (the formal name of the partisans had always been the People's Liberation Army and Partisan Detachments of Yugoslavia). Although the capture of the former capital of Yugoslavia was cause for celebration, relations between the partisans and Russians quickly deteriorated. Reports began to reach Tito, who was in northeastern Serbia, that Russian soldiers were raping, and in some cases then murdering, Serb women. While rape was considered a criminal offense in the Soviet army, there were very few prosecutions. Tito was furious. As the Russians moved farther west, the number of incidents of rape and looting increased dramatically. Once they reached German soil, their full fury was unleashed. In the first few days of May 1945, after Berlin had fallen, Soviet troops were allowed to go on a three day rampage; it is estimated that some 100,000 German women were raped by the victors. As for the whole scale looting of German homes, the vast majority of Soviet soldiers felt it was just compensation for their having to endure the dangers and hardships of war. Tito and the partisan leadership were happy to see the Soviet army move north toward Germany.

While the Soviets aided the partisan war effort on the ground, assistance from the western allies came from the air. The Royal Air Force (RAF) and the U.S. Army Air Force bombed German targets throughout Yugoslavia mainly in the latter stages of the war. (Industrial targets in Germany, northern Italy, the Rumanian oil fields, as well as concentrations of troops and armor that directly faced Allied lines took priority and were therefore the primary focus of Allied bombers.) In 1944, the American 463rd Bombardment Group (Heavy) flying B17 bombers out of Foggia, Italy attacked targets such as the marshalling yards within Croatia at Brod and Zagreb. Other missions included striking the airfields at Banja Luka, and bridges at Belgrade and Sarajevo. One particularly successful raid occurred on April 16, in which 35 bombers destroyed the ammunition depot at Belgrade without losing a single aircraft.[13] Brigadier Maclean himself watched the Flying Fortresses annihilate a concentration of German armor near the town of Leskovac in southern Serbia. While only 20 of the Group's 156 missions flown that year involved targets in Yugoslavia, every raid helped to weaken the Germans, thereby strengthening the partisans.

By late 1944, the German army in Bosnia-Hercegovina was moving north toward Zagreb. This slow fighting retreat would prove costly. Relentlessly attacked by partisan units, German casualty rates were very high during this period. By the spring of 1945, it was clear that the NDH would fall. It was only a matter of time.

Yet even at this late date, the concentration camp at Jasenovac continued to operate. On April 20, one last large group consisting of Serb women and children were murdered by the guards. As camp officials prepared to flee for their lives, they, like their Nazis counterparts, sought to erase all traces of their crimes. As part of this effort, the remaining prisoners were ordered to exhume thousands of buried corpses, since not all bodies had been disposed of by means of the crematorium. For three weeks, the air around the camp was filled with a putrid smell as the large pyres burned.[14]

As of April 22, 1945, there were 1,060 prisoners left alive in the Jasenovac complex. On that morning, the Ustasha guards moved most of the people into a large factory building and nailed boards across the door and windows. Knowing that they were about to be killed, several hundred inmates decided to try to break out. The desperate prisoners smashed through the door and climbed out the windows. As they ran, inmates seized bricks, hammers, iron bars or whatever they could find to use against the heavily armed guards. Some 600 prisoners took part in the escape attempt (the other 450 were either too sick or too weak to rebel). In a few sections of the camp, vicious hand to hand fighting raged for several minutes, as prisoners dashed for the east gate and freedom. The Ustasha, firing bursts from their machine guns, shot approximately 540 of those attempting to break out. In all, sixty people managed to clear the compound and escape from Croatia's most notorious death camp.[15]

Among the lucky few to escape was Ilija Ivanovic, the boy who would later write an account of what he witnessed in this hellish place. His skills as a barber and locksmith had allowed him to survive almost three years in the camp. He was eventually reunited with his mother and three younger siblings, but found that his father had been murdered by the Ustasha. The prisoners that remained in the camp were soon killed and before the guards fled, they destroyed the buildings, and burned the camp to the ground. When the partisans arrived on May 2, ten days after the uprising, they found only blacken ruins. The exact number of people killed at Jasenovac may never be known, although most sources place the number between 600,000 and 700,000.16 Since the war, however, some Croatians have asserted that this figure is exaggerated; while there have been others, along with many Serbs, that claim it is too low. As for the number of Jewish victims, approximately 18,500 were murdered at the camp during the war.17

Two days after the uprising at Jasenovac, the partisans entered what remained of the women's camp at Stara Gradiska. Unfortunately, the compound was empty as the Ustasha had moved the remaining prisoners to the main Jasenovac facility in November 1944. According to the latest data, about 12,200 women and children were killed at Stara Gradiska, but the figures are still incomplete.18 The people that suffered and died in these concentration camps have not been forgotten. Today, near the small town of Jasenovac, on the site where the vast complex once stood, the public is reminded of what happened there. A building houses a small museum, and a locomotive engine and box car used to transport human beings to the camp sit nearby. In 1965 a massive stone flower monument was erected to honor those that died an untimely death at the hands of a brutal regime.

While the partisans were taking control of large areas within the NDH, across the Adriatic in northern Italy their fellow communist guerrillas were assaulting German convoys as well as those of Italian Fascist troops still loyal to the Republic of Salo. As the Allied armies were closing in after having fought their way up the Italian peninsula, Mussolini sensed that the end was near for his Italian Social Republic. On April 25, he disbanded what remained of his armed forces. Rather than fall into the hands of the U.S. Army driving north from Bologna, he decided to attempt an escape. As he prepared to leave, he suggested to his wife that she take the children and cross the border into Switzerland. Knowing that his family might be subjected to retaliation if taken by partisans, he advised her that, "If they [the partisans] try and stop you or harm you, ask to be handed over to the English."[19] Shortly before dawn on April 26, Mussolini began to drive up the West shore of Lake Como. As Winston Churchill recorded:

> Accompanied by a handful of supporters, he attached himself to a small German convoy heading towards the Swiss frontier. The commander of the column was not anxious for trouble with Italian Partisans. The Duce was persuaded to put on a German great-coat and helmet. But the little party was stopped by Partisan patrols; Mussolini was recognized and taken into custody. Other members, including his mistress, Signorina Petacci, were also arrested. On Communist instructions the Duce and his mistress were taken out in a car the next day and shot. Their bodies, together with others, were sent to Milan and strung up head downwards on meat- hooks in a petrol station on the Piazzale Loretto, where a group of Italian Partisans had lately been shot in public.
>
> Such was the fate of the Italian dictator.[20]

Farther to the north, the Soviet army had completely encircled Berlin. On the evening of April 29, Hitler, sitting in his bunker with the Russians only a mile away, was informed that Mussolini had been shot. He was also told of the subsequent humiliating treatment to which the body had been subjected. This only reinforced his determination to commit suicide the next day and leave no remains for the Russians. As he told an SS aide, "After my death I don't want to be put on exhibition in a Russian wax museum."[21] He then gave orders that following his death his body was to be burned. On April 30, 1945, with the Soviets only a few hundred yards from the bunker, Adolf Hitler took his own life. The worst mass murderer in human history was no more.

As the Russians were in the final stages of capturing the Nazi capital, Yugoslav partisans were advancing north along the coast to take the Italian city of Trieste. The port city lies on the border of Italy, Slovenia, and Croatia and has always had a mixed population. It would be the Italian citizens, however, that would suffer at the hands of the partisans as they sought revenge for the Fascist division and occupation of Yugoslavia. The partisans entered the city on April 30. Two days later, the 2nd New Zealand Division arrived and accepted the surrender of the German garrison. Trieste was now a divided metropolis, with the British in control of one section and the partisans dominating the other. A tense standoff developed between the two armies, in part, because Tito laid claim to the entire city, believing it should be part of Yugoslavia. An additional bone of contention involved the indiscriminate shooting of Italian officials, policemen, and any German soldiers unlucky enough to still be within the partisan controlled area. Estimates of the number of those killed range from 2,000 to 20,000. After receiving no support from Stalin for his claim to the city, in mid June, Tito backed down and ordered his men to withdraw. Occupied by British and American troops until 1954, Trieste was formally annexed by Italy in February of that year.

The End of the Ustasha Regime

The bloody war that had engulfed a continent was rapidly coming to an end. General Alfred Jodl signed the instrument of unconditional surrender at General Eisenhower's headquarters in Rheims, France at 2:41 A.M. on May 7. General Walter Bedell Smith, Eisenhower's chief of staff, accepted the surrender on behalf of the western Allies. Even though General Ivan Susloparov affixed his signature as a representative of the Soviet high command, the Russians insisted upon staging a separate signing ceremony in Berlin two days later. May 8, 1945 officially marked VE Day (Victory in Europe). All over the world people celebrated the downfall of the Nazi *Reich*.

It was also on this date that the partisan army entered Zagreb. Tito discouraged his troops from taking revenge upon the population of the Croatian capitol. As a Croat himself, he understood that not everyone in the NDH was guilty of supporting the Ustasha government. Looking to the future of a unified Yugoslavia, the last thing he wanted was to allow a massacre of Croatian civilians. This would serve only to further encourage ethnic hatred and make unification more difficult. The standards were different when it came to dealing with the Ustasha. Earlier in the war, Tito had invited these militiamen, along with soldiers of the regular army, to desert their positions and join the partisan movement. Few questions were asked of those that chose to do so. Now, however, in the last days of the war, revenge was taken against captured Ustasha soldiers. Those found guilty of committing war crimes were summarily executed, including several dozen Catholic priests.[22]

Yet Tito's revenge against the Ustasha had its limits. In keeping with his ideas of national reconciliation, Communist propaganda tended to minimize massacres by the Ustasha and instead emphasize atrocities committed by the foreign Fascist invaders. This is not to suggest that the partisans were willing to let the leaders of the NDH escape responsibility for their actions. In the eyes of Tito and his comrades, the Zagreb officials were guilty of treason, guilty of collaboration with the enemy, and directly responsible for the deaths of hundreds of thousands of people.

As the partisans approached the outskirts of Zagreb, Ante Pavelic and the Ustasha leaders first looted the treasury and then fled the city. They raced north through Slovenia, hoping to reach Austria where they could surrender to the British army rather than to the partisans or Russians. Along the way they were joined by 40,000 retreating German soldiers, Slovene collaborators, Serb Chetniks, and a large number of civilians, all of whom were terrified of falling into the hands of the vengeful partisans. In total approximately 134,000 soldiers and civilians were included in the retreating columns.[23]

On May 15, 1945, the refugees reached the Austrian border town of Bleiburg. At the request of the partisans, however, the British refused to allow them to cross the border. These "quislings"[C] were to be handed over to the partisans to be dealt with as they saw

---

[C]The term has come to mean "traitor" it refers to Vidkun Quisling the collaborationist prime minister of Norway. Following the liberation of Norway he was tried and executed for cooperating with the Nazis.

fit. In response to the appeals of desperate Ustasha officers, the British authorities replied, "All Croatian forces are to surrender and return to Yugoslavia. If Croatian troops resist and fight their way through, British tanks and airplanes will open fire!"24 While a few managed to slip across the border, the vast majority were captured by the partisans. Retribution was swift as thousands were massacred in the fields near Bleiburg. The rest endured marches of hundreds of miles to prison camps; anyone who could not maintain the pace was shot.

It has been estimated that between 45,000 and 55,000 former Ustasha and Croatian army soldiers were killed at Bleiburg or while on the march to prison.25 Yet it was a different story for many of the Ustaha leaders. Most of them avoided capture, among them Pavelic himself, Interior Minister Artukovic and two Jasenovac commanders, Maks Luburic and Dinko Sakic.

Not so fortunate were Slavko Kvaternik and Education Minister Mile Budak. Budak was put on trial in Zagreb, quickly found guilty and executed. Kvaternik, who held the title of marshal, and had first publicly proclaimed the establishment of the Ustasha state, was tried as a collaborator along with five other Croats in 1947. All were sentenced to be executed. Also receiving a death sentence in the same trial was the German ambassador Siegfried Kasche. The seven men were hanged on June 7, 1947.

Kasche was not the only German tried for his actions in Yugoslavia. The two commanders-in-chief, southeast, General Alexander Loehr and his replacement Maximilian von Weichs, each stood trial after the war. Loehr, who had pressed the Italians to deport Jews from their occupation zone in Greece, was convicted by a Yugoslav court and executed. Field Marshal von Weichs was indicted for war crimes by a U.S. military tribunal, but was subsequently released on the grounds of ill health.

What was the fate of the two most powerful Nazis involved with Croatian Jews in the Italian zone of occupation? *Reichsfuehrer SS* Himmler, who was responsible for the deaths of millions, cheated the hangman. He was captured by the British in May 1945. At the time of his arrest he had been attempting to disguise himself by shaving off his small mustache, and discarding his distinctive black SS uniform in favor of that of an army private. His identity was soon discovered, however, when his forged papers were inspected by British soldiers. During a medical exam, he bit into a cyanide capsule he had carefully concealed and died instantly. Foreign Minister Ribbentrop had been the diplomatic face of the Third Reich and negotiated treaties with European countries, the terms which would never be honored by his government. He had hoped to gain favor with Hitler by gaining possession of the Jews in the Italian zone. Ribbentrop was tried at the Allies' joint military tribunal at Nuremburg and was hanged on the morning of October 16, 1946.

In the following months, the Yugoslav Communists dealt with other opponents as well. Draza Mihailovic was captured in March 1946. Although the Chetnik leader was formally charged with collaborating with the Germans, the trial was also politically motivated, as Tito wished to remove his major wartime rival. Mihailovic was convicted and shot by a firing squad on July 17, 1946. Archbishop Stepinac was also taken into custody. Among other charges, he was accused of "activities against the people and the state"[26] (i.e. supporting the Ustasha government and its policies). The Archbishop railed against Communism, especially its pronounced hostility toward religion. He denied playing any role in forced conversions and refused to accept any responsibility for the deaths of Serb civilians that had taken place within the NDH. He did, however, reiterate his support for an independent Croatian state, declaring, "The Croat nation unanimously declared itself for the Croatian state and I would have been remiss had I not recognized and acknowledged the desire of the Croatian people enslaved in the former Yugoslavia."[27] While the clergyman did provide aid and shelter to a few Jews, he clearly could have saved thousands of lives had he spoken out forcefully against the governments genocidal actions against minorities. Sentenced to sixteen years in prison, he served only five and spent his remaining years under house arrest in a small town south-west of Zagreb. He died in 1960.

War Criminals on the Run

The majority of Ustasha leaders benefited from the chaos of the last days of the war during which they made good their escapes. Men such as Pavelic and Artukovic used what the Allies called the "ratlines" to elude capture.D The ratlines were run by Fascist sympathizers who provided escaping Nazis and their collaborators with false travel documents, money, and safe houses until they could leave Europe.

One of the most effective ratlines was located in Rome and involved high level Vatican officials. Bishop Alois Hudal, the rector of a seminary for German and Austrian priests, helped many Nazis. The bishop helped Franz Stangl, the commandant of the Treblinka death camp where approximately 900,000 people were killed, find safe haven in Brazil. It was well known that many right wing governments in South America, chiefly Argentina, Chile, and Paraguay, were well disposed to accept fleeing Nazis. Stangl was finally extradited in 1967 and stood trial in West Germany. He was found guilty of war crimes and received a life sentence. The bishop is also said to have aided Adolf Eichmann in his flight to Argentina. It would be left to the Israelis to bring this mass murderer to justice in 1960.

Hudal wrote to Argentina's President Juan Peron asking him to issue entrance visas for 3,000 Germans and 2,000 Austrians whom he described not as fugitives from justice, but rather as men that had fought against Bolshevism.[28] Peron allowed Nazis to enter his country due to his sincere admiration for the Third Reich as well as self interest as he was determined to use fleeing German scientists and engineers to improve Argentina's industrial sector. The arriving men often found jobs and housing easy to come by, and rapidly adjusted to life in their new country. Historians estimate that between 1945 and 1949 about 2,000 Nazis made their way to Argentina.[29]

The actions of Archbishop Huda did not go entirely unnoticed; in 1947, the media began to report on his activities. Vatican offi-

---

DThe term, pronounced "rattlins," originally referred to the horizontal ropes on sailing ships that, when strung between shrouds, form ladders for sailors to climb to the tops of the masts. Should the ship sink, those sailors unfortunate enough to still be aboard often climbed the ropes in a desperate effort to survive. The term gradually came to mean any escape route used by desperate men.

cials, fearing a scandal, knew that something had to be done. In 1951, at the insistence of the Vatican, he was removed from his post as rector.

Most Ustasha fugitives were aided from Rome by Father Krunoslav Draganovic. Draganovic, a former professor of theology in Zagreb, was a staunch Catholic and fierce Croatian nationalist. As one of the preeminent figures within the Collegio San Girolamo degli Illirici (College of Saint Jerome of the Illyrians), he was in a good position to aid his fellow countrymen. Well aware that some of his former colleagues had been killed or were now languishing in Communist run camps, Draganovic was only too eager to help when Ante Pavelic appeared in Rome in April 1946. It was decided however that it was still too risky for the *paglavnik* to attempt to leave Europe. Although the Croatian cleric later denied it, William Gowen of the United States Army's Counter Intelligence Corps (CIC), was convinced at the time that Draganovic was working closely with the former dictator.[30]

It is no surprise that Pavelic found himself on a list of wanted war criminals as he was responsible for the deaths of hundreds of thousands of people. Following the war, as millions were on the move, Allied intelligence agencies created lists of wanted men who might try to escape by blending in with the masses. War criminals that were wanted in one or more countries were referred to as "Blacks." Those considered Nazi collaborators were called "Grays" (a third term "Whites" was used to denote victims of Nazi persecution). By one estimate, the British classified as many as 4,000 Ustasha members as either Blacks or Grays.[31] In the autumn of 1947, Pavelic had secretly traveled back to Rome awaiting transport to South America. On September 13, armed with a false passport provided by Draganovic, one "Pablo Aranyos" boarded an Italian ship bound for Buenos Aires. Upon his arrival in Argentina, Pavelic was emplyed by Juan Peron as a security advisor.

A committee sponsored by the Argentinean government estimated that as many as fifty-two senior Ustasha officials reached that country following the war, with a total of 115 Ustasha members by 1947.[32]

Although Father Draganovic enjoyed the Vatican's protection, the government of Yugoslavia requested his extradition the same year he helped Pavelic escape. During the war, Draganovic served as an army chaplain at the Jasenovac camp, while holding the rank of lieutenant colonel in the Ustasha.[33] He was charged with aiding in the forced conversions of Serbs. Additionally, as the Vice Chief of the Ustasha's Bureau of Colonization (which had jurisdiction over the redistribution of property seized from dead or deported Serbs), he was accused of seizing large quantities of food from Serb peasants on Mt. Kozara in Bosnia in 1942. He did not deny the charges, asserting only that he had not physically been in the towns and villages in question when the forced conversions took place. In 1967, Draganovic unexpectedly appeared in Yugoslavia. There is speculation that he had been lured back to his native county by Tito's secret police (UDBA). While the details remain unknown, it appears a deal was struck with government officials. Possibly in exchange for information, Draganovic was not prosecuted and allowed to live quietly in Sarajevo.

Although it appeared for a time that most Ustasha leaders would never be brought to trial, the Communist victors had not given up. They did not forget the atrocities that had taken place or the men responsible. In the post war decades, while the UDBA collected intelligence on capitalist countries of the west, it also sought to locate those high ranking members of the Ustasha who had gone into hiding around the world. The primary target, of course, was Ante Pavelic. Following the ouster of Juan Peron from power in 1955, Pavelic retired to the town of Casero near Buenos Aires. His charmed life in Argentina came to an abrupt end in April 1957. An anonymous assassin, who was never caught, shot the former dictator twice. Although severely wounded, and left for dead, Pavelic did not die. Upon his recovery, he stated his belief that the man, or men, responsible must have been agents of Marshal Tito.[34] Some months later, the new Argentinean government agreed to consider a Yugoslav extradition request. Pavelic, not waiting for the government's decision, quickly left the country. He soon found a safe haven in Spain, but died of his wounds in December 1959.

Pavelic's subordinate, the infamous Maks Luburic, would also meet a violent end at the hands of the UDBA. Luburic, one of the commandants of Jasenovac (and the mentor of another—Dinko Sakic), had found refuge in Spain, where he was active in right wing organizations attempting to destabilize the government of Yugoslavia. On April 20, 1969, his body was found on the floor of his villa; he had been bludgeoned and stabbed to death.

Although it would take another thirty years, justice would finally catch up with Sakic as well. He had been living in Argentina until that country granted the extradition request of the independent Republic of Croatia in 1998 (Croatia became an independent country in 1991 with the collapse of Yugoslavia). Tried for war crimes against civilians, the former camp commander was convicted in 1999 and sentenced to 20 years imprisonment.

Some Ustasha fugitives managed to make their way to the United States. The highest ranking Ustasha official to do so was Andrija Artukovic. After four years of hiding under assumed names in Italy, Switzerland, and Ireland, in 1948, the former interior minister felt it was time to leave Europe. After taking the alias Anic, he, along with his wife and five children, left Ireland on July 15, 1948. He settled in Los Angeles, California, where he worked as an accountant for his brother's contracting firm. In 1951, his true identity was revealed and the Yugoslav government requested his extradition on the charge of murder. After eight years of legal wrangling (most of the evidence was circumstantial), their request was denied on the basis that they had provided insufficient grounds for such action. As these were the Cold War years, the U.S. government was not eager to work closely with Tito and his state. Artukovic, who now lived openly under his real name, claimed that he was not responsible for any murders and that if atrocities had taken place during the war, they had arisen out of a bitter "civil war" between Croats and Serbs.[35] Almost thirty years later, after again pressing U.S. officials to move against him, the Yugoslavs finally met with success. In 1986, Artukovic, at this point an old man, was extradited, stood trial, and was convicted of murder. Although he received the death sentence, it was not immediately carried out due to his poor health. He died in a prison hospital in 1988.

1   West, <u>Tito</u>. p.155.
2   Lindsay, p.93.
3   Goldstein, p.148.
4   Goldstein, p.149.
5   Museum of Tolerance Multimedia Learning Center, [home page on-line]; available from http://www.motlc.wiesenthal.org; Internet; accessed October 8, 2003.
6   Ibid.
7   John Clearwater, "SS Manhunt for Marshal Tito," *WW II*, Februar 1999, p.62.
8   Antonio J. Munoz, <u>For Croatia and Christ: The Croatian Army in World War II 1941-1945</u>. (Bayside, New York: Axis Europa Books, 1996), p.13.
9   West, <u>Tito</u>. P.168.
10 Ibid., p.169.
11 Lindsay, p.111.
12 West, <u>Tito</u>. p.167.
13 The 463rd Bombardment Group (H), [home page on-line]; available from http://www.463rd.org Internet; accessed September 8, 2005.
14 Zdenko Lowenthal, ed., <u>The Crimes of the Fascist Occupants and their Collaborators against Jews in Yugoslavia</u>. (Belgrade: Federation of Jewish Communities of the Federative People's Republic of Yugoslavia, 1957), p.19.
15 Isaac Kowalski, ed., Anthology on Armed Jewish Resistance: 1939-1945. (Brooklyn, New York: Jewish Combatants Publishers House, 1984), p.476.
16 Tomasevich, p.726.
17 Mihovilovic interview by author, July 12, 2005.
18 Ibid.
19 John Toland, <u>Adolf Hitler</u> (Garden City, New York: Doubleday and Company, 1976), p.879.
20 Winston S. Churchill, <u>The Second World War, vol. VI, Triumph and Tragedy</u> (Boston: Hughton Mifflin Company, 1953), p.460.
21 Toland, p.887.
22 West, Tito. p.210.
23 Goldstein, p.155.
24 Munoz, p.73.
25 Goldstein, p.155.

26 Ibid., p.157.
27 West, <u>Tito</u>. p.213.
28 Teja Fiedler, "Nazis Auf Der Flucht," Stern, 24 March 2005, p.136.
29 Ibid., p.134.
30 Aarons, p.79.
31 Ibid., p.205.
32 Richard Breitman, and others, <u>U.S. Intelligence and the Nazis</u> (New York: Cambridge University Press, 2005), p.211.
33 Ibid.
34 Paul Meskil, Hitler's Heirs (New York City: Pyramid Books, 1961), p.63.
35 Ibid., p.153.

CONCLUSION

THE ITALIAN MILITARY AND FOREIGN MINISTRY MEMBERS WHO conspired to save the lives of Croatian Jews all survived the war (with the notable exception of General Amico who was not actually privy to the original plan). They continued with their lives and careers as they had before the conflict.

After the war, Count Luca Pietromarchi, the man in charge of the Occupied Territories Department of the Foreign Ministry, became Italy's Ambassador to Turkey and then Ambassador to the Soviet Union. In 1965, he wrote a book entitled *The Soviet World*. Roberto Ducci, Head of the Croatian office at the Foreign Ministry, who had defended Italian actions on behalf of Jews in a 1944 article, held a number of government posts over the next four decades. In 1964, he became Italy's ambassador to Yugoslavia. He served in the same capacity in London in the 1970s.

While the men who saved the lives of Jewish refugees did not do so with the expectation of being rewarded or celebrated for their deeds, at least one was acknowledged for his efforts. Following the war, the *carabinieri* General Giuseppe Pieche, who pointed out that the Germans were actually murdering Jews despite the euphemisms they used, was recognized by the Italian-Jewish community for his attempts to bring the truth to light.

Perhaps the most interesting post war experience concerning an Italian official involved in saving the Croatian Jews was that of General Mario Roatta. On November 17, 1944, the former commander of the Second Army was arrested. He was charged by the High Commission for Sanctions against Fascism with graft, international terrorism, and conspiracy to commit murder.[A] The charges stemmed from the general's questionable actions prior to the war. Roatta was accused of assisting the Ustasha in their assassination of the Yugoslav King Alexander (which also resulted in the death of France's foreign minister Jean-Louis Barthou) in 1934 and of having the Rosselli brothers, Carlo and Nello murdered in 1937.

On the evening of March 4, 1945, as his trial was beginning, the general complained that he felt ill and was transferred to a military hospital. Later that same night, Roatta simply walked out of the hospital. Roatta's *carabinieri* guards, who undoubtedly sympathized with the general's plight, were conveniently absent from their posts. Three days later, a leftist crowd of some 15,000 people held a rally at the coliseum to protest the general's "escape." The trial proceeded without the defendant and Roatta was eventually sentenced to a term of life in prison *in abstentia*. In the meantime, the general had arrived in Spain where he lived quite comfortably for several years.

In June 1946, as Cold War tensions rose and in the spirit of national reconciliation, the Italian government announced a general amnesty for Fascists. The new law greatly reduced the prison terms of those convicted over the previous two years. By the 1960s, the political climate in Italy had changed dramatically and Roatta decided to return to his homeland. He died there in 1968.

In 1945, much of Europe lay in ruins. Millions of soldiers and civilians had been killed or left homeless. As catastrophic as the war

---

[A]The punishment of Italian Fascists began even before the war ended. In early June 1944, shortly after Rome was liberated, the Allies replaced Badoglio and his ministers. The new government, headed by Prime Minister Ivanoe Bonomi, was made up of a coalition of anti-Fascist political parties. On July 27, 1944 the High Commission for Sanctions against Fascism was created. Over the next two years, the commission handed down thousands of indictments against Fascists even as the war was ongoing in Italy.

had been, it was clear that one group had sustained greater losses than any other: the Jews. Two thirds of European Jews had been murdered in what would soon come to be known as the Holocaust. As in other parts of the continent, the implementation of Nazi racial policies, combined with the anti-Semitic zeal of collaborationist governments in Serbia and Croatia, utterly devastated the Jewish population of Yugoslavia. Of the 76,000 Jews in prewar Yugoslavia, only 16,000 survived.[1] Of these, roughly 8,000 were in Serbia and 8,000 in Croatia (including Bosnia-Hercegovina). Included in this last figure are the people interned and protected by the Italians.

Within the borders of the NDH, there had been approximately 40,000 Jews. By war's end, 25,000 had been killed by the Ustasha, and 7,000 deported by the Germans.[2]

Of the 3,500 Jewish men and women from Rab who joined the partisans, approximately 500 fell in battle between July 1943 and May 1945. Although their deaths were tragic, it is of utmost significance that they died fighting. They had been given a chance to strike back at an enemy that had targeted them for annihilation. The Italian military had allowed them to survive, and the partisans gave them the opportunity to fight for themselves and their country.

Although Fascist nations in Europe shared a common ideology, their histories and cultures were, of course, quite different. While Italy and Croatia were technically partners, each had its own distinctive domestic and foreign policy objectives. When it came to the Jews, Italy saw them as posing no particular threat and allowed them to live in relative peace. In Croatia, however, they were viewed as outsiders who threatened to contaminate the newly created state and therefore had to be eliminated. One need only look at the vast statistical difference in the number of Jewish survivors between the two countries. At the time of the German occupation of Italy in 1943, the number of Italian Jews stood at 40,000 (some 17,000 mostly foreign Jews had been forced to leave the country after the 1938 laws were enacted). There was roughly the same number of Jews in Croatia. Yet by the end of the war, eighty percent of Italian Jews were still alive while eighty percent of Croatian Jews had been murdered.

Due largely to the treatment they had received during the war, many Jews in the newly reconstituted Yugoslavia began to think about emigrating. Following the creation of the state of Israel in 1948, several thousand made the decision to leave and join fellow Jews in a new country. In total 7,739 people (or approximately half the country's post war Jewish population) departed in order to help build a Jewish homeland.[3] They would never have been able to make this journey without the Italians.

In understanding how the Italian Military and Foreign Ministry were able to save Croatian Jews, multiple factors must be taken into account. The personality of Benito Mussolini played an important role. The fact that the dictator was not an ardent anti-Semite allowed hope to emerge that Jews who found their way into the Italian zone might indeed survive. Mussolini's feelings about Jews seems to have ranged from admiration to indifference. Although he saw himself as a practical politician and cooperated with his Axis partner in many areas, he was not about to involve his country in the full scale annihilation of the Jews. Although once he aligned himself and his nation with the Nazis, he felt it necessary to enact anti-Jewish laws, these statutes were unevenly enforced and categories for exemptions were created. Italian Jews clearly suffered between 1938 and 1945. Many were humiliated as they were forced from jobs, expelled from schools, and had their careers cut short. Yet compared to what was about to befall Jews elsewhere in Europe, Italian Jews would later consider themselves lucky.

Mussolini's willingness to be swayed by the arguments of his generals also helped the Jews. The Italian leader had at first agreed to allow the Germans to deport the Croatian Jews with his "Nulla Osta" scrawled across the top of Ribentrop's memo. Having made that decision, however, he issued no specific date or timetable under which the army would be bound to carry out such a plan. This, of course, gave time to the diplomats and military personnel to influence their leader to reverse his decision and oppose the German scheme.

Finally, the dictator's management style must be taken into account. While he had always devoted long hours to the affairs of state earlier in his career, he became less attentive to details as his health began to deteriorate during the war years. Mussolini suffered from a severe ulcer and, in the opinion of Italo Balbo, a member of the Fascist Grand Council, he was also slowly dying from the effects of syphilis that he had contracted years earlier.[4] Mussolini's inattentiveness allowed a handful of Italy's officials to assist the Jews without interference from their leader.

The "special relationship" between Adolf Hitler and Benito Mussolini was critical in saving Jews under Italian control. In Hitler's eyes, no other European leader commanded the level of respect as did Mussolini. He was viewed as both a mentor and valued partner (although by the late stages of the war this high regard for *Il Duce* had changed significantly). In the late 1930s, the mutual admiration between the two men was genuine. Hitler respected Mussolini for having established the first Fascist state in Europe, while the Italian was in awe of Hitler's military successes. In territories occupied by the Italians, Nazi officials, including those in the Foreign Ministry, were allowed to press for the deportation of Jews only so far, and in Italy proper, Jews were safe until after the collapse of the dictatorship.

Even Heinrich Himmler, the man responsible for implementing Hitler's genocidal policy against the Jews, knew he had to tread lightly around the Italians when broaching the subject of these "enemies." Privately, he viewed the Italians as unreliable partners who lacked the ruthless nature necessary to eliminate the Jews. He criticized Mussolini for not creating a force similar to his SS, a military unit that was not only fiercely loyal to the state, but also feared on the battlefield (Italy's Fascist militia lacked the training to be effective front line troops and its members never inspired the type of fear that was associated with the *Waffen SS* (the combat arm of the organization). Nevertheless, the *Reichsfueher SS* instructed his subordinates to proceed with caution when dealing with the Italians. In May 1942 he reminded the SS police chief in occupied Serbia:

> Bear in mind that you are a higher SS and Police Leader of Adolf Hitler's Reich, of the Fuehrer, whom a close and cordial friendship unites with the congenial Duce Benito Mussolini. Of course we find a lot to complain about in the behavior of individual Italians; in similar form they will

object to things we do. That makes no difference. We are allies and only as such strong.[5]

It was a combination of all these factors that placed the Italians in a unique position to aid the Jews.

The Croatian Jews were assisted by another group of people as well. Early in the war, when the Nazi leadership deemed it essential not to offend Italian sensibilities, Mussolini's troops were able to protect the Jews. That situation changed dramatically in September 1943 with the announcement that Italy had for all intents and purposes surrendered to the Allies. The fate of the Jews of Croatia was once again uncertain. At the time of the armistice, the Croatian Jews were more fortunate than those under Italian protection elsewhere in Europe, as they were near areas in which Communist partisans were operating. Once the Italian army was gone, the lives of the Croatian Jews entirely depended upon the good will of Tito's guerrillas. Unlike with some irregular forces fighting the Nazis in places such as Poland and the Ukraine, Jews were welcomed to fight with the Yugoslav partisans. The Jews were also extremely lucky that the Communists arrived on the island of Rab when they did. Had they landed only a few days later, they would have found the island occupied by the Germans. Had this been the case, no evacuation of the refugees would have been possible, and the fate of the Jews would have been sealed.

Several key factors must be considered when explaining why the Italian military and diplomatic corps acted to protect the Jews of Croatia from the Nazis and Ustasha. Many Italians resented German arrogance. Especially galling were the condescending attitudes of German officers who, having absorbed years of Nazi indoctrination, felt they were far superior to all other peoples of Europe, including Italians. These beliefs caused friction between the two Axis nations throughout the war. (It is somewhat ironic that these same Italians believed themselves to be superior to Slavs in every way, especially in terms of culture and history.) As the war progressed, the Italian military commands grew increasingly aware of their second class status in relation to the far more successful

German military machine. This, too, caused many to be hypersensitive to any and all perceived insults to their competence and fighting prowess.

In the Balkans, the Italian military felt it had to project an image of strength to friend and foe alike. One way of achieving this goal in the NDH was by refusing to hand over the Jews either to the Ustasha or to the Nazis. By rebuffing Ustasha demands, the Italians demonstrated that they, not the government in Zagreb, were the ultimate authority in their section of Croatia. By refusing to cooperate with the Nazis, the point was made that they would not automatically submit to Nazi requests. In the eyes of the Italian generals, the idea, however unrealistic, that the two nations were equals in the war, had to be upheld. The Italians did not want the local population to perceive Italy as no more than a paper tiger subservient to the Nazi powers. This, of course, would weaken Italian prestige in the eyes of the Chetniks as well as Serbian civilians in general.

Lastly, and perhaps most importantly, Italians aided the Croatian Jews simply out of compassion. This altruism was first seen with the interventions on the part of a few enlisted men and junior officers to stop the murderous rampage of the Ustasha. As time went on, this humanitarianism spread up the chain of command to reach the highest echelons of the military establishment and the top of the Italian Foreign Ministry. The diplomats encouraged the military to defend Jews and Serbs from the Ustasha and then actively opposed repeated German requests for the deportation of Jews who had crossed into the Italian sphere of influence. While both military officers and Foreign Ministry officials knew that Ustasha brutality served only to drive more people into the arms of the partisan enemy, this concern was clearly secondary to the humanitarian concerns in the minds of these men.

Survivors such as Imra Rochlitz credited the Italians with saving not only his own life, but the lives of thousands of others at a time when their prospects for survival were bleak. Jews were forced to put their faith in the Italian army since they had no alternative. Following General Roatta's visit to the internment camp at

Kraljevica on November 27, 1942, at which time Roatta reassured the Jews they would be safe, five of the internees wrote him a letter. They included three businessmen, a university professor, and the director of the Croatian Bank. Their letter stated:

> We all placed ourselves at the specified time under the protection of the Italian army, with complete confidence in the nobility of soul and the humane feelings of the Italian soldiers and the Italian people. After the declarations made by Your Excellency we are convinced that the protection accorded us is made more effective by our internment in this camp, where we are under the immediate guard of the Italian army. These days will leave an indelible memory in our minds, and nothing will ever erase from our hearts the eternal gratitude we feel to the Italian army. Italy has in us sure and true friends, who will endeavor through our activity to serve the interests of this noble land. [6]

Having nowhere else to turn, the Croatian Jews were forced to trust the Italians to keep them safe. It is a tribute to the Italian character that in the end that trust was not misplaced.

1   Dawidowicz, p.392.
2   Cornwell, p.253.
3   Tomasevich, p.607.
4   Neville, p.170.
5   Steinberg, p.205.
6   Poliakov, p.145.

General Sources

Books

Aarons, Mark, and John Loftus. <u>Ratlines: How the Vatican's Nazi networks betrayed Western Intelligence to the Soviets</u>. London: William Heinemann Ltd., 1991.

Beschloss, Michael. <u>The Conquerors: Roosevelt, Truman and the Destruction of Hitler's Germany, 1941-1945</u>. New York: Simon and Schuster, 2002.

Bosworth, R.J.B. <u>Mussolini's Italy: Life Under the Fascist Dictatorship, 1915-1945</u>. New York: The Penguin Press, 2006.

Breitman, Richard, Norman J.W. Goda, Timothy Naftali, and Robert Wolfe. <u>U.S. Intelligence and the Nazis</u>. New York: Cambridge University Press, 2005.

Carpi, Daniel. "Rescue of Jews in Italian Occupied Croatia." In Yisrael Gutman and Efaim Zuroff ed., <u>Rescue Attempts during the Holocaust: Proceedings of the Second Yad Vashem International Historical Conference, Jerusalem, April 8-11, 1974</u>. Jerusalem: "Ahva" Cooperative Press, 1977.

Churchill, Winston S. <u>The Second World War, vol.III, The Grand Alliance</u>. Boston: Houghton Mifflin Company, 1950.

----- <u>The Second World War, vol.VI, Triumph and Tragedy</u>. Boston: Houghton Mifflin Company, 1953.

Cornwell, John. <u>Hitler's Pope: The Secret History of Pius XII</u>. New York: Viking, 1999.

Davidson, Basil. <u>Scenes from the Anti-Nazi War</u>. New York: Monthly Review Press, 1980.

Dawidowicz, Lucy. <u>The War Against the Jews 1933-1945</u>. New York: Bantam Books,1975.

Domenico, Roy Palmer. <u>Italian Fascists on Trial</u>. Chapel Hill, North Carolina: University of North Carolina Press, 1991.

Erickson, John, and Ljubica Erickson. The Eastern Front in Photographs. London: Carlton Books Ltd., 2001.

Gibson, Hugh, ed. The Ciano Diaries 1939-1943: The Complete, Unabridged Diaries Of Count Galeazzo Ciano Italian Minister For Foreign Affairs 1936-1943. Garden City, New York: Doubleday and Company, 1946.

Goldstein, Ivo. Croatia: A History. Translated by Nikolina Javanovic. London: Hurst and Company, 1999.

Hibbert, Christopher. Mussolini: The Rise and Fall of Il Duce. New York: Palgrave MacMillan, 2008.

Ivanovic, Ilija. Witness to Jasenovac's Hell. Translated by Alexsandra Lazic. Mt Pleasant, Texas: Dallas Publishing Company, 2002.

Jowett, Philip. The Italian Army 1940-45 (3) Italy 1943-45. Oxford: Osprey Publishing Ltd., 2001.

Klein, Gerda Weissman. All But My Life. New York: Hill and Wang, 1957.

Kowalski, Isacc, ed. Anthology on Armed Jewish Resistance: 1939-1945. Brooklyn, New York: Jewish Combatants Publishers House, 1984.

Linsay, Franklin. Beacons in the Night: With the OSS and Tito's Partisans in Wartime Yugoslavia. Stanford, California: Stanford University Press, 1993.

Lochner, Louis, ed. The Goebbels Diaries 1942-1943. Garden City, New York: Doubleday and Company, 1948.

Lowenthal, Zdenko, ed. The Crimes of the Fascist Occupants and their Collaborators against Jews in Yugoslavia. Belgrade: Federation of Jewish Communities of the Federative People's Republic of Yugoslavia, 1957.

Manhattan, Avro. The Vatican's Holocaust. Springfield, Missouri: Ozark Books, 1986.

----- Terror Over Yugoslavia: The Threat To Europe. London: Watts and Company, 1953.

Meacham, Jon. Franklin And Winston: An Intimate Portrait Of An Epic Friendship. New York: Random House, 2003.

Meltzer, Milton. Rescue: The Story of How Gentiles Saved Jews in the Holocaust. New York: Harper Trophy, 1988.

Merridale, Catherine. Ivan's War: Life and Death in the Red Army, 1939-1945. New York: Metropolitan Books Henry Holt and Company, 2006.

Meskil, Paul. Hitler's Heirs. New York City: Pyramid Books, 1961.

Michaelis, Meir. Mussolini and the Jews: German-Italian relations and the Jewish Question in Italy 1922-1945. Oxford: The Claredon Press, 1978.

Morley, John. F. Vatican Diplomacy And The Jews During The Holocaust 1939-1943. New York: KTAV Publishing House, Inc., 1980.

Munoz, Antonio. For Croatia and Christ: The Croatian Army in World War II 1941-1945. Bayside, New York: Axis Europa Books, 1996.

Neville, Peter. Mussolini. London: Routledge, 2004.

Paolicelli, Paul. Under The Southern Sun: Stories of the Real Italy and the Americans It Created. New York: Thomas Dunne Books, 2003.

Poliakov, Leon, and Jacques Sabille. Jews Under the Italian Occupation. New York: Howard Fertig, 1983.

Publications International Ltd. The Holocaust Chronicle: A History In Words And Pictures. Lincolnwood, Illinois: Publications International Ltd., 2003.

Shelah, Menachem. "Italian Rescue of Yugoslav Jews" In Ivo Herzer ed., The Italian Refuge: Rescue of Jews During the Holocaust. Washington, D.C.: Catholic University Press, 1989.

Smith, Danny. Wallenberg: Lost Hero. Springfield, Illinois: Temlegate Publishers, 1987.

Steinberg, Jonathan. All or Nothing: The Axis and the Holocaust 1941-43. London: Routledge, 1990.

Thomas, N. and K. Mikulan. Axis Forces In Yugoslavia 1941-5. Oxford: Osprey Publishing Ltd., 1995.

Toland, John. Adolf Hitler. Garden City, New York: Doubleday and Company, 1976.

Tomasevich, Joso. War and Revolution in Yugoslavia, 1941-1945: Occupation And Collaboration. Stanford, California: Stanford University Press, 2001.

West, Rebecca. Black Lamb And Gray Falcon: A trip Through Yugoslavia. New York: Penguin Books, 1940.

West, Richard. Tito And The Rise And Fall Of Yugoslavia. New York: Carroll and Graf Publishers, Inc., 1994.

Zucotti, Susan. The Italians and the Holocaust: Persecution, Rescue, and Survival. Lincoln, Nebraska: University of Nebraska Press, 1987.

----- Under His Very Windows: The Vatican and the Holocaust in Italy. New Haven, Connecticut: Yale University Press, 2000.

Journal and Magazine Articles

Clearwater, John. "SS Manhunt for Marshal Tito." *WWII*, Februar 1999, p.62.

Fiedler, Teja. "Nazis Auf Der Flucht." *Stern*, March 24, 2005, p.136.

Fowler, William. "Battle of France 1940." *War Monthly*, Issue 36, March 1977, p.8.

Loker, Zvi. "The Testimony of Dr. Edo Neufeld: The Italians and the Jews of Croatia." *Holocaust and Genocide Studies* volume 7, number 1 (Spring 1993): pp.67-76.

Shelah, Menachem. "Kroatische Juden zwischen Deutschland und Italien 1941-1943." *Vierteljahrshefte Fuer Zeitgeschichte* (April 1993): pp.175-195. Trans. [from German] Heidi Schiefer.

Verax, "Italiani ed ebrei in Jugoslavia." *Politica Estera*, (1944): pp. 21-29.

Walston, James. "History and Memory of the Italian Concentration Camps." *The Historical Journal*, 40,1 (1997): pp.169-183.

Oral Interviews

Kos, Julija, Chief Librarian—Jewish Community of Zagreb. Interview by author, July 13, 2005, Zagreb, Croatia.

Mihovilovic, Dorde, Curator—Jasenovac. Interview by author, July 12, 2005, Jasenovac, Croatia.

Videotaped Interviews

The following people recorded their experiences with the "Survivors of the Shoah Visual History Foundation."

Paul A., March 14, 1997. Walnut Creek, California, U.S.A. Interview Code 27046.

Desiree E., December 20, 1995. Fullerton, California, U.S.A. Interview Code 10450-1.

Boris N., January 30, 1996. Durban, South Africa. Interview Code 08682.

Dr. Alex R., September 30, 1997. Atlanta, Georgia, U.S.A. Interview Code 34338.

Lucy S., September 7, 1996. Nantucket, Massachusetts, U.S.A. Interview Code 19228-3.

Videotapes

The Righteous Enemy. Produced and directed by Joseph Rochlitz. 84 min.
   Parstel Ltd. Films, 1987. Video.

Government Documents

National Archives and Records Administration (NARA), Collection of
Foreign Records Seized Record Group 242.
Micro. No. T-120, Roll 5784, Frs. H299623 and 299624.
Micro. No. T-120, Roll 5784, Fr. H299660.
Micro. No. T-120, Roll 5785, Fr. H300887 and H300888.
Micro. No. T-586, Roll 424, Fr. 12278.
Micro. No. T-586, Roll 424, Fr. 12304.
Micro. No. T-821, Roll 405, Fr. 749.
Micro. No. T-821, Roll 405, Frs. 821 and 822.
Micro. No. T-821, Roll 405, Frs. 829 and 830.
Micro. No. T-821, Roll 405, Fr. 860.

Document 173. Ministero Degli Affari Esteri, Documenti Diplomatici
   Italiani, Serie 1939-1943 volume X (7 Febbraio-8 Settembre 1943),
   Libreria Dello Stato Roma MCMXC.
Document 680. Ministero Degli Affari Esteri, Documenti Diplomatici
   Italiani, Serie 1939-1943 volume X (7 Febbraio-8 Settembre 1943),
   Libreria Dello Stato Roma MCMXC.
Le Operazioni Delle Unita Italiane in Jugoslavia (1941-9143),
   Documento n. 94. Stato Magiore Esercito, Ufficio Storico, Roma 1978.
"Relations concerning operations of the Ministry of Foreign Affairs to
   help the Jewish community (1938-1943)". Trans. [from French]
   Jean-Yves Widmeyer, Italian Ministry of Foreign Affairs Library.
State Committee for the Investigation of War Crimes of the Occupiers
   and their Collaborators, July 21, 1947. Trans. [from Serbo-Croatian]
   George Radich, Croatian State Archives.

Internet Sources

"Archbishop Damaskinos," The International Raoul Wallenberg
   Foundation. Home page on-line. Available from
   http://www.raoulwallenberg.net; Internet; accessed October 13, 2006.
Centropa, "Excerpts from Jews in Yugoslavia-Part 1," Centropa Reports.

Home page on-line. Available from http://www.centropa.org/reports; Internet; accessed May 26, 2005.

Museum of Tolerance Multimedia Learning Center. Home page on-line. Available from http://www.motlc.wiesenthal.org; Internet; accessed October 8, 2003.

National Museum of the United States Air Force. Home page on-line. Available from http://www.nationalmuseum.af.mil; Internet; accessed August 7, 2007.

The University of Oklahoma College of Law: A Chronology of U.S. Historical Documents. Home page on-line. Available from http://www.law.ou.edu/history/germwar.shtml; Internet; accessed April 16, 2007.

The 463rd Bombardment Group (H). Home page in-line. Available from http://www.463rd.org; Internet; accessed September 8, 2005.

INDEX

223